1 MONTH OF
FREE
READING

at

www.ForgottenBooks.com

By purchasing this book you are eligible for one month membership to ForgottenBooks.com, giving you unlimited access to our entire collection of over 1,000,000 titles via our web site and mobile apps.

To claim your free month visit:

www.forgottenbooks.com/free921832

ISBN 978-0-260-00808-4
PIBN 10921832

For support please visit www.forgottenbooks.com

gains made possible by them were valuable and lasting. By agreeing to count only three-fifths of the slaves, the great principle of representation in the People's House of Congress in proportion to population was gained. By allowing the importation of negroes until 1808, there accrued to Congress the control of commerce. The third compromise, the giving of all the States equal representation in the States' House of Congress, although adopted to win the assent of the smaller States, is one of the great distinctive features of our plan of government.

Since 1789, the United States Constitution has developed in two ways: by addition and amendment and by judicial interpretation and construction of law. Both of these processes have, in their operation, been subject to the modifying influence of changes in prevailing political ideals.

Of such varying governmental tendencies three phases have been distinguished. The first has been called the aristocratic tendency, which prevailed from 1789 to 1857. This period was marked by distrust of the people, who could not vote directly for President or for Senators. It was typified by George Washington, an aristocrat. Socially, its representatives were the Southern planters and the no less aristocratic Northern merchants. Economically, it emphasized property rights. The second tendency, which prevailed from 1857 to the latter part of the century, for want of a better name may be called the plutocratic tendency. It manifested itself in great industrial development, in the formation of "trusts," in the building up of great railroad systems, and in the restraint of trade, with attendant financial disturbances and contests between capital and labor. Politically, it was the age of the laws." Governmentally, it was marked by the preponderance of Congress. The third may be called the democratic tendency. It is the age of the Interstate Commerce Commission and the Sherman "Anti-Trust" law for economic protection, and of Civil Service regulations and commission plans of city government for administrative betterment. Increasing confidence in the political judgment of the people is shown by the popular election of Senators and by such methods of direct legislation as the initiative and the referendum. Governmentally the age exalts the Executive Department of the Federal Government, for the President is the only representative of all the people.

The development of the Constitution by amendment shows three phases. The first deals with the rights of citizens of States as against the United States, and includes Amendments 1-11. The second deals with the citizens of the United States and their rights as against the States, and includes Amendments 13, 14, and 15. The third deals with administrative changes and includes Amendments 12, 16, and 17. Viewed as to their relation to the original Constitution these seventeen amendments fall into two classes—additions and changes. The additions include Amendments 1-10, 11, 13, 15. The 12th, 16th, and 17th Amendments, on the contrary, are changes, dealing respectively with the choosing of the President and Vice-President, the levying of Federal taxes, and the election of Senators.

More important than the growth of the Constitution by amendment has been its development through its use as a standard of legislative, executive, and judicial action. To be able to use the Constitution as such a standard, its very nature as well as the meaning of its various phrases must be understood.

Almost immediately after the adoption of the Constitution a controversy arose as to its nature. One party held that it had created an indissoluble union, a nation; the other that it was only a compact between sovereign States. As time went on, this constitutional issue became complicated by the economic and moral questions involved in slavery. The Constitution tacitly recognized slavery as a State institution. In 1787, slavery existed, but was dying out in both the North and the South. The invention of the cotton gin in 1791, however, caused the revival of slavery and made the South an agricultural section, opposed to a protective tariff. The strife grew increasingly bitter, with the extension of slavery as the burning question. Did the United States have the right to regulate a State institution? This issue of national versus State sovereignty came finally in 1861 to the arbitrament of arms on the question of secession. The War between the States, which settled the constitutional, economic, and moral questions involved in slavery, decided that the Constitution had created an indissoluble union.

The meaning of the Constitution as a document rests on judicial interpretation and construction of law. Acts of executive officers, laws passed by Congress, and many of those passed by State legislatures are likely, sooner or later, to be challenged as to their constitutionality. When such a case arises, the justices of the Supreme Court are given an opportunity to interpret some part of the Constitution. Many phrases in the Constitution have not yet been thus interpreted because no cases have arisen involving their meaning.

The United States Government has frequently had to act in ways that would not seem warranted by a strict interpretation of the Constitution. In such cases the doctrine of implied powers is put forward in justification. In 1791, Alexander Hamilton urged Congress to charter a Bank of the United States to handle the funds of the government. His friends of the Federalist party at once became liberal constructionists of the Constitution, holding that the power to create a bank was implied. On the other hand, the State rights party became literal constructionists, opposing the bank because the word "bank" did not appear in the Constitution. The latter party was forced to abandon its attitude of strict interpretation of the Constitution when, in 1803, its leader, Thomas Jefferson, purchased Louisiana from France. Jefferson personally believed that the purchase was unconstitutional, although he acquiesced in Albert Gallatin's justification of it as an exercise of the treaty-making power, which also serves as the justification of all subsequent additions of territory to the United States. There are other instances of the extension of the power of the Federal Government through a liberal interpretation of the Constitution: among them, the control of navigable waters, of railroad rates, and of corporations as extensions of the power to control commerce; and the issue of paper money during the War between the States as a means of national defence.

The story of the origin of the Constitution and of its interpretation by the courts is told in *The American Plan of Government*. This book shows how a plan of government adopted 127 years ago to give the people of thirteen little republics a central government strong enough to protect them from internal dissension and foreign aggression has been found sufficient for the management of the business of a nation which uses commercial and industrial machinery not dreamed of in the constitution-making era.

No similar book is in existence.

Commentaries upon the Constitution are either profound studies of historical development or unwieldy compendiums in which groups of legal decisions are summarized for the use of lawyers in search of precedents. This book gives the reader the real meaning of the Constitution, a meaning which cannot be obtained by reading the original document because a collection of rules cannot be understood except by reference to cases in which they have been enforced.

The two great popular books on our government are De Tocqueville's *Democracy in America* written by a Frenchman in 1830 and Bryce's *American Commonwealth* by an Englishman in 1888. The one is a glowing treatise on ideals of popular government, illustrated by governmental conditions in the United States. The other is an elaborate comparison of American institutions with the English method of government. The *American Plan of Government*, on the contrary, shows what our plan of government actually is by quoting the words of legal decisions which are precedents for future action when the meaning and purpose of our political institutions shall be in doubt.

GEO. GORDON BATTLE.

NEW YORK, May, 1916.

PREFATORY NOTE

THE judicial decisions quoted in this book may be found in the published reports of the Federal and State Courts of appellate jurisdiction. These reports are in all well-equipped law libraries and in many public libraries.

Court decisions were originally collected and published by volunteer reporters as a business enterprise. These reporters considered themselves authors and therefore put forth their books under their own names. For example, A. J. Dallas published *Dallas' Reports*, here referred to as "Dallas' Rep.," which include the decisions of the Pennsylvania Courts from 1754 to 1788 and the first adjudications of the Supreme Court of the United States. Again, William Johnson published as *Johnson's Reports*, here called "Johnson's (N. Y.) Rep.," the decisions of the highest New York Court from 1799 to 1823. The earlier decisions of the courts of Massachusetts were reported by Ephraim Williams, "with references and notes by a gentleman of the bar." From 1822 to 1837, however, Octavius Pickering published *Pickering's Reports* of cases argued in the Massachusetts courts.

The modern practise is to publish the reports of the Supreme Court of the United States in the *United States Reports*, and those of the Federal Circuit Court of Appeals, Circuit Courts and District Courts in the *Federal Reporter*. Likewise, the reports of the courts of each State are published under the name of the State.

...thanks to my valued ... Barth, who has contributed ... book. **I have been helped** greatly by his thoughtful suggestions upon Federal questions.

My friend and collaborator, Mr. Franklyn S. Morse, has contributed much toward the making of this book. It has been bettered by his careful and painstaking literary criticism and by his skilful presentation of American history from the angle of judicial decision.

CHARLES W. BACON.

NEW YORK, May, 1916.

CONTENTS

PART I.

THE MAKING OF THE CONSTITUTION.

PART II.

NATURE OF THE PREAMBLE.

PART III.

ORGANIZATION OF THE FEDERAL CONGRESS.

PART IV.

LEGISLATIVE GOVERNMENT IN THE UNITED STATES.

CONTENTS

PART V

THE DISTRIBUTION OF LEGISLATIVE GOVERNMENT IN THE UNITED STATES RIGHTS AS GRANTED BY THE CON- STITUTION AND ITS AMENDMENTS

CONTENTS

PART VI.

EXECUTIVE GOVERNMENT IN THE UNITED STATES.

PART VII.

JUDICIAL GOVERNMENT IN THE UNITED STATES.

PART VIII.

THE FEDERAL COMPACT.

PART I

The Making of the Constitution

CHAPTER I

Colonial Constitutions. Virginia, founded in 1607, had, under the provisions of its charter of 1609, a law-making body, called the General Assembly or House of Burgesses. The "Foure Great and Generall Courts of the Governor and Company of the Mattachusetts Bay in New England" were authorized to be held every year under that colony's charter of 1628. Connecticut had an assembly of free men under its colonial charter of 1662, which was retained as the State constitution until 1818. North Carolina had its House of Commons. Rhode Island had its law-making body under the charter which Charles the Second had granted to Roger Williams and others in 1663, and which also served as a State constitution until 1843. Each of the other colonies had its own legislative body. Every Englishman in Colonial America held stoutly that his local assembly stood in exactly the same relation to the King of England as did the parliament of the Kingdom. This claim was set forth in the following words in Resolution IV of the Declaration of Rights made by the First Continental Congress in 1774:

That the foundation of English liberty, and of all free government, is a right in the people to participate in their legislative council; and as the English colonists are not represented, and from their local and other circumstances,

3 .

cannot properly be represented in the British parliament, they are entitled to a free and exclusive power of legislation in their several provincial legislatures, where their right of representation can alone be preserved, in all cases of taxation and internal polity, subject only to the negative of their sovereign, in such manner as has been heretofore used and accustomed.—*Resolution IV. of Bill of Rights of the First Continental Congress.*

The United Colonies of New England. The colonists of New England soon discovered the need of united action both against the Indians, and more importantly, against the Dutchmen at New Amsterdam and Fort Orange (New York and Albany), who claimed all the territory west of the Connecticut River and north of the Delaware. A league of mutual protection, therefore, was made in 1643 by the colonies of New Plymouth, Massachusetts Bay, Connecticut, and New Haven, under the name of "The United Colonies of New England." This confederation had many of the functions of a nation. It had a general council of two commissioners from each colony, which met once every year "to hear, examine, weigh, and determine all affairs of war, or peace, leagues, aydes, charges, and numbers of men for war, division of spoyles, or whatsoever is gotten by conquest, receiving of more confederates, or Plantations into Combination with any of these Confederates, and all things of like nature, which are the proper concomitants, or consequences of such a Confederation, for amity, offence, and defense, not intermeddling with the Government of any of the Jurisdictions, which, by the third Article, is preserved intirely to themselves." The New England Confederation exercised these national functions and was a sovereign nation in everything except the name for nearly twenty years. After

not again feel the need for concerted action until the middle of the eighteenth century, when it became uncertain whether France or England was to control America. The French had a powerful colony in Canada and a string of military posts from Fort Duquesne, where Pittsburgh is now located, along the Ohio River and down the Mississippi to its mouth. They were allied with many of the most powerful Indian tribes of the great hinterland of America. The contest between France and Great Britain for colonial supremacy, already begun in India, soon took form in America in an effort on the part of the French to conquer New England and New York, whose harbors, free from ice all the year, were of immense commercial value. In 1754, during a crisis in this struggle for the mastery of a continent, a conference was held at Albany, at which delegates from all the northern colonies deliberated upon the means of protection against their enemies. Benjamin Franklin, a delegate from Pennsylvania, suggested a general union of all the colonies of English America under a president to be appointed by the British crown and a council representing the different provinces. The plan did not develop into a national reality because the southern colonies were not willing to share the expense of defending the northern colonies. Nevertheless the Albany Conference is important in that it produced a plan for the establishment of an American nation. The idea of American nationality had been born.

... When the French had been
... at the end of the French and
... occurred to British states-
... colonies might properly be
... protection they had received.
... that the home government was
... given to them for services rendered.
... indignation when parliament, in
... passed the Stamp Tax law, which imposed
... on stamp, parchment, or paper used for licenses
... carry on special businesses, wills, deeds of real estate,
... in suits at law, and other legal documents.
... colonists said and believed that the preamble or
... story statement in the act to the effect that it
... necessary to raise the money in order to protect
... colonies, was a mere subterfuge. They saw in
his tax only an attempt by the parliament of Great
Britain to usurp a taxing power which belonged
only to the assemblies of the different colonies.
Massachusetts, Rhode Island, Connecticut, New York,
New Jersey, Pennsylvania, Delaware, Maryland, and
South Carolina sent delegations to the Stamp Act
Congress, which met at New York in October, 1765,
to protest "that *the people of these colonies* are not, and,
from their local circumstances, cannot be, represented
in the House of Commons in Great Britain," and "that
the only representatives of the people of these colonies
are persons chosen therein by themselves, and that no
taxes ever have been, or can be, constitutionally imposed on them, but by their respective legislatures."
Thus the idea of a possible American nation, which
may have been in the minds of the members of the
Albany Conference, grew rapidly in the ten following
years into the conception of an American political body

—the people of the colonies—a phrase restated nearly a quarter of a century later, possibly by accident, in the preamble of the more famous document, the Constitution: "We, the People of the United States."

The protest of the Stamp Act Congress was followed by the repeal of the obnoxious measure; and for a time everything was peaceful and harmonious between the mother country and the colonies. Unluckily, however, the British parliament, in 1767, enacted a law to make "a more certain and adequate provision for defraying the charge of the administration of justice, and the support of civil government" in the colonies, by levying taxes on glass, lead, painter's colors, tea, and paper, imported from Great Britain into any of the colonies. The stamp tax had been opposed by the colonists because it had imposed taxes which, like the internal revenue taxes of the present day, were to be collected directly from the people. The British statesmen who proposed the new measure, thought that it would not be objectionable because the taxes were to be levied on goods brought from England, which the colonists would not have to buy if they did not wish. The colonists did not see it in that light. They objected very generally to any taxing laws enacted by parliament, and particularly to a taxing law, which, by providing royal governors and judges with salaries not granted by the colonial legislatures, would make those officials altogether too independent.

Committees of Correspondence. Colonial opposition, centering at length upon the tea tax, culminated in the Boston "Tea Party," at which cargoes of tea were dumped into the waters of Boston harbor. Parliament, as thoroughly angry as a body corporate ever can be, forthwith punished the offending New England

... began by enacting the Boston Port Bill which pro-
... all vessels from discharging or taking on cargoes at
... Two months afterward parliament made
the ... government more hated ... that were pass-
... of passing the Massachusetts Government Act,
which reduced the richest and most populous community in New England to the condition of a conquered
province. On the same day, by the administration of
... Act, the same body revived a statute which
... been enacted in the reign of Henry the Eighth
... the trial in England of treasons committed abroad.
... statute when first adopted had been intended to
... government officers from abusing their powers
... places. It was now revived to frighten
... Hancock, Quincy and the Adamses into
holding their tongues from protest against tyranny.
The only effect of all this was the organization in
each colony of a Committee of Correspondence,
which made a special business of keeping alive the
agitation against the measures which parliament had
adopted.

The First Continental Congress. On June 17, 1774,
the Massachusetts House of Representatives resolved
that a meeting of these Committees of Correspondence
was highly expedient and necessary "to consult upon
the present state of the colonies, . . . and to deliberate
and determine upon wise and proper measures . . .
for the recovery and establishment of their just rights
and liberties, civil and religious, and the restoration of union and harmony between Great Britain
and the colonies." The Committees which met at
Philadelphia in September, 1774, in pursuance of this
call, constituted the First Continental Congress. Delegates were present from all the colonies except

Georgia. The members voted that "the Congress do confine themselves, at present, to the consideration of such rights as have been infringed by acts of the British Parliament since the year 1763," and thereupon adopted a set of resolutions commonly called the Bill of Rights. In this document they denounced as "impolitic, unjust, and cruel, as well as unconstitutional, and most dangerous and destructive of American rights," the following: The Boston Port Bill, the Massachusetts Government Act, the Administration of Justice Act, and the Quebec Act, which, much to the indignation of all the colonies, had closed the Mississippi valley against settlement. Although no word indicating a desire for independent existence is to be found in the whole document, it was evident that there was an American nation which intended to have its rights or know the reason why.

Provincial Governments. Events moved rapidly from this time. Massachusetts established a Provincial Congress in October, 1774. The battles of Lexington and Bunker Hill were fought in April and June, 1775. General Washington took command of the Continental army at Cambridge and began the siege of Boston, which surrendered to his masterly strategy in March, 1776. In August, 1775, the American provinces were declared by royal proclamation to be in a state of rebellion. Royal governors and judges everywhere took to their heels, and in the twinkling of an eye, the authority of King George the Third vanished from his once loyal colonies. Makeshift governments of one kind or another were set up by the provincials that had been deserted by royal officials who were bound by oath and in honor to uphold the law. These governments, if they may be so called, sent delega-

form of government. It had acquired this meaning when the Constitution was adopted, and this is the one which must be attached to it when used in that instrument or in laws of Congress. What is that meaning? It means one of the commonwealths or political bodies of the American Union, and which, under the Constitution, stand in certain specified relations to the national government, and are invested as commonwealths with full power, in their several spheres, over all matters not expressly inhibited.

The Nation of the United States.   The United States was born into the world at the same moment as its component States. The united action of the States in declaring their independence created the United States. No one knows just what might have been the powers of the original nation, if it had stayed where the Declaration of Independence put it. We do know, however, that it would have had the powers of a nation. The meaning of that word was given by the Supreme Court of the United States in the opinion of Justice Brown in the case of *Montoya vs. United States*[1] in the following words:

The word "nation" as ordinarily used presupposes or implies an independence of any other sovereign power more or less absolute, an organized government, recognized officials, a system of laws, definite boundaries and the power to enter into negotiations with other nations.

The Continental Congress.   The United States is, perhaps, the only nation which ever fought out and won a great war without any government worthy of the name. The Declaration of Independence was the notice which it served upon other nations that it had assumed the position of a sovereign power. This declaration of sovereignty was made good in the campaigns which, so far as serious fighting was concerned, ended with the surrender of Yorktown in 1781, though the final treaty of peace was not signed until two years afterward. From July 4, 1776, until May 2, 1781, the United States, under the direction of a Congress composed of delegates from as many of the thirteen States as were willing to pay their expenses and salaries, carried on a continental war, established a navy, negotiated treaties of commerce and alliance, borrowed money, issued paper currency, and erected courts of admiralty which judged conflicting claims to prizes made by American ships of war. The States were as independent of each other and of the United States as they were of the rest of the world. Each State could send to the Congress as many delegates as it chose; but it could cast only one vote, and nothing could be done without the unanimous vote of all the States. Even the unanimous vote of all the States imposed no obligation which a State government could be forced to recognize. Everything depended upon the honor and good will of the local authorities, on which little reliance could be placed. It is a fact that the Revolutionary War was fought from beginning to end on credit, and the mystery of it is that credit was extended to a nation so loosely organized.

The Articles of Confederation. On June 11, 1776, four days after the question whether the colonies should declare their independence was first taken up, the Continental Congress resolved that "a committee be appointed to prepare and digest the form of a confederation to be entered into between these colonies." This committee framed the scheme of government called

... which is not ... States in Con- ... of rights and ... ht h... not pro- ... and powers ... obey its orders. ... for the common ... be defrayed out ... be supplied by the ... their lands, build- ... that Congress ... share of the ... did not mean ... into a default- ... what might be due to

... the articles was a ... ...ment form of gov- ... ... developed the ... ...uses of the Union ... the times, or the ... ...formed but little ... seemed to ... fears, and it appears ... ... delegates in Congress, the ... ... Remains a State would have no representative. The Treaty of Peace between the Colonies and Great Britain, which was signed September 3, 1783, and which marked the close of the Revolution, could not be ratified until January 14, 1784, because of the absence of so many representatives, and then there were but twenty-three members present. In April, 1783, there were present twenty-five members from eleven States, nine being represented by two each. Three members—therefore one-eighth of the whole—could negative any important measure.[1]

Edmund Randolph, afterward President Washington's Attorney-General, said in substance in one of his addresses in the Constitutional Convention:

The Confederation was made in the infancy of the science of constituting, when the inefficiency of requisition was unknown; when no commercial discord had arisen among the States; . . . when no foreign debts were urgent; when the havoc of paper money had not been foreseen; when treaties had not been violated; and when nothing better would have been conceded by States jealous of their sovereignty.

But it offered no security against foreign invasion, for Congress could neither prevent nor conduct a war; nor punish infractions of treaties or of the law of nations; nor control particular States from provoking war. The federal government had no constitutional power to check a quarrel between separate States; nor to suppress a rebellion in any one of them; nor to establish a productive impost; nor to counteract the commercial regulations of other nations; nor to defend itself against the encroachments of the States.[2]

[1] Andrews, *Manual of the Constitution*, p. 38.
[2] Madison's *Journal*, Albert Scott & Co., Chicago, 1893, pp. 59, 60.

Ordinance of 1787. The one supreme achievement of the Confederation was the adoption on July 13, 1787, by the Confederate Congress of "An ordinance for the government of the territory northwest of the river Ohio." This instrument of government recognized the supreme power of the United States over its own landed property. It gave the territorial legislature power to enact laws which should not violate a number of well-defined political principles that are set forth in an enumeration of the rights of the inhabitants of the territory. It is the first American national document which declared unreservedly that neither slavery nor involuntary servitude should exist, otherwise than in the punishment of crime.[1]

The Constitution of the United States. On January 21, 1787, the Congress of the Confederation adopted the following resolution which had been introduced by Rufus King, a delegate from Massachusetts, who afterward was one of the first two United States Senators from New York:

RESOLVED: That it is expedient that on the second Monday in May next, a convention of delegates, who shall have been appointed by the several States, be held at Philadelphia, for the sole and express purpose of revising the Articles of Confederation, and reporting to Congress and the several legislatures such alterations and provisions therein, as shall, when agreed to in Congress and confirmed by the States, render the Federal Constitution adequate to the exigencies of government and the preservation of the Union.[2]

The different state legislatures appointed delegates, giving them authority to take part in the Convention,

[1] Ordinance of 1787, Article VI.   [2] 4 Journals of Congress, 724.

which began its sittings on May 25, 1787, and adjourned on September 17, 1787, after having framed what Mr. Gladstone once called "the most remarkable document ever struck forth at a given time by the brain and purpose of man."

In 1793, John Jay, the first Chief Justice of the United States, in the opinion which he rendered in the great case of *Chisholm vs. Georgia*,[1] explained the position which this instrument of government occupies among American institutions. He said:

All the country now possessed by the United States was then a part of the dominions appertaining to the crown of Great Britain. Every acre of land in this country was then [prior to the Revolution] held mediately or immediately by grants from that crown. All the people of this country were then subjects of the King of Great Britain, and owed allegiance to him; and all the civil authority then existing or exercised here, flowed from the head of the British empire. They were in a strict sense fellow subjects and in a variety of respects one people. . . . The revolution, or rather the declaration of independence, found the people already united for general purposes, and at the same time providing for their more domestic concerns by State conventions and other temporary arrangements. From the crown of Great Britain, the sovereignty of their country passed to the people of it; and it was then not an uncommon opinion that the unappropriated lands which belonged to that crown, passed not to the people of the colony or State within whose limits they were situated, but to the whole people. . . .

The people nevertheless continued to consider themselves, in a national point of view, as one people; and they continued, without interruption, to manage their national concerns accordingly; afterwards, in the hurry of the war

[1] 2 Dallas' Rep., 470.

... exercised
... sovereignty and
... vested with be-
... United State do
... then we set the
... country, and it
... a Constitution
... State governments
... State constitutions

... United State
... the United

People's Law of the United States now consists of the written plan of government prepared by the Convention of 1787 and seventeen amendments which have been added under the provisions of the amending clause.

The first ten amendments, usually called the Bill of Rights, state in separate articles as additions to the Constitution, the rights, privileges, and immunities of citizens of the States.

The Eleventh and Twelfth Amendments limit the power of the Federal courts in actions against States and correct the defects in an impossible plan of choosing Presidents and Vice-Presidents of the United States.

The three amendments adopted at the close of the Civil War are additions to the Constitution rather than alterations.

The Sixteenth Amendment permits national taxation of incomes derived from any source, including real estate.

The Seventeenth Amendment provides for the election of United States Senators by the people instead of by State legislatures.

... ... deals with the Constitution and its ... ... logical, rather than in chronological ... ... The Constitution has been changed from time ... ... have arisen, but the order in which ... ... have arisen has been purely accidental ... ... here is to insert these amendments in the places where they logically belong so that the reader ... may easily gain a comprehensive view of the Constitution as it is.

It presents the Constitution as it has been interpreted and explained by the courts and by commentators of established reputation. The court decisions referred to may be found in any well-equipped law library. The titles of such decisions mostly explain themselves. It may be well, however, to note that such titles as *Johnson vs. Smith*, applied to a lawsuit tried before a jury, inform the world that some person named Johnson is suing some other person named Smith. A similar title applied to a decision of the Supreme Court of the United States would mean that "Johnson," having lost his case in the court where it was first tried, has asked the higher court to examine the record of that trial and set the judgment aside because wrongfully rendered. The titles *Ex Parte Johnson*, *In re Johnson*, or *Matter of Johnson*, indicate that somebody named Johnson has asked a court to examine into proceedings which affect his personal interests. For instance, an imprisoned person thinks he has been wrongfully put in jail, his proper course is to ask the courts to order him released. The petition to the judge in such a case is entitled "Ex Parte," or "In re," or "Matter of." A person who believes that he has lost some of his rights as a citizen through the unlawful acts of a public official can gain the attention of the courts in a proceeding in the name of the State or of the United States upon a statement signed by him. Such a proceeding, for example, might be entitled *The People of the State of New York, Ex rel.* (on the relation of) *Johnson, against John Smith, Police Commissioner, etc.* In a Federal case, the title would be *United States of America, Ex rel. Johnson.* Cases against certain things, such as ships, or articles of merchandise forfeited because of attempts to defraud the revenue, are known as actions *in rem*, which means "against a thing." The owners of vessels coming to our harbors are unknown to those who may supply them with provisions and other articles. Hence the law holds the ships responsible. The owners of goods which have been smuggled through the custom-house are seldom known. Therefore the action of forfeiture is brought against the goods which are to be forfeited.

PART II
Nature of the Preamble

CHAPTER III

The opening paragraph of the Constitution is usually called the Preamble, which means preface or introduction, because it states the purposes for which our government was established. It does not give the national government any rights or powers at all. The Supreme Court so ruled in the case of *Jacobson vs. Massachusetts*,[1] in which the point was made that a State law compelling people to be vaccinated as a preventive treatment against smallpox was unconstitutional because it tended to subvert and defeat a purpose of the Constitution of the United States. Justice Harlan said:

Although that Preamble [of the Constitution of the United States] indicates the general purposes for which the people ordained and established the Constitution, it has never been regarded as the source of any substantive power conferred on the Government of the United States or on any of its Departments. Such powers embrace only those expressly granted in the body of the Constitution and such as may be implied from those so granted. Although, therefore, one of the declared objects of the Constitution was to secure the blessings of liberty to all under the sovereign jurisdiction and authority of the United States, no power can be exerted to that end by

[1] 197 U. S. Rep., 11.

the United States, unless, apart from the Preamble, it is
found in some express delegation of power or in some power
to be properly implied therefrom.

**We, the People of the United States, in Order to
form a more perfect Union, establish Justice, insure
domestic Tranquility, provide for the common defense,
promote the general Welfare, and secure the Blessings
of Liberty to ourselves and our Posterity, do ordain
and establish this *Constitution* for the United States
of America.**

We, the People of the United States.   The phrase "We,
the People of the United States," has made the United
States a nation instead of a mere league of friendship
between a number of independent States. "With the
strictest propriety, . . . classical and political," said
Justice James Wilson of the national Supreme Court
in his opinion in the great case of *Chisholm vs. Georgia,* [1]
"our national scene opens with the most magnificent
object which the nation could present. '*The People
of the United States*' are the first personages introduced. Who were those people? They were the
citizens of thirteen States, each of which had a
separate Constitution and government, and all of
which were connected together by Articles of Confederation."

According to the first census, the free population of
the States of the United States in 1790, just after the
Constitution went into effect, was about 3,250,000.
Of these, 2,345,844 were of English origin. There were
188,589 Scotch people and 44,273 Irish. The Dutch,
most of whom lived in New York, numbered 56,623.

[1] 2 Dallas' Rep., 419.

in the Middle States; but in the South almost all the colored people were slaves.[2] Whether or not these negroes were part of the people of the United States was an open question which was not judicially answered until 1857.

The great case of *Dred Scott vs. Sanford*[3] involved the validity of a law made by Congress in 1820 and called the Missouri Compromise Act because it settled in part the dispute over the admission of Missouri to the Union as a slave State. This act, which remained in force until 1854, provided that after the admission of Missouri, slavery should be excluded from all States formed out of the rest of the Louisiana Purchase, north of the parallel of 36° 30'.

In 1834, Dred Scott, a negro slave owned by an army surgeon, was taken by his master to a military post in the State of Illinois, which had been carved out of the Northwest Territory and admitted to the Union as a free State in 1818. Two years later, the negro was taken to a place on the west bank of the Mississippi in what is now the State of Iowa. This place was north of 36° 30'—the dead line of slavery. A few years afterward, having been brought to Missouri, a slave State, he brought an action for his freedom against his master's widow in the courts of that State,

[2] *A Century of Population Growth in the United States*, 1790-1900, p. 116. Government Printing Office, Washington, D. C., 1909.
[1] *Ibid.*, p. 83.　　　　　　　　　[3] 19 Howard's Rep., 393, 404.

...

In defining the phrase, Chief Justice Taney, who gave the opinion of the Court, said:

The words "people of the United States" and "Citizens" are synonymous terms and mean the same thing. They both describe the political body who, according to our republican institutions, form the sovereignty, and who hold the power and conduct the government through their representatives. They are what we familiarly call the "sovereign people," and every citizen is one of this people, and a constituent member of this sovereignty.

CHAPTER IV

PURPOSES OF THE CONSTITUTION

In Order to form a more perfect Union. Under the Confederation, the States seem to have done what they could to show the world that the United States was lacking in everything which makes nationality worth while. "Flushed with the enjoyment of sovereign power [the States] increased instead of diminishing measures incompatible with their relations to the Federal government."[1] New York and Pennsylvania, which had good, deep-water harbors, levied customs duties on merchandise going to New Jersey, which had none. Virginia and South Carolina exploited North Carolina in the same way. There was every chance that the young nation would break up unless a more perfect union could be made.

The new Constitution established that more perfect union. The Supreme Court so declared in its decision of the case of *Texas vs. White.*[2]

In 1851, the United States had paid over to the State of Texas five million dollars in United States five per cent. bonds in settlement of a disputed boundary claim. A few of these bonds were in the treasury of the State of Texas when the Civil War began in 1861.

[1] Madison's *Journal*, Intro., p. 34. Albert Scott & Co., Chicago, 1894.

In January, 1862, after Texas had seceded, the State legislature authorized the sale of these bonds to provide funds for the military purposes of the Confederate States. In March, 1865, after the collapse of the Confederacy, but before the actual close of the Civil War, one hundred and thirty-five of these bonds of a par value of $135,000 were delivered to Mr. White, one of the defendants in this case, pursuant to a contract of sale, and he in turn sold and delivered these bonds to other persons. In 1866, a Texas State Convention adopted an ordinance authorizing a lawsuit for the recovery of these bonds or their value, and the governor brought action against Mr. White for that purpose. The question which the Supreme Court of the United States had to decide was whether the State of Texas ever had authorized the sale of the bonds. The Court sustained the demand of the governor on the ground that the Confederate State government which had authorized the sale of the bonds, had had no valid or legal existence, and had been able to do no valid or legal act, such as authorizing a sale of State property, because it had been arrayed in arms against the *more perfect Union* created by the Constitution. Chief Justice Salmon P. Chase said:

The Union of the States never was a purely artificial and arbitrary relation. It began among the Colonies and grew out of common origin, mutual sympathies, kindred principles, similar interests, and geographical relations. It was confirmed and strengthened by the necessities of war, and received definite form, and character, and sanction from the Articles of Confederation. By these, the Union was solemnly declared to "be perpetual." And when these Articles were found to be inadequate to the exigencies of the country, the Constitution was ordained "to form a

interfere in the internal troubles of any State. Hence the Constitution makers were under a bounden duty to give to the new government power to keep the peace in a State. It was lucky they included this purpose, because the Whiskey Rebellion in Western Pennsylvania, an organized protest against the internal revenue tax on whiskey, which broke out in 1794, would have spread along the back country from New York to Georgia if the Federal Government had not had power "to insure domestic tranquility." Also, the clauses of the Constitution which made this purpose effective, gave President Lincoln and Congress power to take measures to restore domestic tranquillity in the Southern States which attempted to secede in 1861.

In order to . . . provide for the common defence. The old plan of government also had failed in this: whereas the Articles of Confederation had provided only that

' 2 Dallas' Rep., 419.

each of the States should pay its proportionate share
of the expenses of defense against foreign attacks, no
method of compelling a State to pay its part of the
cost had been provided. The Constitution makers
knew how much this defect had meant. Many of them
had served in the Continental Congress during the Revolution and could remember that the States, with few
exceptions, either had been slow in providing their
quotas of men and supplies, or had failed altogether
to obey the requisitions made upon them.

Our government really was on trial until it had
survived the rude test of the Civil War. Other nations
were not sure that the Federal Union which had been
created to meet the emergencies of the little United
States of 1787, would stand the strain when nearly a
compact half of the States of the greater Union of 1861
wanted to break it up. It stood the test mainly because
the statesmen of that era found in the Constitution
some national powers available for the common defense,
which the framers of that instrument did not grant in
specific words to the central government. One of the
most important of these discoveries was the power to
issue paper money in order to meet the expense of the
common defense of the nation.

In order to . . . . promote the general Welfare. There
had been fairly good times during the Revolution
because the people were united by a common danger
and were inclined to deal fairly with one another. There
had been little or no competition from abroad and a
few simple industries had been established and were
prosperous. After the war was over, things were different. Each of the States asserted its rights by making it almost impossible for outsiders to trade with its
citizens. Foreign governments imposed ruinous port

duties upon American goods, and foreign merchants flooded our markets with manufactures at prices which American producers could not meet. "While London merchants enjoyed the benefits of free trade with the States, American oil was taxed £18 per ton and tobacco 16 pence a pound in Liverpool."[1] It was quite generally agreed that the Confederation had been a failure, because under it the "united States in Congress assembled" had had no control over the States in commercial matters. That being the case, the natural thing to do was to give the new central government all powers needful for the regulation of foreign and domestic commerce.

Among the first acts of the first administration of President Washington was the negotiation of a commercial treaty with Great Britain, which seems to have been a little, but not much, better than nothing, and a customs revenue law which imposed protective duties on goods imported from foreign countries. The treaty and the law were regulations of commerce with a foreign country and were consistent with the Constitution. Some of the States, however, were inclined to try out conclusions with the nation, if a way could be found; for the power to regulate commerce by tariff legislation cut into the revenue-raising powers of the local governments. Maryland, for example, soon after the beginning of the nineteenth century enacted a law which required all importers of foreign articles to pay an annual license fee. A Baltimore merchant who had imported merchandise without a license was tried and convicted on a charge of misdemeanor. He took his case to the United States Supreme Court on the ground

[1] McMaster's *History of the People of the United States*, vol. i, pp. 246, 248.

3

the Maryland law was unconstitutional. The
[...] Court, thereupon, ruled that a State law im-
[...] any restriction upon dealing in imported goods
[...] regulation of commerce with foreign nations which
[...] has power to make, that power, by the Con-
[...] being vested for the general welfare in the
[...] States. This was the case of *Brown vs. Mary-
[...]* Chief Justice Marshall said in part:

[...] oppressed and degraded state of commerce previ-
[...] the adoption of the Constitution can scarcely be
[...]. It was regulated by foreign nations with a
[...] to their own interests; and our disunited
[...] to counteract their restrictions were rendered im-
[...] by want of combination. Congress, indeed, posses-
[...] power of making treaties; but the inability of
[...] government to enforce them had become so
[...] as to render that power in a great degree useless.
[...] who felt the injury arising from this state of things,
[...] who were capable of estimating the influence of
[...] on the prosperity of nations, perceived the
[...] of giving the control over this important sub-
[...] a single government. It may be doubted whether
[...] the evils proceeding from the feebleness of the
[...] government contributed more to that great revolu-
which introduced the present system, than the deep
[...] conviction that commerce ought to be regulated
[...] ngress.

*order to . . . secure the Blessings of Liberty to
[...]res and our Posterity.* The right to life has been
[...]ed as the right to live, to marry, and govern the
[...], without interference; the right to liberty, as
[...]ight to do and believe at will; and the right to
[...]ursuit of happiness as the right to earn a living

Wheaton's Rep., 419.

in the way each man likes best.   In this sentence in
the Preamble, the Constitution makers announced that
the instrument of government they were creating had
for one of its objects the preservation of these blessings
of liberty.   Elsewhere in the Constitution, they made
provision for a few of the rights of the States and of the
citizens of the States.   The people of the United States
added to the Constitution ten amendments, known as
the Bill of Rights, which prohibit the national government from interfering with the "blessings of liberty."

The "blessings of liberty" thus secured to the people of the United States by their fundamental law, were
explained by the Supreme Court in the case of *Allgeyer
vs. Louisiana.*[1]   This case hinged upon the constitutionality of a Louisiana statute which prohibited all persons
from doing in that State any act placing insurance on
property in any marine insurance company which had
not complied with certain State regulations concerning
such companies.   Allgeyer & Co. had mailed a letter
to the Atlantic Insurance Company of New York,
advising them that a shipment of cotton had been
made in accordance with the terms of an open marine
policy which it had issued.   The Supreme Court of
Louisiana said that this was a violation of the statute.
The firm carried the case to the Supreme Court at
Washington on the ground that the State law was
unconstitutional in that it deprived them of their liberty
without due process of law.   And the Supreme Court
agreed with them.   Justice Peckham, in giving the
decision, defined the word "liberty" as follows:

The Supreme Court of Louisiana says that the act of
writing within that State, the letter of notification, was an

[1] 165 U. S. Rep., 578.

act therein done to effect an insurance on property then in the State, in a marine insurance company which had not complied with its laws, and such an act was, therefore, prohibited by the statute. As so construed we think the statute is a violation of the Fourteenth Amendment of the Federal Constitution, in that it deprives the defendants of their liberty without due process of law. The statute which forbids such an act does not become due process of law, because it is inconsistent with the provisions of the Constitution of the Union. The liberty mentioned in that amendment means not only the right of the citizen to be free from the mere physical restraint of his person, as by incarceration, but the term is deemed to embrace the right of the citizen to be free in the enjoyment of all his faculties; to be free to use them in all lawful ways; to live and work where he will; to earn his livelihood by any lawful calling; to pursue any livelihood or avocation, and for that purpose to enter into all contracts which may be proper, necessary, and essential to his carrying out to a successful conclusion the purposes above mentioned.

PART III
Organization of the Federal Congress

CHAPTER V

Art. I., Sec. 1. All legislative Powers herein granted shall be vested in a Congress of the United States, which shall consist of a Senate and House of Representatives.

The word "Congress" was first applied to the meeting at New York, in 1765, of representatives from the provinces of Massachusetts, Rhode Island, Connecticut, New York, New Jersey, Pennsylvania, Delaware, Maryland, and South Carolina, to protest against the Stamp Act. The First Continental Congress began its sessions at Philadelphia on September 5, 1774. The Second Continental Congress assembled in the same place on May 10, 1775. The Declaration of Independence refers to the "Representatives of the united States of America in General Congress assembled" and the Articles of Confederation speaks of the "United States of America in Congress assembled." It was natural, therefore, when the framers of the Constitution met in Convention that the term "Congress" should be inserted in the Constitution as representing the legislative branch of the government of the United States; but prior to that time, it was a comparatively new term in the history of legislation.[1]

[1] Summarized from Watson, *On the Constitution*, vol. i., p. 122. Chicago, Callaghan & Co., 1910.

"Free government," said Judge Vann of the New York Court of Appeals in his opinion in the case of *Matter of Davies*,[1] "consists of three departments, each with distinct and independent powers, designed to operate as a check upon those of the other two coordinate branches. The legislative department makes the laws, while the executive executes and the judiciary construes and applies them. Each department is confined to its own functions and can neither encroach upon nor be made subordinate to those of another without violating the fundamental principle of a republican form of government."

Congress cannot make any law which is not authorized by some clause of the People's Law. In *Hayburn's Case*,[2] a wounded Revolutionary soldier asked the Federal Circuit Court of Pennsylvania to examine into his claims to a pension under the provisions of an Act of Congress which declared that the circuit courts of the United States should act as pension examining boards. The court to which this application was made refused to perform the duties imposed by this act on the ground that Congress had no power under the Constitution to make a law requiring the courts to perform duties, which are administrative, not judicial, in character, and sent a letter to President Washington, in which the judges explained that the Constitution does not authorize Congress to pass a law under which a judicial body is to perform an executive function. They said:

Congress have lately passed an act to regulate, among other things, "the claims to invalid pensions." Upon due consideration, we have been unanimously of opinion, that

---

[1] 168 New York Rep., 89, 101.   [2] 2 Dallas' Rep., 411.

under this act, the Circuit Court held for the Pennsylvania District could not proceed: . . . Because the business directed by this act is not of a judicial nature. It forms no part of the power vested by the Constitution in the courts of the United States; the Circuit Court must consequently have proceeded without constitutional authority.

Art. I., Sec. 2. The House of Representatives shall be composed of Members chosen every second Year by the People of the several States, and the Electors in each State shall have the Qualifications requisite for Electors of the most numerous Branch of the State Legislature.

The two-year term of members of the House of Representatives was the result of a compromise in the Constitutional Convention. The delegates who thought members ought not to sit more than one year had to admit that such a term would be too short in the case of members from Georgia, some of whom would not have undertaken the six weeks' journey from Savannah to Philadelphia if they had had to return ten months later to stand for reëlection. Those who thought a longer term of office desirable had to agree that a member would be less likely to disregard the wishes of his constituents if he knew that he would have to ask for their votes within two years.

By the People of the several States. The People of the United States, by whom members of the House of Representatives are chosen, are the citizens of the States of the United States. This rule was established by the Supreme Court, in 1857, in the case of *Dred Scott vs. Sanford.*[1]

[1] 19 Howard's Rep., 393. *See* above.

Fourteenth Amendment. Sec. 1. (In part.) All persons born or naturalized in the United States, and subject to the jurisdiction thereof, are citizens of the United States and of the State wherein they reside.

The Fourteenth Amendment, adopted in 1868, increased the number of the "People of the United States" by making all persons, including negroes, born or naturalized here and under this jurisdiction, citizens of the United States and of the States in which they reside. The condition of colored people under the law had been undefined. In some States, they had been citizens. In others, where slavery had prevailed, they had been classed with domestic animals.

And the Electors in each State shall have the Qualifications requisite for Electors of the most numerous Branch of the State Legislature. Each State fixes the qualifications of the voters who choose the members of the most numerous branch of its legislature and the Constitution declares that those voters shall be electors of members of the National House of Representatives. The Constitution does not give the States any right or power to control elections of members of Congress. The Supreme Court passed upon this very question in the case of *Ex Parte Yarbrough.*[1] Jasper Yarbrough and seven others had been found guilty in the United States Court of Georgia upon indictments which charged them with having intimidated and otherwise prevented one Berry Saunders, a negro citizen, from voting at an election for member of Congress. They immediately petitioned the Supreme Court to order their release under a writ of habeas corpus on the ground that Congress

[1] 110 U. S. Rep., 651.

had no power to enact the law regulating State elections at which representatives in Congress were chosen. Their contention was that such power vested exclusively in the States, which, under this clause, fix the qualifications of electors of the most numerous branch of the State legislature, who were thereby qualified for voting at elections of members of Congress. Justice Miller, who delivered the opinion of the Court, said:

The States in prescribing the qualifications of voters for the most numerous branch of their own legislatures, do not do this with reference to the election of members of Congress. Nor can they prescribe the qualification for voters for those *eo nomine*. They define who are to vote for the popular branch of their own legislature, and the Constitution of the United States says the same persons shall vote for members of Congress in that State. It adopts the qualification thus furnished, as the qualification of its own electors for members of Congress.

Art. I., Sec. 2. (Continued.) No Person shall be a Representative who shall not have attained to the Age of twenty-five Years, and have been seven Years a Citizen of the United States, and who shall not, when elected, be an Inhabitant of that State in which he shall be chosen.

No Person shall be a Representative. In the case of *Minor vs. Happersett*,[1] the Supreme Court decided that no woman can sit in the House of Representatives. On October 15, 1872, Mrs. Virginia Minor, a native born, free, white citizen of Missouri, over twenty-one years of age, applied to one Happersett, the local registrar of voters, to register her as a lawful voter. He refused on the ground that she was not a "male citizen of the United States." She sued him for damages. The State court gave judgment in his favor. The case then was taken to the Supreme Court of the United States on the ground that Mrs. Minor, as a native born citizen of the United States, had, under the Constitution as changed by the Fourteenth Amendment, the privilege of voting, which the State of Missouri was forbidden to abridge. Obviously, if a female person were entitled to the suffrage, she would be a person who could be a representative in Congress. Chief Justice Waite said:

Being unanimously of the opinion that the Constitution of the United States does not confer the right of suffrage upon any one, and that the constitutions and laws of the several States which commit that trust to men alone are not necessarily void, we affirm the [State court] judgment.

Who shall not have attained to the Age of twenty-five Years. No person can sit as a member of the House of Representatives until he is twenty-five years old. He cannot take the oath of office while under this age limit.

In the case of *Smith vs. Brown,*[1] which was heard before the House Committee on Elections in 1868, it appeared that Mr. Brown was under twenty-five when elected. He did not take his seat, however, until the second session of the Congress to which he had been elected. He was then over the constitutional age and his right to membership was admitted.

And been seven Years a Citizen of the United States. Seven years probably was fixed upon as the period of

[1] House Election Case, 2 Bart., 403.

citizenship qualification, because the First Congress under the Constitution was to meet in December, 1790, just seven years after the Peace of Paris of 1783, which had ended the Revolutionary War. The foreign soldiers who had fought in the War for Independence and had then settled here and become citizens of States were thus made eligible for this high national office.

"The term citizen," according to the opinion in the case of *Amy vs. Little*,[1] "is derived from the Latin word, *civis*, and in its primary sense signifies one who is vested with the freedom and privileges of a city. . . . When the term came to be applied to the inhabitants of a state, it necessarily carried with it the same signification with reference to the privileges of the state, which had been implied by it with reference to the privileges of a city, when it was applied to the inhabitants of the city; and it is in this sense that the term, citizen, is believed to be generally, if not universally understood in the United States."

Under the Fourteenth Amendment "all persons born or naturalized in the United States and subject to the jurisdiction thereof are citizens of the United States." A person of the Chinese race is eligible according to the decision in *United States vs. Wong Kim Ark*,[2] in which a Chinaman born in the United States insisted that he was a citizen.

In 1873, Wong Kim Ark was born in San Francisco, where his mother and father had a permanent home and were in business. In 1890, the family went back to China on a visit, and on July 26, of that year, the young man came back to San Francisco, where he was detained and ordered deported, under the Exclusion Act, as a Chinese laborer. He sued out a writ of

[1] 11 Kentucky Rep., 326. [2] 169 U. S. Rep., 649.

habeas corpus, a process by which a court investigates the legality of an imprisonment. The case went on appeal to the Supreme Court, where a majority of the justices ruled that he could not be deported because he was a citizen. Justice Gray stated the opinion of the Court as follows:

The evident intention and the necessary effect of the submission of the case to the decision of the Court upon the facts agreed upon by the parties, were to present for determination the single question, stated at the beginning of the opinion, namely, whether a child born in the United States of parents of Chinese descent, who at the time of his birth, are subjects of the Emperor of China, but have a permanent domicile and residence in the United States, and are there carrying on business, and are not employed in any diplomatic or official capacity under the Emperor of China, becomes at the time of his birth a citizen of the United States. . . . This Court is of opinion that the question must be answered in the affirmative.

The liberties, rights, privileges and immunities which belong to each citizen of the United States quite as much as the coat on his back are his property because it is his law that he shall possess them. But just as it is true that he may have them, so it is also true that he may lose them by his own act. He holds them by keeping within his law which gives and regulates his possession. He may lose them by going outside of his law of possession and becoming an outlaw.

In old times, the felon lost his life and forfeited his goods; that is, he forfeited the law or right by which he held his possessions. When punishments became more humane, forfeiture of property was abolished and only a few of the rights of the citizen; chiefly the right to vote, were declared forfeited. Some other rights (for example, the right to maintain actions in courts of law) were forfeited by the man who broke the rules of the law; for the law never shielded those who defied it. Nowadays, the right of the convict to the protection of the laws is suspended so long as he is in prison. When he comes out, he may again have the equal protection of the laws, guaranteed by the Fourteenth Amendment. His right to vote, however, is forfeited unless, by special clemency, it be restored by the power which took it away.

The citizen who voluntarily goes away from the United States and stays away, abandons his right to the protection of his own nation. At the time of the Franco-Prussian War of 1870, and for some time afterward, many prosperous Americans who had made their homes in France for years and a number of French people who had been naturalized in the United States and then had returned to their native places, applied for protection to our minister to France.

Minister Washburne applied to Hamilton Fish, then Secretary of State, for instructions and received the following reply[1]:

The Court of Claims, adopting the language of one of my predecessors, Mr. Seward, has decided it to be the law and usage of nations that one who takes up his residence in a foreign place and there suffers an injury to his property by reason of belligerent acts committed against that place by another foreign nation must abide the chances of the country in which he chooses to reside, and his only chance, if any, is against the government of that country in which his own sovereign will not interest himself.

Two years later, a number of Frenchmen who had

[1] Diplomatic Correspondence of the United States, Secretary Fish to Minister Washburne, April 28, 1871.

been naturalized in the United States and then had returned to their old homes, were required to serve in the French army. They asked the United States Minister to interfere on the ground that, as citizens of the United States, they could not legally be compelled to perform military service for another country. Incidentally, some of the people who complained were the sons of naturalized Americans who had resided in France with their families for nearly forty years. This time Secretary Fish went more deeply into the question as follows[1]:

If, on the one hand, the government assumes the duty of protecting his rights and privileges, on the other hand, the citizen is supposed to be ever ready to place his fortune and even his life at its service, should the public necessities demand such a sacrifice. If, instead of doing this, he permanently withdraws his person from the national jurisdiction; if he places his property where it cannot be made to contribute to the national necessities; if his children are born or reared upon a foreign soil, with no purpose of returning to submit to the jurisdiction of the United States, then, in accordance with the principles laid down by Chief Justice Marshall, and recognized in the Fourteenth Amendment, and in the Act of 1868, he has so far *expatriated* himself as to relieve this government from the obligation of interference for his protection. . . . Each case as it arises must be decided on its own merits. In each, the main fact to be determined will be this,—has there been such a practical expatriation as removes the individual from the jurisdiction of the United States? If there has not been the applicant will be entitled to protection.

The United States always has recognized the right of expatriation as "a natural and inherent right of all, indispensable to the enjoyment of the rights of life, lib-

[1] Ibid. pp. 156, 157.

erty, and the pursuit of happiness." Chief Justice Marshall stated the law on this point in the case of *Murray vs. Schooner 'Charming Betsey*,'[1] in which the facts were as follows: Jared Shattuck, born in the United States, had, while a child, removed with his parents to St. Thomas in the Danish West Indies, where he remained. He traded there as a Danish subject, married and bought land there, and took an oath of allegiance to the crown of Denmark. In 1800, he bought a schooner, the *Jane* from Baltimore, at St. Thomas, loaded her with American produce and sent her out from Guadeloupe as a Danish vessel. She was captured on the high seas by a French privateer and was captured again by Captain Murray of the frigate *Constellation*, then employed in enforcing the Act of Congress of April 27, 1800, which suspended commercial intercourse between the United States and France, and declared forfeited all vessels employed in illicit commerce owned by persons residing in the United States. Captain Murray took the schooner to Martinique and began court proceedings to have her condemned and sold as a prize. At this juncture, Mr. Shattuck filed in court a claim that the ship and cargo belonged to him as a Danish burgher, and so were not subject to seizure under the Non-Intercourse Act. This claim had to be recognized, if under all the circumstances he had ceased to be a citizen of the United States and had become a subject of the King of Denmark. The Court decided that he was a Danish subject. Chief Justice Marshall said:

Jared Shattuck is not a person under the protection of the United States. The American citizen who goes into a

---

[1] 2 Cranch Rep., 64.

4

military

... ner

... of his

... municipal

... a right

... of the

... considered as

... completely

... himself the

... may not

... for any crime

... not intended

... of the pro-

... territory of the

...

... *be an Inhabitant of*

... **"An 'inhabitant'**

... second section of

...," it is said in the

... who is *bona fide* a

... the requisitions of

... privileges and advan-

...

... been defined to mean one of

... the United States, one of the

... of the United States.   In

... *Riley*, which was decided in the

... Court in 1804, the question at issue was

... of Columbia was a "State" within

... that word as used in the Constitution.

... Marshall and.

... the Judiciary Act] obviously uses

... to that term as used in the

Constitution, it becomes necessary to inquire whether [the District of] Columbia is a State in the sense of that instrument. The result of that examination is a conviction that the members of the American confederacy only are the States contemplated in the Constitution.

Art. I., Sec. 2. (Continued.) Representatives and direct Taxes shall be apportioned among the several States which may be included within this Union, according to their respective Numbers, which shall be determined by adding to the whole Number of free persons, including those bound to Service for a Term of Years, and excluding Indians not taxed, three fifths of all other Persons. The actual Enumeration shall be made within three Years after the first Meeting of the Congress of the United States, and within every subsequent Term of ten Years, in such Manner as they shall by Law direct. The Number of Representatives shall not exceed one for every thirty Thousand, but each State shall have at Least one Representative; and until such Enumeration shall be made, the State of New Hampshire shall be entitled to chuse three, Massachusetts eight, Rhode-Island and Providence Plantations one, Connecticut five, New-York six, New Jersey four, Pennsylvania eight, Delaware one, Maryland six, Virginia ten, North Carolina five, South Carolina five, and Georgia three.

The House of Representatives in the First Congress was organized according to the program prescribed in this clause. The qualified electors in each State, except North Carolina and Rhode Island, which joined the Union afterward, chose the number of members allotted to them. This First Congress, which met at New York in April, 1789, passed the Act under which the census

foreign country, although he ... ...
allegiance to that country ... ; or if he ... ...
act changing his condition entitled ... protecting the
own government; and if, with ... ... the second
law, he should be oppressed under it, ... years,
to claim that protection, and ... ... inhab-
American governm ... ...
a ju ... ...
chang ...

subject of a foreign ... ...monly
... ...
... ... the United ... ... the Su-
... ... city *of*
... ... assem ...ly then
... ... Depar ... ... cities
... ... inhab-

And who shall ... ...
half State ... all of the ... ... were to
on a State ... ...
the ... ... The ... ... Huntington
case a ... ... the ity had
men ... ... that its
its ... and ... ... metropolitan
tags which ... ... Court

The Act ... ... law which ... ... that the
the ... ... minded per-
... ... the ... ... had not
... ... to the city ... ... with the
... church of the city ... ... easily
... ... at E ... the ... ... therefore
... ... the ... ... the ity
... I was sure there w ... ... because a
... ... the ity then
... ... had

been taken. Chief Justice Howard of the Supreme Court of Indiana said in the decision of this case that the city was right, basing his opinion upon the following definition of the word "census."

The statute mentions the census to be taken by the mayor in connection with the census taken by the United States. Even if it were not mentioned in such connection, we should know that the census provided for in the statute, to be taken by the mayor of the city, must be an official enumeration of the people, and as such a public record. The standard definitions are to this effect. Webster says that a census is "An official registration of the number of the people." The *Century Dictionary:* "An official enumeration of the inhabitants of a State or country. . . ." The *Standard Dictionary:* "An official numbering of the people of a country or district." Burrill, *Law Dict.:* "In the Roman law, a numbering or enrollment of the people, with a valuation of their fortunes." Black, *Law Dict.:* "The official counting or enumeration of the people of a State or nation, with statistics." Bouvier, *Law Dict.:* "An official reckoning or enumeration of the inhabitants and wealth of a country."

Representatives and direct Taxes shall be apportioned among the several States which may be included within this Union, according to their respective Numbers, which shall be determined by adding to the whole Number of free persons, including those bound to Service for a Term of Years, and excluding Indians not taxed, three fifths of all other Persons. "Those bound to service for a term of years" were indentured servants, who had been brought to the colonies in large numbers under contracts to labor for a term of years to repay the cost of their passage. The words "three fifths of all other persons" refer to slaves then held in large numbers in the South. This

clause was the result of a compromise in the Federal
Convention. The slaveholders insisted that the negroes
were inhabitants who ought to be counted in the census
enumerations which were to be made. The Northern
men would not consent to a plan which would have
given a few hundred slave owners as large a number of
Congressmen as many thousand farmers and merchants
in the free States. They were able to agree upon a
compromise chiefly because the Southern delegates felt
safe in accepting a plan limiting the amount of taxes
which could be assessed upon their real estate, in the
same proportion as it diminished the representation of
their States in the House of Representatives. Justice
Paterson said in his opinion in the case of *Hylton vs.
United States* :

This provision was made in favor of the southern States.
They possessed a large number of slaves; they had extensive
tracts of territory, thinly settled, and not very productive.
A majority of the States had but few slaves, and several
of them a limited territory, well settled, and in a high state
of cultivation. The southern States, if no provision had
been introduced in the Constitution, would have been
wholly at the mercy of the other States. Congress in such
case might tax slaves, at discretion or arbitrarily, and land
in every part of the Union after the same rate or measure;
so much a head in the first instance, and so much an acre
in the other. To guard them against imposition in these
particulars was the reason of introducing the clause in the
Constitution, which directs that representatives and direct
taxes shall be apportioned among the States according to
their respective numbers.

Fourteenth Amendment. Sec. 2. Representatives
shall be apportioned among the several States, accord-

ing to their respective numbers, counting the whole number of persons in each State, excluding Indians not taxed. But when the right to vote at any election for the choice of electors for President and Vice President of the United States, Representatives in Congress, the Executive and Judicial officers of a State, or the members of the Legislature thereof, is denied to any of the male inhabitants of such State, being twenty-one years of age, and citizens of the United States, or in any way abridged, except for participation in rebellion, or other crime, the basis representation therein shall be reduced in the proportion which the number of such male citizens shall bear to the whole number of male citizens twenty-one years of age in such State.

The basis of apportionment in the original Constitution went to the scrap heap when slavery was abolished as a part of the outcome of the Civil War. Therefore it was necessary to formulate a new plan of computation. This was accomplished by the Fourteenth Amendment, adopted in 1868, which made all persons born or naturalized in the United States, and subject to its jurisdiction, citizens of the United States, and omitted all reference to "those bound to service for a term of years" and to "three-fifths of all other persons." There could be no indentured servants and no slaves, because involuntary servitude, except as punishment for crime, and slavery had been prohibited by the Thirteenth Amendment, adopted in 1865.

Every one knows that there are restrictions on the rights of citizens of the United States to vote at State and National elections. New York requires the citizen, before voting, to register and sign his name. Massachusetts and some other States have educational qualifications, such as ability to read any section of the State Constitution or understand it when read or give a reasonable interpretation of it. Such restrictions do not deny or abridge the right of citizens of the United States to vote "on account of race, color, or previous condition of servitude."[1]   The validity of an educational test was challenged in Mississippi, in the case of *Dixon vs. State*.[2]   In this case, a man who had been convicted of murder asked the Supreme Court to set aside the verdict on the ground that the State Constitution under which the law for the punishment of murder had been passed, was void because inconsistent with the provisions of the Fourteenth Amendment. Chief Justice Cooper took occasion in the course of the decision of this case to say that such educational qualifications are proper:

All these provisions, if fairly and impartially administered, apply with equal force to the individual white and negro citizen.   It may be, and unquestionably is, true that, so administered, their operation will be to exclude from the exercise of the elective franchise a greater proportionate number of colored than of white persons.   But this is not because one is white and the other colored, but, because of superior advantages and circumstances possessed by the one race over the other, a greater number of the more fortunate race is found to possess the qualifications which the framers of the Constitution deemed essential for the exercise of the elective franchise.

Direct Taxes shall be apportioned among the several States which may be included within this Union, according to their respective Numbers.   In the days of the Constitution makers, there was a reason why direct

fair thing then was to charge up such taxes, if needed, against each of the States, making the thickly settled communities carry the heavier part of the burden and putting the lighter share on those which were sparsely inhabited.

There has been little direct taxation in our national history. The first direct tax, authorized in 1798 in anticipation of a war with France, apportioned to the States a tax of two million dollars assessed upon "dwelling houses, lands, and slaves,"[1] which in some States were classed by law as real estate. A second national direct tax of three million dollars was levied in 1813, and apportioned to the States.[2] The third direct tax[3] of six million dollars, apportioned in 1815 among the States on "all lands, lots of grounds with their improvements, dwelling houses and slaves," grew out of the War of 1812. There was no further need of direct taxes until the beginning of the Civil War. Sales of public lands and low customs and internal revenue duties produced a national income so large that the government once divided a surplus among the States. In 1861, however, Congress voted to raise twenty million dollars by a direct tax on real estate,[4] apportioned to the States. Since the Civil War, Congress has not enacted any laws taxing real estate and

[1] 1 U. S. Stats., 597.
[3] 3 U. S. Stats., 164.
[2] 3 U. S. Stats., 33.
[4] 12 U. S. Stats., 294.

apportioning the amount among the States. The reason is that, as wealth is distributed in modern times, the commercial States of the North, in proportion to population, are more prosperous in money values than the great agricultural States of the South, although the people on an average may be as comfortable in one section as in the other.

Soon after the Constitution went into operation the courts were called upon to explain just what a direct tax is. On June 5, 1794, Congress enacted a law taxing "carriages for the conveyance of persons, which shall be kept by or for any person for his or her own use, or to be let out for hire or for the conveyance of passengers." Daniel Lawrence Hylton, who owned and kept for hire one hundred and twenty-five chariots, refused to pay the tax, on the ground that, as it was assessed directly on carriages, it was a direct tax and unconstitutional because not apportioned among the States according to population. The proceedings which followed constitute the case of *Hylton vs. The United States*,[1] which is one of the monuments of American law. Justice Samuel Chase said in this case:

It appears to me that a tax on carriages cannot be laid by the rule of apportionment, without very great inequality and injustice. For example, suppose two States equal in census, to pay eighty thousand dollars each, by a tax on carriages of eight dollars on every carriage, and in one State there are one hundred carriages, and in the other one thousand. The owners of carriages in one State would pay ten times the tax of owners in the other. A, in one State, would pay for his carriage eight dollars; but B, in the other State, would pay for his carriage eighty dollars. . . . I am inclined to think, but of this I do not give a judicial

[1] 3 Dallas Rep., 171.

opinion, that the direct taxes contemplated by the Constitution are only two, to wit, a capitation or poll tax, simply, without regard to property, profession, or any other circumstance, and a tax on land. I doubt whether a tax by a general assessment of personal property, within the United States, is included within the term direct tax.

Justice Paterson, in his opinion in the same case, said more distinctly:

I never entertained a doubt that the principal, I will not say, the only objects, that the framers of the Constitution contemplated as falling within the rule of apportionment, were a capitation tax and a tax on land.

Art. I., Sec. 2. (Continued.) When vacancies happen in the Representation from any State, the Executive Authority thereof shall issue Writs of Election to fill such Vacancies.

All vacancies which result from the death, resignation, or removal of a representative, or from his acceptance of an office incompatible with that of representative, may be filled on this plan.

Art. I., Sec. 2. (Continued.) The House of Representatives shall chuse their Speaker and other Officers, and shall have the sole Power of Impeachment.

"In designating the presiding officer of the House, 'the Speaker,' the Convention," says Watson, *On the Constitution*, "follows the rule which prevailed in the [British] House of Commons. The presiding officer of the Colonial Congress was called 'The President.' Each political party in the House nominates its candidates for Speaker, Clerk, Sergeant-at-Arms, Door Keeper,

Postmaster, and Chaplain, in caucus. The successful candidates of the caucus are then nominated by their respective parties at a meeting of the members of the House and the candidates of the dominant party are elected to their respective offices."[1]

The sole Power of Impeachment. "Impeachment, in the United States," according to Watson, "is an accusation in writing, by the House of Representatives, presented to the United States Senate, against a civil officer of the government. . . . The power of impeachment is of great importance. It is intended to reach civil officers occupying influential positions in the government and who are not punishable under ordinary statutes, because general legislation does not reach such cases."[2]

The House of Representatives has arbitrary power to impeach government officials. A grand jury cannot find a valid indictment except upon some evidence that the accused person has committed a crime. But the national House of Representatives can file charges against any Federal officer without any evidence at all; and, even in that case, the Senate must receive the articles of impeachment and sit in judgment upon the accused.

[1] Watson, *On the Constitution*, i., 203.
[2] *Ibid.*, 207.

CHAPTER VI

THE SENATE OF THE UNITED STATES

Art. I., Sec. 3. The Senate of the United States shall be composed of two Senators from each State, chosen by the Legislature thereof, for six Years; and each Senator shall have one Vote.

This section was superseded in 1913 by the Seventeenth Amendment.

Seventeenth Amendment. The Senate of the United States shall be composed of two Senators from each State, elected by the people thereof, for six years; and each Senator shall have one vote. The electors in each State shall have the qualifications requisite for electors of the most numerous branch of the State legislatures.

The Senate is a sort of diplomatic body, whose members represent their States near the seat of the Federal Government. It always has been in a special way the guardian of the rights of the States rather than of the rights of the people, who have their own representatives in their own legislative body.

The Senate . . . shall be composed of two Senators from each State, chosen by the Legislature thereof, for six years. (Art. I., Sec. 3.)

The Senate . . . shall be composed of two Senators from each State, elected by the people thereof, for six years. (Seventeenth Amendment).   The makers of the Constitution seem to have thought that the Senators were to be diplomatic officers of the States, who ought not to be responsible to many masters because they were to be entrusted with diplomatic secrets of great importance. They were quite sure that the people were not to be trusted.   They felt that the lives and property of those who had something to lose would be a deal safer if the many did not have too much to say in the public business.   Twentieth-century Americans have learned to trust to the wisdom and prudence of the people.

The longer term of office gave the Senate an advantage over the other branch of Congress.   For example, on March 3, 1903, Congressman Cannon, afterward Speaker of the House, reported as one of a Committee of Conference that an appropriation bill would have to be so amended as to pay to one of the States a sum of money to which, in the opinion of the House of Representatives, it had no honest claim.   The reason was that the Congress was to come to an end at midnight of that day and one of the Senators had said that, if the appropriation amendment was not agreed to, he would keep on talking until the Congress and the appropriation bill died together.   The Senator could talk as long as he chose, because there is no time limit set upon senatorial speakers; and by talking, he could prevent the passage of a law which had to be enacted in order to enable the nation to keep faith with its creditors.   The Senator might not have been so aggressive if he had had to look forward to popular election as each member of the House always must do.   Mr. Cannon's protest on this occasion is worth remembering.   He declared with emphasis that the Senate should change its procedure, or that another body, "backed up by the people, will compel that change; else this body, close to the people, shall become a mere tender, a bender of the pregnant hinges of the knee to submit to what any one member of another body may demand of this body as a price for legislation."[1]

Each Senator shall have one vote. James Madison commented as follows on this clause of the Constitution:

It is well known that the equality of the States in the Federal Senate was a compromise between the larger and the smaller States, the former claiming a proportional representation in both branches of the Legislature, as due to their superior population; the latter, an equality in both, as a safeguard to the reserved sovereignty of the States, an object which obtained the concurrence of members from the larger States.[2]

The electors [of Senators] in each State shall have the qualifications requisite for electors of the most numerous branch of the State legislatures (Seventeenth Amendment). This part of the amendment, made necessary by the changed method of election, repeats word for word the clause which prescribes the qualification of electors of members of the House of Representatives.

Art. I., Sec. 3. (Continued.) Immediately after they [the senators] shall be assembled in Consequence of the first Election, they shall be divided as equally as may be into three classes. The Seats of the Senators of the first Class shall be vacated at the Expiration of

[1] Ex-Congressman McCall, on "The Power of the Senate," *Atlantic Monthly*, October, 1903.
[2] Madison's *Works*, iv., 429, 430.

the second Year, of the second Class at the Expiration of the fourth Year, and of the third Class at the Expiration of the sixth Year, so that one-third may be chosen every second Year.

This plan, taken from the first constitution of the State of Pennsylvania, is a method of keeping the Senate supplied with new ideas at regular intervals. It prevents inconvenient and irregular law-making, which would be quite possible if the whole personnel of the Senate, like that of the House of Representatives, could be changed at each election.

Art. I, Sec. 3. (Continued.) And if Vacancies happen by Resignation, or otherwise, during the Recess of the Legislature of any State, the Executive thereof may make temporary Appointments until the next Meeting of the Legislature, which shall then fill such Vacancies.

Seventeenth Amendment. (Continued.) When vacancies happen in the representation of any State in the Senate, the executive authority of such State shall issue writs of election to fill such vacancies: *Provided*, That the legislature of any State may empower the executive thereof to make temporary appointment until the people fill the vacancies by election as the legislature may direct.

Under the Seventeenth Amendment, the plan of filling vacancies in the Senate is the same as in the case of vacancies in the House of Representatives, except that the legislature of any State may give the governor power to make temporary appointments so that the office may not be vacant while the people are taking time to decide who is to serve them in this vastly important position.

Seventeenth Amendment. (Continued.) This amendment shall not be so construed as to affect the election or term of any Senator chosen before it becomes valid as part of the Constitution.

The Senators, when voting upon the proposed amendment, insisted that all of their number duly elected in the old way, should be allowed to finish their terms of office.

Art. I., Sec. 3. (Continued.) No person shall be a Senator who shall not have attained to the Age of thirty Years, and been nine Years a Citizen of the United States, and who shall not, when elected, be an Inhabitant of that State for which he shall be chosen.

The age limit of Senators was fixed at thirty years in order to insure the decorum of the more select branch of Congress. Henry Clay, however, was appointed to the Senate when under thirty, and did not reach the required age until after he had served the term for which he had been appointed.

A Senator must have been a citizen nine years before he takes the office. Albert Gallatin, one of the ablest of our Secretaries of the Treasury, who came here from Switzerland in 1780, and moved to Pennsylvania in 1785, was chosen a United States Senator in 1793, and served in the Senate until February 28, 1794, when it was decided that he was not qualified because he had not been a citizen nine years.[1]

[1] Watson, *On the Constitution*, i., 248.

General Ames, who was born in Maine, was elected to the Senate from Mississippi in 1870, by the "carpetbagger" government then in control of that State. He had gone to that State in 1868 to fill the position of provisional governor under the Reconstruction Act, and in 1869 had been appointed by the President military commander of the District of Mississippi. He was holding these offices when elected. His right to sit in the Senate was challenged on the ground that, when chosen to office, he still was an inhabitant of Maine where he always had kept his residence. The case was referred to a committee which reported against him, but the Senate overruled the Committee and he served his term.[1]

Art. I., Sec. 3. (Continued.) The Vice President of the United States shall be President of the Senate, but shall have no Vote, unless they be equally divided.

Alexander Hamilton said in *The Federalist*[2]:

Two considerations seem to justify the ideas of the Convention in this respect. One is, that to secure at all times the possibility of a definite resolution of the body, it is necessary that the President should have only a casting vote. And to take the senator of any State from his seat as senator, to place him in that of President of the Senate, would be to exchange, in regard to the State from which he came, a constant for a contingent vote.

Art. I., Sec. 3. (Continued.) The Senate shall chuse their other Officers, and also a President pro tempore, in the Absence of the Vice President, or when he shall exercise the Office of President of the United States.

[1] Watson, *On the Constitution*, I., 249.　　　　[2] No. 68.

⁄ The other officers of the Senate are the Secretary, Chief Clerk, Executive Clerk, Sergeant-at-Arms, Door Keeper, and Chaplain. They are elected like the officers of the House of Representatives.

It has grown into a general practice for the Vice President to vacate the senatorial chair a short time before the termination of each session in order to enable the Senate to choose a president *pro tempore*, who might already be in office if the Vice President in the recess should be called to the chair of state. The practice is founded in wisdom and sound policy, as it immediately provides for an exigency which may well be expected to occur at any time, and prevents the choice from being influenced by temporary excitements or intrigues arising from the actual existence of the exigency.[1]

Art. I., Sec. 3. (Continued.) The Senate shall have the sole Power to try all Impeachments. When sitting for that Purpose, they shall be on Oath or Affirmation. When the President of the United States is tried, the Chief Justice shall preside: And no Person shall be convicted without the Concurrence of two thirds of the Members present. Judgment in Cases of Impeachment shall not extend further than to removal from Office, and disqualification to hold and enjoy any Office of honor Trust or Profit under the United States: but the Party convicted shall nevertheless be liable and subject to Indictment, Trial, Judgment and Punishment, according to Law.

This clause gives the Senate power to hear and decide impeachment cases. The Chief Justice presides when the President is on trial, because it would be improper

[1] Story, *On the Constitution*, Sec. 741.

General Ames, who was born in M
to the Senate from Mississippi in 187(
bagger" government then in contr(
He had gone to that State in 1868 t
of provisional governor under the Re
and in 1869 had been appointed l
military commander of the District of
was holding these offices when elect(
sit in the Senate was challenged on
when chosen to office, he still was
Maine where he always had kept hi:
case was referred to a committee whicl
him, but the Senate overruled the C
served his term.[1]

Art. I., Sec. 3. (Continued.) The
the United States shall be President (
shall have no Vote, unless they be e(

. Alexander Hamilton said in *The Fe*

: Two considerations seem to justify th
vention in this respect. One is, that to
the possibility of a definite resolution of t
sary that the President should have on
And to take the senator of any State
senator, to place him in that of Presid(
would be to exchange, in regard to the
he came, a constant for a contingent vc

Art. I., Sec. 3. (Continued.) The $

... the Senate are the Secretary,
Clerk, Sergeant-at-Arms, Door
... They are elected like the of-
... Representatives.

... general practice for the Vice Presi-
... chair a short time before the
... in order to enable the Senate
... tore, who might already be in
... in the recess should be called
... The practice is founded in wisdom
... ediately provides for an exigency
... ed to occur at any time, and pre-
... being influenced by temporary excite-
... from the actual existence of the

... (Continued.) The Senate shall have
... try all Impeachments. When sitting
... they shall be on Oath or Affirmation.
... of the United States is tried, the
... shall preside: And no Person shall be
... the Concurrence of two thirds of the
... Judgment in Cases of Impeach-
... not extend further than to removal from
... disqualification to hold and enjoy any Office
... Trust or Profit under the United States: but
... convicted shall nevertheless be liable and
... ment, Trial, Judgment and Punishment,
... Law.

... gives the Senate power to hear and decide
... The Chief Justice presides when
... because it would be improper

Sec. 741.

on its face to let the Vice President take part as a judge in a trial which might end in promoting him to the place of the person impeached.

An impeachment case begins with the presenting of charges in the House of Representatives. This body then adopts a resolution to impeach, and prepares the articles of impeachment, which set forth in form the charges against the accused person. These are presented to the Senate, which summons the person against whom the proceedings are brought to appear before it on a certain day. The Senate hears the evidence against the defendant and his defense. The Senators then decide by vote whether the accused person is guilty or not guilty.

The punishment of impeached officials is both severe and merciful. The stigma of removal from office and disqualification to hold any position of honor is about as much as a person with any sense of self-respect can possibly endure. At the same time, his life or liberty is not put at the mercy of a political body.

Robert W. Archbald, a Federal Circuit Court Judge serving as a judge in the United States Commerce Court, was impeached in 1912. He was charged with having used his official power and position to obtain business favors and concessions from companies which had litigation before the Commerce Court. The judgment of the Senate was that he was guilty of this misconduct; and he was removed from office and forever disqualified to hold any office of honor, trust, or profit under the United States.

An excellent monograph upon "Impeachment," by Wrisley Brown, Esq., an Assistant Attorney General of the United States, has this to say of the efficacy of this method in assuring the good conduct of public officials:

The impeachment prescribed by our Constitution weighs well the evil to be redressed and adjusts the ordained relief to the occasion. It is the expression of the sober will rather than the restive whim of the people. It restrains judicial tyranny without overawing the authority of the courts. It regulates the conduct of the judges without disturbing the poise and balance of their judgments. It strikes directly at the judicial fault without destroying the judicial independence that is essential to the preservation of our constitutional jurisprudence. This great body of fundamental law must be maintained intact. It absorbs the changing needs of changing times, yet does not change. Upon it, the stability and the integrity of our institutions rest. Upon it our civil liberties depend. And without it, our republican government could not long endure.

CHAPTER VII

THE CONGRESS AS A LEGISLATURE

Art. I., Sec. 4. The Times, Places and Manner of holding Elections for Senators and Representatives, shall be prescribed in each State by the Legislature thereof; but the Congress may at any time by Law make or alter such Regulations, except as to the places of choosing Senators.

Americans of the first days of independence were quite touchy on the subject of the right of each of the States to manage its own affairs without any meddling by any general government which might be created. Their representatives in the Federal Convention knew as well as they could know anything that the proposed Constitution could not have the ghost of a chance for acceptance, if the States were not allowed to say how, when, and where elections should be held. On the other hand, they saw clearly that the new government would have to have some control over elections of Federal law-makers so as to be sure that Senators and Representatives should be elected in case the States failed to call elections to fill those offices. Therefore they gave Congress the power mentioned in this section. Justice Miller said in *Ex Parte Yarbrough*:[1]

[1] 110 U. S. Rep. 651.

every elector voting for as many names as the State was entitled to representatives in that House, worked injustice to other States which did not adopt that system, and gave an undue preponderance of power to the political party which had a majority of votes in the State, however small, [it] enacted that each member should be elected by a separate district, composed of contiguous territory. . . . And to remedy more than one evil arising from the election of members of Congress occurring at different times in the different States, Congress, by the Act of February 2, 1872, thirty years later, required all the elections for such members to be held on the Tuesday after the first Monday in November, in 1876, and on the same day of every second year thereafter.

The frequent failures of the legislatures of the States to elect Senators at the proper time, by one branch of the legislature voting for one person and the other branch for another person, and refusing in any manner to reconcile their differences, led Congress to pass an Act which compelled the two bodies to meet in joint convention, and fixing the day when this should be done, and requiring them so to meet on every day thereafter and vote for a Senator until one was elected. . . .

Now the day fixed for electing members of Congress has been established by Congress without regard to the time set for election of State officers in each State, and but for the fact that the State legislatures have, for their own accommodation, required State elections to be held at the

Art. I., Sec. 4. (Continued.) The Congress shall assemble at least once in every Year, and such Meeting shall be on the first Monday in December, unless they shall by law appoint a different Day.

The politicians of the constitutional era were mostly farmers, who had plenty of time to spare in winter, but were busy from planting time to harvest. It suited them exactly to leave home in October, serve in Congress until the following March, and then go back to their fields and meadows. That is the way Congressmen and Senators usually spent their time. When there was a war on hand or some great emergency had to be provided for, an extra session was called; but this did not happen very often.

Art. I., Sec. 5. Each House shall be the Judge of the Elections, Returns and Qualifications of its own Members, and a Majority of each shall constitute a Quorum to do Business; but a smaller Number may adjourn from day to day, and may be authorized to compel the Attendance of absent Members, in such Manner, and under such Penalties as each House may provide.

Our people have put down in black and white many things which the older nations maintain by custom. This section, for example, is a very exact statement of the corporate privileges which each House of the British Parliament enjoys by the unwritten Constitution of the United Kingdom.

A Majority of each House shall constitute a Quorum to do business. A "quorum," as the word is commonly used, means the number of members of a body or corporation competent to transact business by its law or constitution. Hence an Act of Congress, in order to be valid, must be passed at a meeting at which a majority of the members are present. In the case of *United States vs. Ballin*,[1] the validity of the McKinley Tariff Act of 1890 was challenged by a New York importing firm on the ground that no quorum was present in the House of Representatives when it was voted on. It was shown to the Court that, when the roll was called on the question, the Clerk of the House reported to the Speaker: yeas, 138; nays, 0; not voting, 189. Thereupon the Speaker read from a list, noted by the Clerk at his suggestion, the names of seventy-four members who were present in the Hall of Representatives when their names were called. The Speaker then stated that such members present and refusing to vote, together with those recorded as voting, showed a total of 212 members present, constituting a quorum to do business. He then declared that the bill had passed the House. The importing firm contended that the Speaker had no right to declare present members who had not voted at the calling of the roll; that those only were legally present who had answered when their names were called; that there was no quorum present when the vote was taken; that, therefore, the McKinley bill never had been passed. They urged that a consignment of worsted goods upon which duties had been levied under the McKinley bill should have been assessed at lower rates of duty under the Wilson Tariff Act of 1883. The case was heard first in the Circuit Court at New York City, which decided against the government and in favor of the importers. On appeal to the Supreme Court, however, the judgment of the Circuit Court was reversed in a decision, in which Justice Brewer said in part:

[1] 144 U. S. Rep., 5.

The Constitution provides that "a majority of each [House] shall constitute a quorum to do business." In other words, when a majority are present the House is in a position to do business. Its capacity to transact business is then established, created by the mere presence of a majority, and does not depend upon the disposition or assent or action of any single number, or fraction of the majority present. . . . But how shall the presence of a majority be determined? The Constitution has prescribed no method of making this determination, and it is therefore within the competency of the House to prescribe any method which shall be reasonably certain to ascertain the fact. It may prescribe answer to roll-call as the only method of determination; or require the passage of members between tellers, and their count as the sole test; or the count of the Speaker or the clerk, and an announcement from the desk of the names of those who are present. Any one of these methods, it must be conceded, is reasonably certain of ascertaining the fact, and as there is no constitutional method prescribed, and no constitutional inhibition of any of these, and no violation of fundamental rights in any, it follows that the House may adopt either or all, or it may provide for a combination of any two of the methods. This was done by the rule in question; and all that that rule attempts to do is to prescribe a method for ascertaining the presence of a majority, and thus establishing the fact that the House is in a condition to transact business. As appears from the Journal, at the time this bill passed the House there was present a majority, a quorum, and the House was authorized to transact any and all business. It was in a condition to act on the bill if it desired.

Art. I, Sec. 5. (Continued.) Each House may determine the Rules of its Proceedings, punish its Members for disorderly Behaviour, and, with the Concurrence of two thirds, expel a Member.

The supreme law-making body of the nation is, of course, beyond the reach of any law except the People's Law, the Constitution itself, to which the Houses owe their existence. The People's Law authorizes each House to decide how its business is to be done and to regulate the behavior of its members.

Each House may determine the Rules of its Proceedings. The House of Representatives, with more than four hundred members, has been forced to adopt rules to prevent discussion. More than 30,000 bills and resolutions are offered at each Congress. Most of these are killed in the committee rooms. A few hundred which must be passed to keep the government going, are reported for the consideration of the assembled members, and are put through practically without debate because the Speaker will recognize only those members who are scheduled to address the House for or against the bills before it. These autocratic rules were introduced in 1889, when Thomas B. Reed of Maine was the Speaker of the House. His rules have been criticized as arbitrary and tyrannical, but are still in force. "How absolutely necessary his code was," said A. Maurice Low in the *North American Review* of February, 1902, "is shown from the fact that his Democratic successor substantially made the Reed rules his own; and still later, when the swing of the pendulum once more placed the House in control of the Republicans, the Republican majority saw no good reason why any change should be made in the rules." The Senate has its own rules, which are based upon a manual prepared by Thomas Jefferson for his own use during his Vice Presidency from 1797 to 1801. These rules permit unlimited debate upon any subject under consideration—a method which works fairly well in a deliberative assembly of less than one hundred members.

Each House may . . . punish its Members for dis-
orderly Behaviour, and, with the Concurrence of two thirds,
expel a Member. This clause of the Constitution gives
a limited judicial power to each of the Houses of Congress. They are constitutional courts to the extent that
they can punish their own members for disorderly
behavior and can expel a member. This provision
counterbalances the exemption of Representatives and
Senators from arrest by order of the courts during their
attendance in Congress.[1]

Art. I., Sec. 5. (Continued.) Each House shall keep
a Journal of its Proceedings, and from time to time
publish the same, excepting such Parts as may in
their Judgment require Secrecy; and the Yeas and
Nays of the Members of either House on any question shall, at the Desire of one fifth of those Present,
be entered on the Journal.

These are commands which the Constitution expressly lays upon the law-making departments of the
national government. Mr. Justice Miller, in his book
On the Constitution[2] says of this provision:

Whether wise or unwise, [it] is a fruitful source of a
great waste of time. It may be very well doubted whether
the call of the yeas and nays in the House of Representatives,
which necessarily consumes a great deal of time, is not
resorted to more for that purpose than any other, thereby
frequently defeating a measure which a majority of the
House is prepared to pass. It may be of some advantage in
the way of compelling members to spread their names upon

---

[1] See Art. I., Sec. 6, Subd. 1.
[2] Miller, *On the Constitution*, p. 197.

the record as having voted for or against any particular proposition, and thereby holding them responsible to the public sentiment of their constituents. Where this is the conscientious object and motive in calling for the yeas and nays, it is probably unobjectionable, and in the enactment of laws of great public importance it is desirable for many reasons that the votes of members should be recorded. No doubt this was the object of the Constitution in authorizing a call of the yeas and nays upon the request of one fifth of the members present, and this requirement of one fifth seems to be a necessity to prevent the frittering away of the time of the legislative body at the request of a single number.

Art. I., Sec. 5. (Continued.) Neither House, during the Session of Congress, shall, without the Consent of the other, adjourn for more than three days, nor to any other Place than that in which the two Houses shall be sitting.

But for this clause, either House, in case of a dispute with the other, could break up the session by adjourning for a long period or to some place other than the Hall of Congress. "If the House could adjourn of its own motion, without the other, for two or three weeks at a time," says Miller, *On the Constitution*, "the obstruction of the public business would be very great, and there would be an impossibility of the coöperative action contemplated by the Constitution. In practice, the three days' limit is reached by one or both branches of Congress very frequently during a long session, when an adjournment is had over from Thursday until Monday."[1]

[1] Miller, *On the Constitution*, p. 197.

Art. I., Sec. 6.   The Senators and Representatives
shall receive a Compensation for their Services, to be
ascertained by Law, and paid out of the Treasury of
the United States.   They shall in all Cases, except
Treason, Felony, and Breach of the Peace, be privileged
from Arrest during their Attendance at the Session of
their respective Houses, and in going to and returning
from the same; and for any Speech or Debate in either
House, they shall not be questioned in any other place.

*The Senators and Representatives shall receive a Com-
pensation for their Services, to be ascertained by Law, and
paid out of the Treasury of the United States.*   The
members of the Continental Congress had had to travel
hundreds of miles over the wretched roads of those days
or take the chances of a sea voyage in war time, in
order to spend months on end in the boarding houses
of Philadelphia while attending to their public duties.
Fairly good pay at regular intervals would have made
these conditions endurable.   But that is what they did
not get.   Some States had been so thrifty and so irregular in the payment of salaries that their representatives often had a very unpleasant time of it.   Other
States had carried financial prudence to the extremity
of remaining unrepresented during long periods.   Experience had shown that Representatives and Senators
ought to be paid by the Nation.   More than this, since,
under the proposed government, each House was to have
a right to compel the attendance of absent members,
it was no more than just to provide that those who
might be compelled to appear in their places should
be paid what it would cost to come and go and live
while at their work.

The only doubtful thing here was that Congress was

the only body which could "ascertain" the compensation its own members should receive. James Madison said in the Federal Convention that "to leave them [Senators and Representatives] to regulate their own wages was an indecent thing."[1]

The scheme made trouble in 1816, when the compensation was raised from six dollars per day of actual attendance to $1,500 per year. The change was so unpopular that most of the members that voted for the bill were defeated at the next election. This was nothing to what happened in 1871, when Congress on the last day of its session raised the salary of members from $5,000 to $7,500 and made it payable from the beginning of the session two years before. The "salary grab" was responsible for the downfall of many hopeful politicians of that day.

The Senators and Representatives . . . shall in all Cases, except Treason, Felony, and Breach of the Peace, be privileged from Arrest during their Attendance at the Session of their respective Houses, and in going to and returning from the same. If this personal privilege had not been granted to members of the new Congress, there might have been endless trouble in those days when arrest and imprisonment for small debts and upon the slightest and most insignificant criminal charges was the usual procedure.

The House of Commons of the British Parliament had contended for this privilege, because British Kings had used the power of arrest as a means of forcing members to vote for measures which the Crown wished to carry through. The makers of the Constitution gave it to Senators and Representatives in Congress in order to preserve the independence of the law-making

[1] Madison's *Journal*, p. 152.

Art. I., Sec. 6. (Continued.) No Senator or Representative shall, during the Time for which he was elected, be appointed to any Civil Office under the Authority of the United States, which shall have been created, or the Emoluments whereof shall have been encreased during such time; and no Person holding any Office under the United States, shall be a Member of either House during his Continuance in Office.

The Constitution declares that Senators and Representatives shall not use their power as law-makers to provide fat jobs for themselves, and it prohibits Federal officials from sitting in Congress. The Constitution makers were creating a government which was to be managed by makers of laws, administrators of laws, and judges of laws. In Great Britain supreme power, then as now, was vested in parliament. If a member of parliament also held office in a subordinate branch of the government, there was no great harm done so long as his constituents were satisfied. But our Constitution vests governmental power in three theoretically equal and coördinate bodies: makers of laws, administrators of laws, and judges of laws. Under our system, therefore, any such overlapping of official authority is unthinkable; with us, no man may use power in one capacity and in another capacity have a right to check that use of power.

Art. I., Sec. 7. All Bills for raising Revenue shall originate in the House of Representatives; but the Senate may propose or concur with Amendments as on other Bills.

Section 7, as a whole, was an attempt to adopt the order of law-making procedure which had been followed in England for at least three hundred years before the United States became independent. The English imprint is especially plain in this clause which says that taxing bills shall begin in the House of Representatives, just as in England all money bills begin in the House of Commons. Here the similarity ends. The Senate, under its right of amendment, often cuts out of a House revenue bill all except the enacting clause, and substitutes a measure of its own. This is what is called a Senate amendment of a House revenue bill.

Art. I., Sec. 7. (Continued.) Every Bill which shall have passed the House of Representatives and the Senate, shall, before it become a Law, be presented to the President of the United States; If he approve he shall sign it, but if not he shall return it, with his Objections to that House in which it shall have originated, who shall enter the Objections at large on their Journal, and proceed to reconsider it. If after such Reconsideration two thirds of that House shall agree to pass the Bill, it shall be sent, together with the Objections, to the other House, by which it shall likewise be reconsidered, and if approved by two thirds of that House, it shall become a law. But in all such Cases the Votes of both Houses shall be determined by Yeas and Nays, and the Names of the Persons voting for and against the Bill shall be entered on the Journal of each House respectively. If any Bill shall not be returned by the President within ten Days (Sundays excepted) after it shall have been presented to him, the Same shall be a Law, in like manner as if he had signed it, unless the Congress by their Adjournment prevent its Return, in which Case it shall not be a Law.

It was generally taken for granted that the sentiment and opinion of the people would be reflected in the House of Representatives and that the Senate would in general be dominated by the larger House. The men who framed the Constitution, however, were men of means who intended to safeguard property rights by preventing irresponsible legislation. They were sure there ought to be some plan whereby the power of the people through their representatives to make such laws as they chose, should be limited or balanced by some other department of authority. That is why they put into the hands of the President of the United States a right to prevent the taking effect of any law which should not have back of it the recorded votes of two-thirds of the members of the Congress.

"It is to be hoped," wrote Alexander Hamilton in *The Federalist*, No. 73, "that it will not often happen that improper views will govern so large a proportion as two-thirds of both branches of the Legislature at the same time; and this, too, in spite of the counterpoising weight of the Executive. It is at any rate far less probable that this should be the case, than that such views should taint the resolutions and conduct of a bare majority. A power of this nature in the Executive, will often have a silent and unperceived, though forcible, operation. When men, engaged in unjustifiable pursuits, are aware that obstructions may come from a quarter which they cannot control, they will often be restrained by the bare apprehension of opposition from doing what they would with eagerness rush into, if no such external impediments were to be feared."

If any Bill shall not be returned by the President within ten Days (Sundays excepted) after it shall have been presented to him, the Same shall be a Law, in like manner as if he had signed it, unless the Congress by their Adjournment prevent its Return, in which Case it shall not be a Law. The President is not obliged to veto or return with objections any bill sent to him by Congress during the ten days before the fourth day of March of every other year. A President who has before him any bills presented less than ten days before that date, can stuff them into the handiest wastebasket, if he does not wish to send in a veto with his reasons. This is what is called the "pocket veto," because the President "pockets" the bill and carries it away with him.

Art. I., Sec. 7. (Continued.) Every Order, Resolution, or Vote to which the Concurrence of the Senate and House of Representatives may be necessary (except on a question of Adjournment) shall be presented to the President of the United States; and before the Same shall take Effect, shall be approved by him, or being disapproved by him, shall be repassed by two thirds of the Senate and House of Representatives, according to the Rules and Limitations prescribed in the Case of a Bill.

This clause puts the same limitations and conditions upon the enactment of orders, resolutions, and votes as the preceding clause does upon the enactment of laws. It was suggested in the Constitutional Convention by James Madison as a means of preventing Congress from enacting bills into laws and dodging the presidential veto by calling them orders or resolutions or votes.

PART IV

Legislative Government in the United States

CHAPTER VIII

Art. I., Sec. 8, Subd. 1. The Congress shall have Power.

The Constitution of the United States is not an instrument which executes itself, but a plan of government which must be executed by the departments which it establishes. In the case of *United States vs. Hudson and Goodwin*,[1] the publishers of a Connecticut newspaper were charged with libel for having on May 7, 1806, published a statement that President Jefferson and Congress had secretly made a present of $2,000,000 to Napoleon Bonaparte to induce him to make peace. In the United States Circuit Court, where the case first came up, the defendants urged that they could not lawfully be punished for criminal libel under the laws of the United States, because the United States had no law punishing that offence. Hence the Supreme Court, in deciding the case, had to determine whether the Constitution gave the United States power to punish attacks upon its sovereignty in the absence of a Federal statute. Justice Johnson said:

The only question which this case presents, is, whether the Circuit Courts of the United States can exercise a common law jurisdiction in criminal cases. . . . The

[1] 7 Cranch's Rep., 34.

legislative power of the Union must first make an act a crime, affix a punishment to it, and declare the court which shall have jurisdiction of the offence.

Art. I., Sec. 8, Subd. 1. (Continued.) To lay and collect Taxes, Duties, Imposts and Excises, to pay the Debts and provide for the common Defence and general Welfare of the United States; but all Duties, Imposts and Excises shall be uniform throughout the United States.

Art. I., Sec. 8, Subd. 2. To borrow Money on the credit of the United States.

The impotent League of Friendship created by the Articles of Confederation had had no power to compel the payment of taxes. The old Congress had never been able, even in the most strenuous crises of the War for Independence, to induce the States to supply their quotas of men and munitions of war. The delegates who met to suggest improvements in the Articles of Confederation knew that the thing most needed was this power of taxation.

The Congress shall have Power To lay and collect Taxes. The Supreme Court, in the case of *State Freight Tax,*[1] explained what taxes are. In 1864 Pennsylvania passed a law which required all transportation companies doing business within the State to pay a tax upon every ton of freight taken up in the State and carried out of it, or taken up outside of the State and brought within it. The Reading Railroad Company, which had been granted an exclusive right to charge tolls upon freight carried by it, refused to pay this tax on coal carried from Pennsylvania to points outside the State on the ground that this was commerce among the States of the United

[1] 15 Wallace's Rep., 232.

States, the regulation of which is exclusively under the control of the national government. The Supreme Court of Pennsylvania decided that, because the railroads had been built on lands which the State had permitted the companies to take from the owners for use as highways, the State had a right to collect tolls or taxes for the use of those highways. The question for the Court to decide was whether the State could, by imposing tolls, tax freight carried in interstate commerce. Thus the Supreme Court had to say what a "tax" is. Justice Strong said:

Tolls and freights are a compensation for services rendered, or facilities furnished to a passenger or transporter. They are not rendered or furnished·by the State. A tax is a demand of sovereignty: a toll is a demand of proprietorship.

The Congress shall have Power To lay and collect . . . Duties. This word "duties" has been accurately defined by the Supreme Court in the case of *Pacific Insurance Co. vs. Soule.*[1] Soon after the Civil War, the Pacific Insurance Company, doing business in California, was compelled to pay internal revenue duties amounting to $7,365 upon its dividends, undistributed cash, and income. The duties were paid under protest, and an action was brought by the company against the Federal collector upon the ground that the duties imposed by the statute were in fact direct taxes which, not being apportioned to each of the States according to population as required by another part of the Constitution, could not lawfully be exacted. The case was taken to the Supreme Court at Washington upon the question whether duties levied upon the income of corporations were taxes on property or were excise

[1] 7 Wallace's Reports, 433.

duties upon the privilege of doing business. If they were
taxes, they were unlawful as direct taxes not apportioned. If they were excise duties, they were lawful.
Justice Swayne, in deciding that these were "duties,"
said:

Duties are defined . . . to be things due and recoverable
by law. The term, in its widest signification, is hardly less
comprehensive than "taxes." . . . If a tax upon carriages
kept for his own use by the owner [as had long before been
decided by the Supreme Court in the case of *Hylton vs.
United States*], is not a direct tax, we can see no ground upon
which a tax upon the business of an insurance company can
be held to belong to that class of revenue charges.

*The Congress shall have Power To lay and collect . . .
Imposts.* This word "imposts" is used in connection
with the inexact word "duties" to denote a charge specially imposed upon goods and merchandise exported
or imported. In the case of *Woodruff vs. Parham,* decided by the Supreme Court of the United States in
1868, it was shown that the City of Mobile, Alabama,
was collecting sums of money from auctioneers by
compelling them to pay a percentage of the value of
merchandise which they imported from other States
and sold at auction. A Mr. Woodruff, an auctioneer,
contended that a tax on the sale of goods imported
from other States was an impost on goods imported
from those States, and as such forbidden by the Constitution. When this case came before the Federal
Supreme Court, Justice Miller wrote a decision in
which he said that a State may tax any property which is
within its borders, no matter where it came from. He
said

In the case of *Brown vs. Maryland*, the word imports, as used in the clause now under consideration, is defined, both on the authority of the lexicons and of usage, to be articles brought into a country; an impost is there said to be a duty, custom, or tax levied on articles brought into the country. In the ordinary use of the terms at this day, no one would, for a moment, think of them as having relation to any other articles than those brought from a country foreign to the United States.

The Congress shall have Power To lay and collect . . . Excises. The word "excise" grated on the ears of our great-great-grandfathers, who remembered that the Stamp tax was an excise. Even now, when the events which made an excise "a hateful tax" are buried under the dust of a century of history, American statesmen like better to talk about "internal revenue," which means exactly the same thing.

The first Federal excise law, passed by Congress in 1791, stirred up the Whiskey Rebellion in Western Pennsylvania. This act, which imposed excise taxes upon spirits distilled within the United States, was denounced as unnecessary and tyrannical by the legislatures of Maryland, Pennsylvania, Virginia, and North Carolina. The farmers in the frontier settlements near the Alleghany Mountains raised great quantities of corn and rye, which could not be shipped to the East at a profit except in the form of whiskey. Like the makers of "moonshine" whiskey of the present day, these men could not or would not see any reason why they should pay a tax on the product which they distilled from grain harvested on their farms. One unlucky deputy collector was seized by a body of armed men who stripped him, cut off his hair, tarred and feathered him. The

United States courts issued warrants for the arrest of those who had committed this outrage; but all the authorities got for their pains was news that the private messenger who carried the process papers had also been tarred and feathered, had lost his watch and horse, and had been left tied to a tree in the woods for five hours. The disorders continued until 1794, when the national government intervened. President Washington issued proclamations commanding the rioters to disperse, and warning all persons against abetting them. He made requisitions upon the governors of Pennsylvania, New Jersey, Virginia, and Maryland for 15,000 troops and got ready to lead this little army in person. The bottom then fell out of the whole movement. David Bradford, its leader, fled to New Orleans. Several insurgents were arrested and bound over for trial, and two of them were convicted of treason. These, however, were afterward pardoned by President Washington.[1]

Internal revenue taxes upon cigars, cigarettes, and tobacco in various forms, wines, malted and distilled liquors, and other articles, have been levied so regularly by the national government that everybody nowadays accepts them as part of the daily business of life.

It is more difficult to understand the reasoning by which excise taxation has been extended to include duties on the privileges which corporations have to engage in business, especially when the amount of the duties is reckoned on the basis of income and not upon the value of property they own. The national corporation income tax law, superseded by the general income tax law of 1913, was really an expansion of the old principle of excise duties. In the case of *Portland Bank vs.*

[1] 26 Federal Cases, 499, No. 15, 443; 2 Dallas' Rep., 335.

Apthorp,[1] it appeared that the State of Massachusetts, in 1812, had enacted a law which required every bank in the State to pay to the State Treasurer within ten days after declaring a semi-annual dividend an excise tax of one half of one per cent of the par value of its capital stock. The Portland Bank neglected to pay this tax after declaring a dividend on January 1, 1813. Thereupon the sheriff of Cumberland County, in the District of Maine, then a part of Massachusetts, seized property of the bank to the amount of the tax. The bank brought an action against him. Chief Justice Parker declared that this tax was an excise duty which the State had a right to levy, saying:

There are other sources of emolument and profit, not strictly called property, but which are rather to be considered as the means of acquiring property, from which a reasonable revenue may be exacted by the legislature. . . . The term *excise* . . . is limited, in our Constitution [Massachusetts] as to its operation, to produce, goods, wares, merchandise, and commodities. This last word will perhaps embrace . . . the privilege of using particular branches of business or employment, as, the business of an auctioneer, of an attorney, of a tavern keeper, of a retailer of spirituous liquors, etc.

The Congress shall have Power To lay and collect Taxes [etc.] to pay the Debts . . . of the United States. The Supreme Court at Washington frequently has been called upon to decide whether the United States can collect money by taxation for any purpose except to pay the debts it is legally bound to pay. In the case of *United States vs. Realty Co.*,[2] the question was upon the constitutionality of the Act of Congress of 1895 which

[1] 7 Massachusetts Rep., 252. [2] 163 U. S. Rep., 427.

appropriated money for bounties to encourage the production of high grade sugars. Could Congress lawfully collect money by imposing customs duties on imported merchandise and then make a free gift of a part of the proceeds to sugar manufacturers? Justice Peckham said:

What are the debts of the United States within the meaning of this constitutional provision? It is conceded and indeed it cannot be questioned that the debts are not limited to those which are evidenced by some written obligation or to those which are otherwise of a strictly legal character. The term "debts" includes those debts or claims which rest upon a merely equitable or honorary obligation and which would not be recoverable in a court of law if existing against an individual. The nation, speaking broadly, owes a "debt" to an individual when his claim grows out of general principles of right and justice; when, in other words, it is based upon considerations of a moral or mere honorary nature, such as are binding on the conscience or the honor of an individual, although the debt could obtain no recognition in a court of law. The power of Congress extends at least as far as recognition and payment of claims against the government which are thus founded. . . . Their recognition depends solely upon Congress, and whether it will recognize claims thus founded must be left to the discretion of that body. Payments to individuals, not of right or of a merely legal claim, but payments in the nature of a gratuity, yet having some feature of moral obligation to support them, have been made by the government by virtue of acts of Congress, appropriating the public money, ever since its foundation.

The Congress shall have Power To lay and collect Taxes [etc.] to . . . provide for the common Defence and general Welfare of the United States. The taxing power for

these purposes has never been exercised so unreasonably as to compel an appeal to the Federal Supreme
Court for a decision upon the meaning of the phrase.
Justice Story, in his *Commentary on the Constitution*,
says[1]:

> The reading . . . which will be maintained in these
> commentaries is that which makes the latter words a quali-
> fication of the former, and this will be best illustrated by
> supplying the words which are necessarily to be understood
> in this interpretation.   They will then stand thus:
> "The Congress shall have power to lay and collect taxes,
> duties, imposts, and excises, in order to pay the debts, and
> to provide for the common defence and general welfare of
> the United States"; that is, for the purpose of paying the
> public debts, and providing for the common defense and
> general welfare of the United States.   In this sense, Con-
> gress has not an unlimited power of taxation; but it is
> limited to specific objects,—the payment of the public
> debts, and providing for the common defense and general
> welfare.

Protective tariff laws, enacted "to provide revenue
for the government and to encourage the industries of
the United States,"[2] have been criticised upon the
ground that the Constitution does not authorize Congress to impose customs duties upon foreign made
goods for the purpose of giving our manufacturers a
better chance in competing in our home markets.   On
the other hand, many eminent statesmen have urged
that it is the bounden duty of Congress "to provide for
. . . the *general Welfare* of the United States" by adjusting the tax burden in such a way as to compel

· [1] 5th ed., Sect. 908.
[2] Enacting Clause of Dingley Tariff Bill, Act of July 4, 1897.

far as it can be called a tax, is an excise duty on the business
of bringing passengers from foreign countries into this, by
ocean navigation, is uniform and operates precisely alike in
every port of the United States where such passengers can
be landed.

*The Congress shall have Power To . . . borrow Money
on the credit of the United States.*   During the Revolution, the power to borrow money was grossly misused by
the Continental Congress and by each of the States in
issuing floods of continental and state paper money
which never was redeemed.   At the very time the Convention was laboring over the work of Constitution
making, there spread over Massachusetts a hot flame of
rebellion caused by efforts to get worthless paper money
out of the way.   Hence, the original draft of this clause
that Congress should have power "to borrow money
and emit bills of credit on the credit of the United States"
found so little favor with the delegates that, by unanimous consent, the words "emit bills of credit" were
cut out.

James Madison, the real leader of the Constitutional
Convention, said then and afterward that this omission
would prevent the United States from issuing legal
tender paper money.   Indeed, until 1863, our government when in need of money had issued bonds or its
promissory notes at 7 30/100 per cent—a rate fixed to
net the holder two cents per day on each $100.   In 1863,
however, Congress authorized an issue of paper money
to pay off the army in the field and to meet the expense
of the Civil War.

The question of validity was not raised at once,
because the North needed the relief which the paper
money gave.   In 1869, however, when there were only

seven Supreme Court justices, a majority of the Court held, in the case of *Hepburn vs. Griswold*,[1] that the act of 1863 was void for unconstitutionality. Chief Justice Chase, in giving the opinion of the Court, said:

No one questions the general constitutionality, and not very many, perhaps, the general expediency of the legislation by which a note currency has been authorized in recent years. The doubt is as to the power to declare a particular class of these notes to be a legal tender in payment of pre-existing debts. . . .

There is another provision in the . . . [fifth] amendment, which, in our judgment, cannot have its full and intended effect unless construed as a direct prohibition of the legislation which we have been considering. It is that which declares that "no person shall be deprived of life, liberty, or property, without due process of law.". . . The . . . question is, whether an act which compels all those who hold contracts for the payment of gold and silver money to accept in payment a currency of inferior value deprives such persons of property without due process of law.

. . . A very large proportion of the property of civilized men exists in the form of contracts. These contracts almost invariably stipulate for the payment of money. And we have already seen that contracts in the United States, prior to the act under consideration, for the payment of money, were contracts to pay the sums specified in gold and silver coin. And it is beyond a doubt that the holders of these contracts were and are as fully entitled to the protection of this constitutional provision as the holders of any other description of property. . . .

We confess ourselves unable to perceive any solid distinction between such an act and an act compelling all citizens to accept, in satisfaction of all contracts for money, half or three-quarters or any other proportion less than the

[1] 8 Wallace's Rep., 603, 619, 624.

... of the value actually ... according to our terms. ... difficult to conceive what ... could take private property ... ... due process of law ... and would not.

We are obliged to conclude that ... in making more ... ... to pay dollars ... ... contracted ... ... made with ... ... the Constitution; and that ... ... by that Constitution.

In 1869, soon after taking office, President Grant appointed two more Supreme Court justices. Two cases involving the constitutionality of the Legal Tender Act of 1863 were advanced for hearing, and this time the *Legal Tender* case ... the Court by a ... justices to four reversed a previous decision. The justices said in these cases that Congress had power under the Constitution to enact any law it considered necessary to execute the Constitution. The opinion written by justice Strong, says in part:

"Closely allied ... the argument considered is that the legal tender ... ... the spirit of the fifth amendment which ... taking private property for public use without just compensation or due process of law. That provision has always been understood as referring only to a direct appropriation and not to consequential injuries resulting from the exercise of lawful power. It has never been supposed to have any bearing upon, or to inhibit laws that indirectly ... A new tariff, ... a ... draft, or a war may ... depreciate ... more than ... indeed, render ... ... due process of law ... They may destroy the ... ... supposed that, because ... ... or a law of a non-intercourse ... ... or a war be declared? ...

... ... 357, 551.

Without extending our remarks further, it will be seen that we hold the acts of Congress constitutional as applied to contracts made either before or after their passage. In so holding, we overrule so much of what was decided in *Hepburn vs. Griswold*, as ruled the acts unwarranted by the Constitution so far as they apply to contracts made before their enactment. That case was decided by a divided court, and by a court having a less number of judges than the law then in existence provided this court shall have. . . .   We are not accustomed to hear them [cases involving constitutional powers] in the absence of a full court, if it can be avoided. . . .   And it is no unprecedented thing in courts of last resort, both in this country and in England, to overrule decisions previously made.

It was generally thought at that time that the decisions sustaining the Legal Tender acts went no further than to declare that the nation in time of war may meet its needs by using its notes and giving them value by making them a legal tender for the payment of debts. But, in 1878, in a time of profound peace, Congress passed another legal tender paper money law. This brought forward the old question in a new form; for, if this law were valid, there could be no doubt that the government at Washington had full power to issue paper money at any time. The question came before the Supreme Court in the great case of *Juilliard vs. Greenman*,[1] in which a New York man sued a citizen of Connecticut for the price and value of one hundred bales of cotton billed at $5,122.90. The buyer admitted that he had bought and received the cotton and said he had paid $22.90 of this sum in coin, and had offered the seller two United States legal tender notes, one for $5,000 and one for $100 in payment of the balance, and

[1] 110 U. S. Rep., 421.

whole of the value actually due, and ... ...

It is difficult to conceive what ... ...

erty without due process of law, ... the law serving.

We are obliged to ...

promises to pay dollars a legal tender, ... than it was to ...

previously contracted, ...

of the Constitution, and that of the government, or in the

stitution. ... ... to furnish

... the government and of

In 1869, soon as ... ... expedient

pointed two more ... ... deter-

involving the constitut ... ... and not a

Act of 1862 were adverse ... ... by the courts.

in ... ...

ju ...

ju ...

un ...

no ...

w ...

CHAPTER IX

Art. I., Sec. 8, Subd. 3.   To regulate Commerce with foreign Nations, and among the several States, and with the Indian Tribes.

All governments exist chiefly for the safety and prosperity of business in the broadest sense of the word. The United States as constituted in 1783 was composed of thirteen States, each of which claimed to be independent and sovereign. These States were neither considerate nor reasonable in their conduct toward the central government or toward one another. "The States flushed with the enjoyment of power, increased, instead of diminishing, measures incompatible with their relations to the federal government."[1]   John Adams, our first minister to England, was an able and skilful diplomatist; but he had to confess that it was not easy to make a treaty which could not be carried out on the part of the United States unless each of the thirteen States was willing to observe its provisions. The new State governments enacted local laws bearing hard upon all outsiders. Certain States which had good harbors imposed customs duties on goods imported by their less fortunate neighbors. "New Jersey, placed between Philadelphia and New York, was likened to a

[1] Madison's *Journal*, p. 29.

some other steamboat men could not see why they also did not have as much right as anybody else to do business on the waters of a river.   Wherefore they took out a Federal license for the coasting trade and went into the steamboat business in opposition to the monopoly, claiming that their coasting trade license gave them a right to use free of tolls, improvements in local navigation made by private persons under State license. Veazie and his associates urged the Supreme Court to protect them in their infringement of Moor's monopoly, on the ground that the local products carried by their boats might ultimately become the subjects of foreign commerce, which should be regulated by the national government.   Justice Daniel refuted this argument as follows:

Commerce with foreign nations must signify commerce which in some sense is necessarily connected with those nations, transactions which either immediately, or at some stage of their progress, must be extra-territorial.   The phrase can never be applied to transactions wholly internal between citizens of the same community, or to a polity and laws whose ends and purposes and operations are restricted to the territory and soil and jurisdiction of such community. Nor can it be properly concluded, that because the products of domestic enterprise in agriculture or manufactures, or in the arts, may ultimately become the subjects of foreign commerce, that the control of the means or the encouragements by which enterprise is fostered and protected, is legitimately within the import of the phrase foreign commerce, or fairly implied in any investiture of the power to regulate such commerce.

The Congress shall have Power To . . . regulate Commerce . . . among the several States.   Without freedom of commerce among the States, the winning of political independence would have been in vain. The existence of the national right to manage domestic commerce became immensely important when Robert Fulton, by applying steam power to navigation, revolutionized transportation methods. When Fulton and Livingston ran steamboats in New York waters under State grants of exclusive privilege, the United States Supreme Court had to decide whether Congress or the States were to regulate domestic commerce.

This question first came to an issue in the New York courts in an action brought by Robert R. Livingston to assert his and Fulton's joint rights under the act of the New York legislature giving to them alone the privilege of running steamboats. This is the case of *Livingston vs. Van Ingen*,[1] in which Chancellor Kent asserted:

Congress, indeed, has not any direct jurisdiction over our interior commerce or waters. Hudson River is the property of the people of this State, and the legislature have the same jurisdiction over it that they have over the land, or over any of our public highways, or over the waters of any of our rivers or lakes. They may, in their sound discretion, regulate and control, enlarge or abridge the use of its waters, and they are in the habitual exercise of that sovereign right. If the Constitution had given to Congress exclusive jurisdiction over our navigable waters, then the argument of the respondents would have applied; but the people never did, nor ever intended to grant such a power; and Congress have concurrent jurisdiction over the navigable waters no further than may be incidental and requisite to the due regulation of commerce between the States and with foreign nations.

This assertion of States rights against the rights of the United States was promptly challenged in the United

[1] 9 Johnson's Rep., 589.

States Supreme Court in the case of *Gibbons vs. Ogden.*[1] Fulton and Livingston had assigned to Aaron Ogden a part of their rights covering the privilege of conducting a steamboat line between Elizabethtown, New Jersey, and New York City. Thomas Gibbons started an opposition line with two steamboats called *The Stoudinger* and *The Bellona*. Ogden brought an action in equity and obtained a temporary injunction. Gibbons answered the bill in equity by urging that his boats were duly enrolled and licensed to engage in the coastwise trade under the laws of the United States; and this he claimed gave him a right superior to Ogden's right under a State law. The New York courts ruled in Ogden's favor. Gibbons then took the case to the Federal Supreme Court, where the New York injunction was annulled on the ground that the Act of Congress under which Gibbons' steamboats had been enrolled and licensed to be employed in the coastwise trade, gave those vessels full authority to navigate the waters of the United States by steam or otherwise, "any laws of the State of New York to the contrary notwithstanding." This decision, rendered by Chief Justice Marshall in February, 1824, is the basis of that long series of decrees which have given Congress *absolute power to regulate* the business of the United States. The significant parts of the decision are:

We are now arrived at the inquiry—what is this power? It is the power to regulate; that is, to prescribe the rule by which commerce is to be governed. This power, like all others vested in Congress, is complete in itself, may be exercised to its utmost extent, and acknowledges no limitations other than are prescribed in the Constitution. . . .

[1] 9 Wheaton's Rep., 1.

If, as has always been understood, the sovereignty of Congress, though limited to specified objects, is plenary as to those objects, the power over commerce . . . among the several States is vested in Congress as absolutely as it would be in a single government, having in its constitution the same restrictions on the exercise of the power as are found in the Constitution of the United States. The wisdom and the discretion of Congress, their identity with the people, and the influence which their constituents possess at elections, are, in this, as in many other instances, as that, for example, of declaring war, the sole restraints on which they have relied to secure them from its abuse. They are the restraints on which the people must often rely solely in all representative governments.

The unlimited power of Congress over all business which crosses State lines extends even to the reversing of decisions of the Supreme Court of the United States.

In 1849, the State of Pennsylvania brought the action of *Pennsylvania vs. Wheeling and Belmont Bridge Company*,[1] in which it asked the Supreme Court to order the destruction of a bridge across the Ohio River from Wheeling, Virginia (now West Virginia), on the ground that it was an obstruction to commerce. Justice McLean, in giving the judgment of the Court that the bridge was an unlawful structure, said:

The Ohio being a navigable stream, subject to the commercial power of Congress, and over which that power has been exerted; if the river be within the State of Virginia, the commerce upon it, which extends to other States, is not within its jurisdiction; consequently if the act of Virginia authorized the structure of the bridge, so as to obstruct navigation, it could afford no justification to the bridge company.

[1] 13 Howard's Rep., 518.

The bridge company paid no attention either to this decision or to an injunction which was issued by Justice Grier of the Supreme Court. It went to Congress, which, in August, 1852, enacted "that the bridges across the Ohio River at Wheeling, in the State of Virginia, and at Bridgeport in the State of Ohio, abutting on Zane's Island in said River, are hereby declared lawful structures, in their present positions and elevations, and shall be so held and taken to be, anything in the law or laws of the United States to the contrary notwithstanding." This law further declared the bridges to be post roads, authorized the company to maintain them in that position, and commanded that all persons navigating the river should so regulate the use of their vessels and boats, and the pipes and chimneys belonging to them, as not to interfere with the elevation and construction of the bridge. This was plainly a reversal of the decision which the Supreme Court had rendered only a few months before. The State of Pennsylvania, apparently thinking the Court would insist upon its rights in the matter, asked the justices to punish the bridge company for disobeying the Court's original decree. At this second hearing of the case,[1] the Court had to consider whether Congress had power to overrule a decision of the judicial department of government. The Supreme Court said it had that power. Justice Nelson said:

The defendants rely upon this act of Congress as furnishing authority for the continuance of the bridge as constructed, and as superseding the effect and operation of the decree of the court previously rendered, declaring it an obstruction to navigation. . . . Since, however, the rendi-

[1] 18 Howard's Rep., 421.

... the contemplation of

... authority of the
... the ... "Anti-
... ...ting combinations
... in restraint of
... been challenged in
... pass these laws
... a very perfunctory
... in disregarding
... with the meaning
...

tracts could be applied to contracts made before it was adopted.   Justice Peckham said:

The language of the act includes *every* contract, combination in the form of trust or otherwise, or conspiracy, in restraint of trade or commerce among the several States or with foreign nations. So far as the very terms of the statute go, they apply to any contract of the nature described.   A contract therefore that is in restraint of trade or commerce is by the strict language of the act prohibited even though such contract is entered into between competing common carriers by railroad, and only for the purpose of thereby affecting traffic rates for the transportation of persons and property. If such an agreement restrain trade or commerce, it is prohibited by the statute, unless it can be said that an agreement, no matter what its terms, relating only to transportation cannot restrain trade or commerce. We see no escape from the conclusion that if any agreement of such a nature does restrain it, the agreement is condemned by this act.

This decision was rendered by a majority of the Court. Four justices, including Justice White, later Chief Justice of the United States, thought the other five were wrong in their idea of the meaning and application of this important statute. A divided court cannot render a final decision on any point. Therefore, two years later (1898), the validity of the Sherman Law was again challenged in the case of *United States vs. Joint Traffic Association.*[1] In this case, it was urged that Congress has no power to punish all contracts in restraint of trade, but only such contracts as are prejudicial to society. The railroad companies belonging to the Joint Traffic Association insisted that their

[1] 171 U. S. Rep., 505.

tion of this decree, the acts of Congress already ro
have been passed, by which the bridge is made a
for the passage of the mails of the United States,
defendants are authorized to have and maintain
present site and elevation, and requiring all po
gating the river to regulate such navigation
interfere with it. So far, therefore, as this brid
obstruction to the free navigation of the river.
previous acts of Congress, they are to be reg
fied by this subsequent legislation; and although
be an obstruction in fact, it is not so in the
law.

No one nowadays disputes the
law-making department to enact the
Trust" Law and other statutes forbid
and monopolies, rebatings, and con
trade. Each of these laws in turn has
the courts, but the power of Congre
has gone unchallenged, except in
way. The questions raised under
laws have been largely concern
and application of the laws
validity. For example, in 180
States vs. Trans-Missouri F
point in dispute was the mea
tract in restraint of trade
combination of railroad c
formed, before the Sherma
purpose of mutual pro

Delaware and Hudson Railroad Company, the Erie Railroad, the Central Railroad of New Jersey, the Delaware, Lackawanna and Western Railroad, the Pennsylvania Railroad, and the Lehigh Valley Railroad, all of which had after the enactment of the law transported in interstate commerce coal produced by coal mining companies in which they were interested as stockholders, were called upon in 1908 to answer in the United States Courts indictments charging violation of this "commodities" clause.[1] Each of the railroad companies interposed by way of defense the contention that the interest which they as stockholders had in the coal companies was not an "interest, direct or indirect" in its products within the meaning of those words as used in the Hepburn Act. Justice White, who had dissented from the decision in the Trans-Missouri case, now announced a new interpretation of the Sherman Law as follows:

It remains to determine the nature and character of the interest embraced in the words "in which it is interested directly or indirectly." . . . If it be true that the mind of Congress was fixed on the transportation by a carrier of any commodity produced by a corporation in which the carrier held stock, then we think the failure to provide for such a contingency in express language gives rise to the implication that it was not the purpose to include it. At all events in view of the far-reaching consequences of giving the statute such a construction as that contended for, as indicated by the statement taken from the answers and returns which we have previously inserted in the margin [notes annexed to the opinion], and of the questions of constitutional power which would arise

[1] U. S. vs. D. and H. R. R. Co., 213 U. S. Rep., 366.

8

if that construction was adopted, we hold the contention of the government not well founded.

We then construe the statute as prohibiting a railroad company engaged in interstate commerce from transporting in such commerce articles or commodities under the following circumstances and conditions: (a) When the article or commodity has been manufactured, mined, or produced by a carrier or under its authority, and at the time of transportation the carrier has not in good faith before the act of transportation dissociated itself from such article or commodity; (b) When the carrier owns the article or commodity to be transported in whole or in part; (c) When the carrier at the time of transportation has an interest, direct or indirect, in a legal or equitable sense in the article or commodity, not including, therefore, articles or commodities manufactured, mined, produced, or owned, etc., by a *bona fide* corporation in which the railroad company is a stockholder. The question then arises whether, as thus construed, the statute was inherently without the power of Congress to enact as a regulation of commerce. That it was, we think is apparent.

Having decided that the Hepburn Act meant less than it said, the Supreme Court was bound to say sooner or later that the Sherman Law did not mean all it said. When the Standard Oil Company and the Tobacco "Trust" were called to the bar of justice, a ruling that the "light of reason" must be used in the interpretation of the Sherman Law did not save them from being condemned to dissolution. Chief Justice White did not find it easy to reconcile the old rulings with the new theory. In the Trans-Missouri and Joint-Traffic cases, the Court had decided only that certain contracts complained of had restrained trade and had produced the injuries which the statute was intended to prevent, and had not, in those cases, committed itself to any hard and fast rule of interpretation.   On this ground, he said that those decisions did not control the Court. In the case of *Standard Oil Co. vs. United States*,[1] he said:

In substance, the propositions urged by the government are reducible to this: That the language of the statute embraces every contract, combination, etc., in restraint of trade, and hence its text leaves no room for the exercise of judgment, but simply imposes the plain duty of applying its prohibitions to every case within its literal language. The error involved lies in assuming the matter to be decided. This is true because as the acts which may come under the classes stated in the first section and the restraint of trade to which that section applies are not specifically enumerated or defined, it is obvious that judgment must in every case be called into play in order to determine whether a particular act is embraced within the statutory classes, and whether if the act is within such classes its nature or effect causes it to be a restraint of trade within the intendment of the act. To hold to the contrary would require the conclusion either that every contract, act, or combination of any kind or nature, whether it operated a restraint on trade or not, was within the statute, and thus the statute would be destructive of all right to contract or agree or combine in any respect whatever as to subjects embraced in interstate trade or commerce, or if this conclusion were not reached, then the contention would require it to be held that as the statute did not define the things to which it related and excluded resort to the only means by which the acts to which it relates could be ascertained—the light of reason—the enforcement of the statute was impossible because of its uncertainty.   The merely generic enumeration which the statute makes of the acts to which it refers and the absence of any definition of restraint of trade as used in the statute leaves room for but

[1] 221 U. S. Rep., 1.

interstate commerce ever could be used to regulate the conduct of individuals. Immorality, dishonesty, violence, murder, and other crimes were offences against the sovereignty of each State, which imposed such punishments as its citizens thought proper. Such local regulation, in the absence of any national control, enabled many persons to avoid punishment for offences which began in one State and ended in another.

This unsatisfactory method of control lasted until the abolition of slavery removed one of the reasons for exclusive local regulation of safety, health, and morals. Then it began to be seen that standards of conduct ought not to follow State lines.

In 1895, Congress enacted a law which prohibited under severe penalties the transportation of lottery tickets from one State to another. In February, 1899, three persons were indicted in the United States Court for sending lottery tickets by Wells-Fargo Express from Dallas, Texas, to Fresno, California. Out of their arrest grew the celebrated *Lottery Case*.[1] The accused persons petitioned the Supreme Court for release by writ of habeas corpus, upon the ground that the Lottery Act was repugnant to and inconsistent with the Constitution of the United States in that it was an exercise of the police power which had not been delegated to the United States, but had been reserved to the States or the people. Justice Harlan, in sustaining the law, said:

We cannot think of any clause of that instrument [the Constitution] that could possibly be invoked by those who assert their right to send lottery tickets from State to State except the one providing that no person shall be deprived of liberty without due process of law. We have said that the

[1] 188 U. S. Rep., 356.

ment aside in an opinion delivered by Justice McKenna, in which the absolute power of Congress in these cases was described as follows:

The question here is whether articles which are outlaws of commerce may be seized wherever found, and it certainly will not be contended that they are outside of the jurisdiction of the National Government when they are within the borders of a State. The question in the case, therefore, is, What power has Congress over such articles? Can they escape the consequences of their illegal transportation by being mingled at the place of destination with other property? To give them such immunity would defeat, in many cases, the provision for their confiscation, and their confiscation or destruction is the especial concern of the law. The power to do so is certainly appropriate to the right to bar them from interstate commerce, and completes its purpose, which is not to prevent merely the physical movement of adulterated articles, but the use of them, or rather to prevent trade in them between the States by denying to them the facilities of interstate commerce. And appropriate means to that end, which we have seen is legitimate, are the seizure and condemnation of the articles at their point of destination in the original, unbroken packages. The selection of such means is certainly within that breadth of discretion which we have said Congress possesses in the execution of the powers conferred upon it by the Constitution.

The power of Congress to suppress the "white slave" traffic under the interstate commerce clause is stated in the case of *Hoke and Economides vs. United States*.[1] In this case, one Effie Hoke, who had been convicted in a United States district court under the Federal law forbidding the transporting of women and girls from one State to another for immoral purposes, and a man

[1] 227 U. S. Rep., 308.

regulate Com- ... the colonial govern- ... peace alliance, and

over them."[1]

This right of unlimited control has been translated into a moral duty of guardianship in the interest of the Indians, especially for their protection against unscrupulous individuals and even against unscrupulous States. For there always has been a general feeling in the newer States that the natives of the soil ought to be made to give place to white men. This sentiment was strong in Georgia, in 1832, when the case of *Worcester vs. Georgia*[2] was decided by the Supreme Court of the United States. The Rev. Samuel A. Worcester, one of the first of our missionaries to the Indians, who had been preaching the gospel and translating the scriptures into the Cherokee language at New Echota in the Cherokee reservation in the western part of Georgia, was arrested and convicted in the Superior Court of Gwinnett County, Georgia, under a State law which declared that no persons should live with the Indians except such as had taken an oath of allegiance to the State, and had been duly licensed by the governor. Mr. Worcester defended himself by proving that he had been licensed to go to the Cherokee reservation by the

[1] *Jaeger vs. U. S.*, 27 Court of Claims Rep., 278, 285.
[2] 6 Peters' Rep., 515.

President of the United States. He showed that our treaties with that nation expressly stipulated that citizens of the United States should not enter the Cherokee territory without passports from the President of the United States or the governor of the State. He then asserted that the laws of Georgia under which he had been convicted were unconstitutional and void because they were an attempt to regulate and control the intercourse with the said Cherokee nation, which by the said Constitution belongs exclusively to the Congress of the United States. In other words, Mr. Worcester said that the Georgia law under which he had been tried was unconstitutional because it was repugnant to the clause in the Constitution which gives Congress power to regulate commerce with the Indian tribes.

He was convicted in the Georgia court, which sentenced him to four years' imprisonment at hard labor. He appealed to the Supreme Court of the United States, which set aside the judgment of the State court in an opinion which does not conceal the indignation of the great Chief Justice who pronounced it.

The governor of Georgia disregarded the mandate of the Supreme Court ordering the release of the missionary, and President Jackson, who hated the Chief Justice cordially, refused to take any action. The missionary was left to the tender mercies of the State authorities, which however pardoned him as soon as their political point had been made. The State of Georgia was satisfied when President Jackson said: "John Marshall has made his decision. Now let him enforce it." The opinion of the Court was in part as follows:

The Cherokee Nation . . . is a distinct community, occupying its own territory, with boundaries accurately described, in which the laws of Georgia can have no force, and which the citizens of Georgia have no right to enter, but with the assent of the Cherokees themselves, or in conformity with treaties and with the acts of Congress. The whole intercourse between the United States and this nation is, by our Constitution and laws, vested in the government of the United States. The act of the State of Georgia, under which the plaintiff . . . was prosecuted, is consequently void, and the judgment is a nullity. . . .

He [Mr. Worcester] was seized and forcibly carried away while under the guardianship of treaties guaranteeing the country in which he resided, and taking it under the protection of the United States. He was seized while performing, under the sanction of the chief magistrate of the Union, those duties which the humane policy adopted by Congress had recommended. He was apprehended, tried, and condemned under color of a law which has been shown to be repugnant to the Constitution, laws, and treaties of the United States. . . .

It is the opinion of this court that the judgment of the Superior Court for the County of Gwinnett, in the State of Georgia, condemning Samuel A. Worcester to hard labor, in the penitentiary of the State of Georgia for four years, was pronounced by that court under color of a law which is void, as being repugnant to the Constitution, treaties, and laws of the United States, and ought, therefore, to be reversed and annulled.

CHAPTER X

Art. I., Sec. 8, Subd. 4. To establish an uniform Rule of Naturalization, and uniform Laws on the subject of Bankruptcies throughout the United States;

Art. I., Sec. 8, Subd. 5. To coin Money, regulate the Value thereof, and of foreign Coin, and fix the Standard of Weights and Measures;

Art. I., Sec. 8, Subd. 6. To provide for the Punishment of counterfeiting the Securities and current Coin of the United States;

Art. I., Sec. 8, Subd. 7. To establish Post Offices and post Roads;

Art. I., Sec. 8, Subd. 8. To promote the Progress of Science and the useful Arts, by securing for limited Times to Authors and Inventors the exclusive Right to their respective Writings and Discoveries.

The American colonists knew that their vast territory would become immensely valuable as soon as it was well peopled. They resented the check upon immigration caused by the refusal of Great Britain to naturalise the immigrants, and said so with blunt directness in the Declaration of Independence. The Continental Congress very early in its history declared that all persons who lived in any of the colonies were members of the local body politic.[1] The Articles of Confederation

---

[1] Andrews, On the Constitution, p. 86.

contained a clause which gave all the free inhabitants of each of the States, "paupers, vagabonds, and fugitives from justice excepted," the status of citizens of the United States.[1] The bankruptcy clause, by affording legal relief for alien debtors, was a further incentive to immigration. Primarily, however, Federal control over bankruptcy is logically a part of the power of Congress to regulate commerce.

The Congress shall have Power To . . . establish an uniform Rule of Naturalisation. The naturalization which this clause provides for is "the act of adopting a foreigner and clothing him with the privileges of a native citizen."[2] It gives him all the privileges of one who is native born, except that he cannot be President or Vice-President. Of the naturalized citizen Chief Justice Marshall, in the case of *Osborn vs. United States Bank*,[3] said:

He [the naturalized citizen] becomes a member of the society, possessing all the rights of a native citizen, and standing in the view of the Constitution on the footing of a native.

This rule was applied by President Buchanan in a famous diplomatic incident just before the Civil War, the story of which is thus told in John Bassett Moore's *Digest of International Law*[4]: "Christian Ernst, a native of Hanover, emigrated to the United States in 1851, when nineteen years of age. In February, 1859, he was

[1] Articles of Confederation, Art. IV.
[2] Boyd *vs.* Nebraska, 143 U. S. Rep., 162.
[3] 9 Wheaton's Rep., 739.
[4] John Bassett Moore's *Digest of International Law*, vol. iii., pp. 573-578.

naturalized, and in the following month procured a
passport and went back to Hanover on a visit. On
arriving in his native village he was arrested and forced
into the Hanoverian army. President Buchanan submitted the case to Attorney-General Black for an opinion. Attorney-General Black advised . . . that it was
the 'natural right of every free person, who owes no
debts and is not guilty of any crime, to leave the country
of his birth in good faith and for an honest purpose,'
and to throw off his natural allegiance and substitute
another in its place; . . . that 'natural reason and
justice,' 'writers of known wisdom,' and 'the practice
of civilized nations' were all 'opposed to the doctrine
of perpetual allegiance,' and that the United States was
pledged to the right of expatriation and could not without perfidy repudiate it; that expatriation 'includes not
only *emigration* out of one's native country, but *naturalization* in the country adopted as a future residence';
that 'naturalization does *ipso facto* [by the fact itself]
place the native and adopted citizen in precisely the
same relations with the government under which they
live, except in so far as the express and positive law of
the country has made a distinction in favor of one or
the other'; that, with regard to the protection of American citizens in their rights at home and abroad, there
was no law that divided them into classes or made any
difference whatever between them; that the opinion
held by 'persons of very high reputation' that a naturalized citizen ought to be protected everywhere except in
the country of his birth had 'no foundation to rest
upon . . . except the dogma which denies altogether
the right of expatriation without the consent of his
native country,' . . . that the Hanoverian government
could justify the arrest of Mr. Ernst only by proving

that the original right of expatriation depended on the consent of the natural sovereign—a proposition, which, said Mr. Black, 'I am sure no man can establish.'

"The views of the President in relation to the case of Christian Ernst and analogous cases were communicated to the American minister at Berlin, July 8, 1859. In this communication the position was maintained that . . . by the treaty with Hanover, which provided that the 'inhabitants' of each country should be permitted to sojourn in all parts of the other, submitting to the laws, every inhabitant of the United States had a right to visit that country and sojourn there in the prosecution of his business, and that no distinction could be made in this regard between a native and a naturalized citizen of the United States. . . .

"On August 20, 1859, the Hanoverian government stated that a 'full pardon' had been granted to Ernst and that he had been 'dismissed' from the military service."

The Congress shall have Power To . . . establish . . . uniform Laws on the subject of Bankruptcies throughout the United States. Congress has not enacted many bankruptcy laws. The law of 1800, repealed in 1803, gave relief only to certain classes of men who actually were engaged in business, and not even then unless the creditors asked the courts to divide the debtor's property among them. The debtor could not himself invoke the help of the law. The next bankruptcy law was passed in 1841, and repealed in 1843. Another, adopted in 1867, remained in force until 1878. The present law was enacted in 1898.

The Constitution calls for "uniform" naturalization rules and "uniform" bankruptcy laws. Chief Justice Waite, sitting as a Circuit Court judge, in the

... the word "money" as

... law account of a general
... of the back
... currency, carried in every and acquiring
... according to their respec-
... therefore to confine ...
... process could reach ...
... throughout the United
... the meaning of that term as used

... From To ... *coin Money*.
... power to coin money was
... from in the case of *United*
... In October 1848, one Peter
... Albany New York, for having
... brought a number of counterfeits
... the United States which he
... In the trial of the case in
... Court, the defendant claimed
... that *money* could not be
... make a law against bringing
... currency from abroad. Justice
... the decision said.

... money and of regulating its value
... the Constitution for the very
... the framers of that instrument, if
... the uniformity and parity of such
... on account of the impossibility
... settling the inequalities
... necessarily incident to different rates

of policy, which in different communities would be brought to bear on this subject.

The Congress shall have Power To . . . regulate the Value thereof [of Money].   Congress has absolute power to decide what metal may be coined into money and what proportion the coined money shall bear to the value of the bullion out of which it is made.   In the *Legal Tender Cases*,[1] Justice Strong said:

The Constitution does not ordain what metals may be coined, or prescribe that the legal value of the metals, when coined, shall correspond at all with their intrinsic value in the market. . . .   Confessedly the power to regulate the value of money coined, and of foreign coins, is not exhausted by the first regulation.   More than once in our history has the regulation been changed without any denial of the power of Congress to change it, and it seems to have been left to Congress to determine alike what metal shall be coined, its purity, and how far its statutory value, as money, shall correspond, from time to time, with the market value of the same metal as bullion.   How then can a grant of a power to coin money and regulate its value, made in terms so liberal and unrestrained, coupled also with a denial to the States of all power over the currency, be regarded as an implied prohibition to Congress against declaring treasury notes a legal tender, if such declaration is appropriate, and adapted to carrying into execution the admitted powers of the government?

The Congress shall have Power To . . . fix the Standard of Weights and Measures.   About 1834, the Pennsylvania assembly enacted a law which made 2,000 lbs. a legal ton.   A man named Holt delivered several hundred tons of coal under a contract with a ship-owning firm, and,

[1] 12 Wallace's Rep., 457, 546.

motion of a convicted counterfeiter that the verdict of the jury be annulled because the indictment for counterfeiting did not charge an intent to pass the bogus money, District Judge Deady of Oregon explained as follows the kind of law he thought should be meted out to a counterfeiter[1]:

In the case of the actual forger or counterfeiter, knowledge of the character of the coin, and the fraudulent intent to put it into circulation, in some way, as genuine, are implied from the fact of the false making, and need not be specially averred. . . . And, if this is not the law, Congress ought to make it so. No one ought to be allowed to trifle with the integrity of the coin of the realm. The circulating medium of a people is the life to its trade and commerce and ought not to be exposed to the danger of corruption from contact or commingling with the spurious coinage of amateur forgers and counterfeiters.

The Congress shall have Power To . . . establish Post Offices and post Roads. Justice Clifford of the Supreme Court traced the origin of the United States post office in his opinion in the case of *Ware vs. United States*[2]:

A general post office was established on the twenty-sixth day of July, 1775, the year before the Declaration of Independence. By that ordinance it was directed that a line of posts be appointed under the direction of the Postmaster General from Falmouth [now Portland, Maine] to Savannah, with as many cross-posts as he shall think fit; and he was authorized to appoint as many deputies as to him might seem proper and necessary. Amendments were made to that ordinance from time to time to the twenty-eighth day of October, 1782, when it was repealed, and a supplemental ordinance was adopted in its place, conferring substantially

[1] U. S. vs. Otey, 31 Federal Rep., 68.   [2] 4 Wallace's Rep., 630.

habeas corpus was then filed with the Supreme Court
of the United States.   This case of *Ex Parte Jackson*[1]
brought squarely before the Court the question whether,
under the power "to establish post offices and post
roads," Congress can order excluded from the mails
any letter or packet upon which the postage has been
paid.   Justice Field, in the decision of this case, said:

The validity of legislation prescribing what should be
carried [by the mails] and its weight and form, and the
charges to which it should be subjected, has never been
questioned. What should be mailable has varied at different
times, changing with the facility of transportation over the
post roads. At one time, only letters, newspapers, magazines, pamphlets, and other printed matter, not exceeding
eight ounces in weight were carried; afterwards books were
added to the list; and now small packages of merchandise,
not exceeding a prescribed weight, as well as books and
printed matter of all kinds are transported in the mail.
The power possessed by Congress embraces the regulation
of the entire postal system of the Country. The right to
designate what shall be carried necessarily involves the
right to determine what shall be excluded. . . .

In excluding various articles from the mail, the object of
Congress has not been to interfere with the freedom of the
press, or with any other rights of the people; but to refuse
its facilities for the distribution of matter deemed injurious
to the public morals.   Thus by Act of March 3, 1873,
Congress declared that no obscene, lewd, or lascivious book,
pamphlet, picture, paper, print, or other publication of
an indecent character, or any article or thing designed or
intended for the prevention of conception or procuring of
abortion, nor any article or thing intended or adapted for
any indecent or immoral use or nature, nor any written or
printed card, circular, book, pamphlet, advertisement, or

[1] 96 U. S. Rep., 727.

notice of any kind, giving information, directly or indirectly, where, or how, or of whom, or by what means, either of the things before mentioned may be obtained or made, nor any letter upon the envelope of which, or postal card upon which indecent or scurrilous epithets may be written or printed, shall be carried in the mail; and any person who shall knowingly deposit, or cause to be deposited, for mailing or delivery, any of the hereinbefore mentioned articles or things . . . shall be deemed guilty of a misdemeanor, and on conviction thereof, shall, for every offence, be fined not less than $100, nor more than $5,000, or imprisonment at hard labor not less than one year nor more than ten years, or both, in the discretion of the judge.

All that Congress meant by this act was, that the mail should not be used to transport such corrupting publications and articles, and that any one who attempted to use it for that purpose should be punished. The same inhibition has been extended to lotteries—institutions which are supposed to have a demoralizing influence upon the people. . . . The only question for our determination relates to the constitutionality of the act; and of that we have no doubt.

The Postmaster General issues what are called "fraud orders," whenever it is called to his attention that schemes to cheat and defraud are being carried on by means of the postal facilities of the United States. In

proper exercise of the faculty of the brain and mind, to largely control and remedy the ills that humanity is heir to.   On May 15, 1900, the Postmaster General issued a fraud order directing the postmaster at Nevada, Mo., where the School of Magnetic Healing was located, to "return all letters, whether registered or not, and other mail matter which shall arrive at your office, directed to said concern [American School of Magnetic Healing] and persons [officers of that institution] to the postmasters at the offices at which they were originally mailed, to be delivered to the senders thereof, with the word 'fraudulent' plainly written or stamped upon the outside," and forbidding him to pay any postal money order to said concern and persons.   The officers of the School of Magnetic Healing brought an action in the United States Court of Missouri against the postmaster at Nevada, asking that he be restrained from carrying out the "fraud order" of the Postmaster General.   The case went on appeal to the Supreme Court at Washington, which decided that, as the scheme was not necessarily fraudulent, the School of Magnetic Healing should have its letters.

In the case of *Public Clearing House vs. Coyne*,[1] in which the Supreme Court sustained the validity of a "fraud order" issued by the Postmaster General in November, 1902, it appeared that an Illinois corporation had used the mails in the course of a scheme to induce people to become members and co-operators in what was called a "League of Equity."   The member who paid three dollars as an enrollment fee and agreed to pay one dollar a month for five years, was to receive a proportionate share of the total paid in during five years by all the members; if he secured three new

[1] 194 U. S. Rep., 497.

members in any one year, he might receive at the end of that year one-fifth of the amount which he would be entitled to at the end of five years, assuming that the growth of the concern continued. The Public Clearing House, upon learning that its mail was to be detained, filed a petition for an injunction in the Federal District Court at Chicago. The postmaster of Chicago interposed the defense that the fraud order had been properly issued to suppress a lottery. The case was referred to a master in chancery (an officer of the Court, who hears testimony and reports to the Court the facts of a case), who reported that the petition ought to be denied. The case was taken to the Supreme Court by an appeal where it was decided in favor of the postmaster. Justice Brown, who prepared the opinion, said:

We do not consider it necessary to enter into the details of the plan, which is a somewhat complicated one, and the success of which obviously depended upon constantly and rapidly increasing the number of subscribers or co-operators. The only money paid in was a small enrollment fee of three dollars and a monthly payment of one dollar for five years. The return to the subscribing member, which is called a realization, is not only uncertain in its amount, but depends largely upon the number of new members each subscriber is able to secure, as well as the number of new members which his co-operators are able to secure. The return to members who have been able to secure a large number of other members, and to pay their own monthly dues, may be very large in comparison with the amount paid in, but the amount of such return depends so largely, and indeed almost wholly, upon conditions which the member is unable to control that we think it fulfills all the conditions of a distribution of money by chance. . . .

In the careful and satisfactory report of the master the plan of the complainant is briefly described "as a plan for securing money from a constantly increasing large number for the benefit of a constantly increasing smaller number, with an absolute certainty that when the enterprise reaches an end for any reason the larger number will lose every dollar they have put into it, and in the meantime the smaller number will have realized such amounts as may have resulted from the growth of the larger number; but no one can predict what that growth will be." . . .

The master found that there had been no false representations of existing facts and no unfair dealing with the co-operators; yet, as we held in *Durland vs. United States*, 161 U. S. 206, the misrepresentation of existing facts is not necessary to a conviction under a statute applying to "any scheme or artifice to defraud," as was observed by Mr. Justice Brewer (p. 313), "Some schemes may be promoted through mere representations and promises as to the future, yet are none the less schemes and artifices to defraud. . . . In the light of this the statute must be read, and so read it includes everything designed to defraud by representations as to the past or present, or suggestions and promises as to the future.   The significant fact is the intent and purpose."

Congress makes regular appropriations for all sorts of public improvements under its authority to lay and collect taxes for the public welfare, to regulate interstate commerce, to establish post offices and post roads, and to do what is necessary and proper to execute the judicial power of the nation.   This group of appropriations constitutes the "Pork Barrel," so called because it is as helpful in winning votes as was the old-time free barrel of pork which candidates for office used to open for voters on election day.   Nowadays, the Congressman who fails to obtain an appropriation of public money to be spent in his district, lessens by so much his chance of re-election.   The constituencies seem to think it the official duty of their representative to engineer a vote of public money which will be spent mostly in wages of those who are employed on local improvements for national purposes.

"Probably out of this provision [giving Congress power to establish post offices and post roads], more than any other," says *Watson On the Constitution*,[1] "there grew one of the most important questions ever presented for discussion under the Constitution. It is the great question of internal improvements; that is, whether there is authority to carry them on under the express or implied powers of the Constitution. Judge Story states the beginning of this controversy as follows: 'Upon the construction of this clause of the Constitution, two opposite opinions have been expressed. One maintains that the power to establish postoffices and post roads can intend no more than the power to direct where postoffices shall be kept, and on what roads the mails shall be carried. Or, as it has been on other occasions expressed, the power to establish post roads is a power to designate or point out what roads shall be mail roads, and the right of passage of way along them, when so designated. The other maintains that, although these methods of exercising the power are perfectly constitutional, yet they are not the whole of the power, and do not exhaust it. On the contrary, the power comprehends the right to make or construct any roads which Congress may deem proper for the convenience of the mail, and to keep them in due repair for such purposes.'"

The power of the nation to spend money on public improvements was a debatable question during the years before the Civil War when the Constitution was finding itself. That time has long gone by. A genera-

[1] Vol. I, 643.

tion which has spent nearly half a billion dollars upon the waterway between the oceans at Panama will not waste its time discussing the power of the United States to put its money into national improvements. "The trend of national sentiment for many years," Mr. Watson adds, "has been in favor of appropriations for such improvements, and perhaps no President for fifty years has vetoed a bill because it carried appropriations which provided for the construction of public works coming within the jurisdiction of the general government and possessing national characteristics. The improvement of lakes, rivers, and harbors by deepening their channels, removing obstructions to navigation, constructing dams and docks, as well as the construction of lines of railway crossing the continent have called for appropriations from the national treasury aggregating fabulous sums, and have all met with the approval of a great majority of the American people and been sustained by the courts."[1]

The Congress shall have Power To . . . promote the Progress of Science . . . by securing for limited Times to Authors . . . the exclusive Right to their . . . Writings. The history of protection by copyright was reviewed in 1834, in the case of *Wheaton vs. Peters,*[2] in which Henry Wheaton, one of the early reporters of the decisions of the Supreme Court, tried to enforce his copyright on the twelve volumes of decisions which bear his name. Richard Peters, who, in 1827, succeeded Mr. Wheaton as court reporter, published a book called *Condensed Reports of Cases in the Supreme Court of the United States,* containing all the decisions of the court since its organization and including those which had appeared in the first volume of *Wheaton's Reports.* Mr. Wheaton

<hr />

[1] Vol. i., 648.   [2] 8 Peters' Rep., 593.

... ... of the supreme
... ... Court at Phila-
... ... that ... Peters be in-
... ... matter contained in
... ... that Mr. Wheaton had
... ... decisions of the United
... ... passed by Congress in 1790 and
... ... protection of the courts. Mr.
... ... argued that this was not a
... ... even if his copyright
... ... not good, he was the true
... ... by the ancient law of
... ... property. This controversy,
... ... three questions concern-
... ... make books, and more
... ... whether any person could, by
... ... acquire a copyright upon
... ... of the Supreme Court had
... ... which Mr. Wheaton had
... Supreme Court was "unani-
... reporter has or can have any
... opinions delivered by this
... thereof cannot confer on any
... right. ... Justice McLean, who de-
... ... the Court explained the broad
... ... as follows:

... ... their right on two grounds
... ... Secondly, under the acts
... ... the first case that a
... ... literary property
... ... the rules of the building
... ... where the copy of a book is
... ... by the author of a book at
... ... Court of King's bench in the great

case of *Miller vs. Taylor*, reported in 4 Burr. 2303. This was a case of great expectation, and the four judges, in giving their opinions, *seriatim*, exhausted the argument on both sides. Two of the judges, and Lord Mansfield, held that, by the common law, an author had a literary property in his works; . . . Mr. Justice Yeates . . . maintained the opposite ground. . . .

The question was brought before the House of Lords, in the case of *Donaldson vs. Beckett and others*, reported in 4 Burr. 2408. The eleven judges gave their opinions on the following points:

1.   Whether at common law an author of any book or literary composition, had the sole right of first printing, and publishing the same for sale; and might bring an action against any person who printed, published, and sold the same without his consent. On this question there were eight judges in the affirmative, and three in the negative.

2.   If the author had such right originally, did the law take it away, upon his printing and publishing such book or literary composition; and might any person afterward, reprint and sell, for his own benefit, such book or literary composition, against the will of the author? This question was answered in the affirmative by four judges and in the negative by seven. . . .

4.   Whether the author of any literary composition, and his assigns, had the sole right of printing and publishing the same in perpetuity, by the common law. Which question was decided in favor of the author by seven judges to four.

5.   Whether this right is in any way impeached, restrained, or taken away by the statute 8 Anne. Six to five judges decided that the right is taken away by the statute. . . .

It would appear from the points decided that a majority of the judges were in favor of the common law rights of authors, but that the same had been taken away by the statute. . . .

From the above authorities, and others which might be

referred to if time permitted, the law appears to be well settled in England, that, since the statute of 8 Anne, the literary property of an author in his works can only be asserted under the statute. . . .

That an author, at common law, has a property in his manuscript, and may obtain redress against any one who deprives him of it, or by improperly obtaining a copy, endeavors to realize a profit by its publication, cannot be doubted; but this is a very different right from that which asserts a perpetual and exclusive property in the future publication of the work, after the author shall have published it to the world. . . .

It is insisted that our ancestors, when they migrated to this country brought with them the English common law as a part of their heritage. . . . It was adopted, so far only as its principles were suited to the condition of the colonies; and from this circumstance we see, what is common law in one State is not so considered in another. . . . If the common law, in all its provisions, has not been introduced into Pennsylvania, to what extent has it been adopted? Must not this court have some evidence on this subject? If no right, such as is set up by the complainants, has heretofore been asserted, no custom or usage established, no judicial decision been given, can the conclusion be justified that, by the common law of Pennsylvania, an author has a perpetual property in the copyright of his works?

These considerations might well lead the court to doubt the existence of this law in Pennsylvania; but there are others of a more conclusive character.

The question respecting the literary property of authors was not made a subject of judicial investigation in England until 1760; and no decision was given until the case of *Miller vs. Taylor* . . . was decided in 1769. Long before this time the colony of Pennsylvania was settled. What part of the common law did Penn and his associates bring with them from England? The literary property of authors, as now asserted, was then unknown in that country. . . .

No such right at the common law had been recognized in England when the colony of Penn was organized. Long afterwards, literary property became a subject of controversy, but the question was involved in great doubt and perplexity; and a little more than a century ago [*i.e.*, prior to 1834], it was decided by the highest judicial court in England, that the right of authors could not be asserted at common law, but under the statute. . . . Can it be contended that this common law right, so involved in doubt as to divide the most learned jurists of England, at a period in her history as much distinguished by learning and talents as any other, was brought into the wilds of Pennsylvania by its first adventurers? Was it suited to their condition? But there is another view still more conclusive. In the eighth section of the first article of the Constitution of the United States it is declared, that Congress shall have power "to promote the progress of science and useful arts, by securing for limited times, to authors and inventors the exclusive right to their respective writings and discoveries." And in pursuance of this power thus delegated, Congress passed the act of the 31st of May, 1790. This is entitled "An Act for the encouragement of learning, by securing the copies of maps, charts, and books, to the authors and proprietors of such copies, during the times therein mentioned." . . .

That Congress, in passing the Act of 1790, did not legislate in reference to existing rights, appears clear from the provision that the author, etc., "shall have the sole right and liberty of printing," etc. Now if this exclusive right existed at common law, and Congress were about to adopt legislative provisions for its protection, would they have used this language? Could they have deemed it necessary to vest a right already vested? Such a presumption is refuted by the words above quoted, and their force is not lessened by any other part of the act. Congress, then, by this act, instead of sanctioning an existing right, as contended for, created it.

The Congress shall have Power To . . . promote the Progress of Science and useful Arts, by securing for limited Times to . . . Inventors the exclusive Right to their . . . . . Discoveries. We know what a patent is; because the term has been defined many times by the courts. For example, Chief Justice Marshall in the case of *Grant vs. Raymond,*[1] defined a patent as "the reward stipulated for the advantages derived by the public from the exertion of the individual and is intended as a stimulus to those exertions. . . . The public yields nothing which it has not agreed to yield; it receives all which it has contracted to receive. The full benefit of the discovery, after its enjoyment by the discoverer for fourteen years, is preserved, and for his exclusive enjoyment of it during that time the public faith is pledged." In the case of *National Hollow Brake Beam Co. vs. Interchangeable Brake Beam Co.*[2] in which Mr. George Westinghouse had to defend his title to a valuable part of the railway air brake which goes by his name, Judge Sanborn said:

A patent is a contract by which the government secures to the patentee the exclusive right to vend and use his invention for a few years, in consideration of the fact that he has perfected and described it and has granted its use to the public forever after.

Trade-marks cannot be copyrighted. In the *Trade-Mark Cases,*[3] the Supreme Court withheld its countenance from a law which made it a crime to use imitated or counterfeited trade-marks. In these cases, three men were before the Court charged with having in their possession counterfeited trade-marks. One, a man

[1] 6 Peters' Rep., 242.   [2] 106 Federal Rep., 693, 701.
[3] 100 U. S. Rep., 82, 94.

named Staffens, had imitations of labels owned and used by G. H. Mumm & Company of Rheims, France, on their champagne; another, named Witteman, counterfeits of trade-marks of the Piper Heidsieck brand of champagne; a third, copies of the trade-marks of a firm which manufactured a special brand of whiskey. These defendants challenged the law under which they had been indicted on the ground that the copyright clause of the Constitution did not include trade-marks. Mr. Justice Miller said in the decision:

The trade-mark may be, and generally is, the adoption of something already in existence as the distinctive symbol of the party using it. At common law the exclusive right to it grows out of its use, and not its mere adoption. By the act of Congress this exclusive right attaches upon registration. But in neither case does it depend upon novelty, invention, discovery, or any work of the brains. . . . If the symbol, however plain, simple, old, or well known, has been first appropriated by the claimant as his distinctive trade-mark, he may by registration secure the right to its exclusive use. While such legislation may be a judicious aid to the common law on the subject of trade-marks, and may be within the competency of legislatures whose general powers embrace that class of subjects, we are unable to see any such power in the constitutional provision concerning authors and inventors, and their writings and discoveries.

10

POWERS OF CONGRESS—POWERS TO REGULATE COMMERCE

Art. 1, Sec. 8, Clause 9. To constitute Tribunals inferior to the supreme Court;

Art. 1, Sec. 8, Clause 10. To define and punish Piracies and Felonies committed on the high Seas, and Offences against the Law of Nations;

Art. 1, Sec. 8, Clause 11 to 16. To declare War, grant Letters of Marque and Reprisal, and make Rules concerning Captures on Land and Water; To raise and support Armies, but no Appropriation of Money to that Use shall be for a longer Term than two Years; To provide and maintain a Navy; To make Rules for the Government and Regulation of the land and naval Forces; To provide for calling forth the Militia to execute the Laws of the Union, suppress Insurrections and repel Invasions; To provide for organizing, arming, and disciplining, the Militia, and for governing such Part of them as may be employed in the Service of the United States, reserving to the States respectively, the Appointment of the Officers, and the Authority of training the Militia according to the discipline prescribed by Congress.

"By the [Judiciary] Act of 1789," according to the *International Encyclopedia*, "the States were divided into thirteen districts, which have increased to seventy-six (1906), each district usually having a judge, a clerk, a marshal, and an attorney, appointed by the Federal government.   The district courts have an extensive jurisdiction embracing jurisdiction over admiralty and maritime causes; suits arising under the revenue laws, the civil rights statutes, and various other legislation; prosecutions for crimes against the United States or for the recovery of penalties under Federal laws; proceedings in bankruptcy."

The Circuit Courts of the United States, originally six in number, later nine, were at first held by justices of the Supreme Court and district judges.   At a later date, twenty-nine circuit judges were appointed.   These courts had power to decide civil cases in which more than $2,000 was involved, and appeals from the District Courts.

Circuit Courts of Appeals were established in 1891 in order to relieve the Supreme Court of a part of its work.

The Federal Court system was revised by the Judiciary Act that went into effect on January 1, 1912. This statute abolished the old Circuit Courts of the United States and gave the District Courts power to hear and decide all suits to which the judicial power of the United States extends.   This act also created a new Circuit Court of Appeals in which district judges may sit.   The Court of Claims, which had been established in 1855, was continued.   The Court of Customs Appeals and the Commerce Court (since abolished) were constituted by the same law.

The Congress shall have Power To . . . define and punish Piracies.   Piracy had not been an unpardonable sin in colonial times.   The high seas had not been policed in those days.   Illicit trade with the Spanish West Indies always had been profitable.   Between this traffic and outright piracy, the line had not been clearly drawn. By 1787, things had changed for the better, but no one

argued that seafaring men had improved enough to
be trusted on distant oceans unless there was at home
a law with teeth of steel to induce them to resist temptation. A little later, when the Spanish provinces of
South America had declared for independence on the
American plan, many sturdy rogues, some of them
citizens of the United States, went privateering on the
high seas under letters of marque granted by the new
infant American republics. Their activities, which did
not fall far short of piracy, soon gave our courts oppor-
tunities to define the words and phrases of this division
of the Constitution.

One infamous villain, for example, gave the Supreme
Court, in the case of *United States vs. Smith*,[1] a chance
to decide, not only that he ought to suffer as a pirate,
but also that piracy is nothing more nor less than
robbery on the high seas. The privateer *Creollo* had
been given letters of marque by the government of
Buenos Aires to fight against Spain. In March, 1819,
Smith, the defendant in this case, and others of her
crew had mutinied at Margarita, and seized an armed
vessel called the *Irresistible*, belonging to the government of Artigas which also was at war with Spain.
The rogues at once had put to sea, where they had
captured and robbed a Spanish vessel. The judges of
the United States Circuit Court of Virginia, being
doubtful whether robbery on the high seas was piracy
within the meaning of this clause of the Constitution,
had submitted the case to the Supreme Court. In
deciding the case, Justice Story said:

Whether we advert to writers on the common law, or the
maritime law, or the law of nations, we shall find that they

[1] 5 Wheaton's Rep., 162.

universally treat of piracy as an offence against the law of nations, and that its true definition by that law is robbery upon the sea.

The Congress shall have Power To . . . define and punish . . . Felonies on the high Seas. This power was given to the national government for the sake of uniformity. "If the laws of the States are to prevail on this subject," said Mr. Madison in the Constitutional Convention, "the citizens of different States will be subject to different punishments for the same offence at sea. There will be neither uniformity nor stability in the law."[1]

A vessel is a little kingdom in which the captain is a despot, having unlimited authority so long as his ship is on the ocean. Seafaring men are a rough lot at best; sometimes they are desperate and unscrupulous. Even now, passengers need sharp laws to protect them against crimes which may be committed ten thousand miles away from a police court. In an era when outrages committed in the Indian Ocean might not be known in New York or Boston for six months or a year or perhaps never, the need of such protection was much greater.

The case of *United States vs. Holmes,*[2] which was tried out in the United States Circuit Court of Massachusetts in 1818, gave Justice Bushrod Washington of the Supreme Court an opportunity to let the world know that the United States would do its full duty in punishing criminal acts of all sorts, committed on the ocean. Two privateers, sailing under letters of marque from Buenos Aires, had captured a Spanish ship and

---

[1] Madison's *Journal*, vol. ii., p. 186, New York, G. P. Putnam's Sons, 1908. [2] 5 Wheaton's Rep., 12.

… Holmes … the … vessel had … overboard … interior court … a right of power under the … signal upon a citizen of the … a foreigner … high seas. Justice Washington …

… a foreign vessel
… board of a vessel
… offender is to be
… under whose
… a citizen or a
… the offence is
… the United States

… of the United States
… on the high seas."
… given in the case of

… William Ross
…
…
…
…
…
…
…
…
…
…

waters of another country and had died before the ship reached a port of the United States. Justice Story of the Supreme Court, sitting at the trial as a Circuit Judge, said:

> I am of opinion that the words "high seas" mean any waters on the sea coast, which are without the boundaries of low water mark; although such waters may be in a roadstead or bay, within the jurisdictional limits of a foreign government. . . . In the present case, the crime was not completed until the vessel was standing out at sea under sail. The mortal stabs were given when the vessel was about a half mile from the shore; but the death did not happen until the vessel had drifted or sailed a considerable distance. I do not, however, deem the difference material. Had the death occurred *instanter*, I think it would have been a homicide on the high seas.

The Congress shall have Power To . . . define and punish . . . Offences against the Law of Nations. One of the accepted principles of international law is that one country must not allow its laws to be used to shield those who commit crimes against another country. For example, in the case of *United States vs. Arjona*,[1] a man named Ramon Arjona was charged in the United States Court in New York City with counterfeiting and having in his possession counterfeited bank notes of a bank in Bolivar, one of the States of the United States of Colombia. Arjona's defense was that the statute of 1884 for the suppression of the counterfeiting in the United States of foreign bank notes was unconstitutional in that Congress had no power to enact such a law. Chief Justice Waite, in the course of the decision, said:

[1] 120 U. S. Rep., 479.

The law of nations requires every national government to use "due diligence" to prevent a wrong being done within its own dominion to another nation with which it is at peace or to the people thereof; and because of this the obligation of one nation to punish those who within its own jurisdiction counterfeit the money of another nation has long been recognized. . . . It was incumbent on the United States as a nation to use due diligence to prevent any injury to another nation or its people by counterfeiting its money or its public or *quasi* public securities. This statute was enacted as a means to that end, that is to say, as a means of performing a duty which had been cast on the United States by the law of nations, and it was clearly appropriate legislation for that purpose. Upon its face, therefore, it defines an offense against the law of nations as clearly as if Congress had in express terms so declared.

The Congress shall have Power To . . . declare War. The framers of the Constitution turned over an ample measure of the powers of war to Congress because Representatives and Senators are delegates of the People and States of the United States whose commercial interests must be staked upon the issues of every conflict. The People pay the bill. Therefore, their representatives in Congress are of right the proper persons to control military affairs.

"The war making power," according to the decision in the case of *Perkins vs. Rogers*,[1] "is, by the Constitution, vested in Congress and . . . the President has no power to declare war or conclude peace except as he may be empowered by Congress. . . . The existence of war, and the restoration of peace are to be determined by the political department of the government, and such determination is binding and conclusive upon

[1] 35 Indiana Rep., 167.

the courts, and deprives the courts of the power of hearing proof and determining as a question of fact either that war exists or has ceased to exist."

In the course of the decision of the case of *Brown vs. United States*,[1] which grew out of one of the incidents of the War of 1812 with Great Britain, Chief Justice Marshall took pains to explain just what happens to commerce when war is declared. A ship owned in Massachusetts, chartered to a British company and loaded with British goods, had put in at New Bedford, where, at the instance of the Federal authorities, the cargo had been claimed as enemy property. An action for forfeiture had been instituted upon the claim that the goods seized were the property of an alien enemy. The case finally reached the Supreme Court of the United States, where Chief Justice Marshall ruled that a declaration of war does not of itself authorize the seizure and condemnation of property of the enemy, but that a special act of Congress must be passed for that purpose. He said:

The declaration of war has only the effect of placing the two nations in a state of hostility, of producing a state of war, of giving those rights which war confers; but not of operating, by its own force, any of those results, such as a transfer of property, which are usually produced by ulterior measures of government.

The Congress shall have Power To . . . grant Letters of Marque and Reprisal. In Revolutionary days, owners of small ships found profitable employment as privateers. A smart sailing master with a good reputation as a fighting man, could get any number of stout fellows to take the chances of the sea against the merchant

[1] 8 Cranch's Rep., 120.

The law of earthly, . the . testimental . Congress issued to use "ducuds pinou" in order to harass the enemy and its own door unto to already suffered. Many an honest Dewitt to Congress das to put in prize money during hilario of last water. Vet, and was sorry when it was over. jurisdiction could not ascertain did their share for the long been hidden. Their captures of muskets, gun-United . . . military supplies often came in the nick any injry . . . Washington had more soldiers than he its money . . . with arms. Privateering now being out of . . . means . . . of the Constitution is obsolete.

United Congress shall have Power To . . . make Rules appointing Captures on Land and Water. This clause gives Congress a right to prescribe what disposition shall be made of property captured in time of war; and the President, as commander-in-chief of the Army and Navy carries out its directions. The case of *The Thomas Gibbons*[1] turned upon President Madison's instructions of August 28, 1812, that privateers should not interrupt any vessels belonging to citizens of the United States, coming from British ports to the United States laden with British merchandise, in consequence of the repeal of the British Orders in Council.

The Thomas Gibbons, one of those very ships, had been brought into the harbor of Savannah by a priva-teer which claimed her as a prize. The Federal District Court sustained the protest of the owners that the ship and cargo were protected from seizure by the terms of the President's proclamation. The appeal of this case to the Supreme Court resulted in a declaration that it is for Congress to lay down, and for the President to enforce, rules concerning "captures on land and water." Justice Story said:

[1] 8 Cranch's Rep., 421.

It is very clear that the President has, under the Prize Act, power to grant, annul, and revoke at his pleasure, the commissions of privateers; and by the act declaring war, he is authorized to issue the commission in such form as he shall deem fit. . . .   In this view, the commission is qualified and restrained by the power of the President to issue instructions.   The privateer takes it subject to such power, and contracts to act in obedience to all the instructions which the President may lawfully promulgate.

The Congress shall have Power To . . . raise and support Armies, but no Appropriation of Money to that Use shall be for a longer Term than two Years.   The Supreme Court has said that in this particular the power of Congress is "plenary and exclusive."   This statement was made in *Tarble's Case,*[1] in which the main question was whether a State court has any right to discharge a soldier from military service by writ of habeas corpus.   One Edward Tarble had enlisted in the United States army in July, 1869.   Soon afterward, his father had petitioned a Wisconsin court to issue a writ of habeas corpus on the ground that, as the boy was under eighteen, he could not legally be enlisted.   The writ was issued and served on his commanding officer, who protested that the State court had no power to release a Federal soldier by this means.   When, in spite of this objection, the release was ordered the case was taken to the Supreme Court of Wisconsin, which ruled that a State court might lawfully decide whether a Federal court had jurisdiction in a case involving the rights and liberties of a citizen of a State.   The military authorities now took the case to the Supreme Court at Washington, and asked that tribunal to decide whether

[1] 13 Wallace's Rep., 397.

... and the Courts were to be dealt with
... Justice Field said:

> ... the National government
> ... armies," and the power
> ... and regulation of the land
> ... these powers falls
> ... control over the subject
> ... determine, without ques-
> ... how the armies shall be
> ... enlistment or forced draft,
> ... be received, and the period
> ... the compensation he shall be
> ... which he shall be assigned. . . .
> ... execution of this power of the
> ... formation, organization, and
> ... any State officials could be
> ... impairing the efficiency, if it did
> ... of the public service.

> ... which Congress may make
> ... support of an army, was estab-
> ... the members of the House
> ... elected every two years. The
> ... Congress must assume respon-
> ... army, since it has to take
> ... the biennial appropriation
> ... Hamilton is said to have
> ... The Federalist" which says:

> ... United States will be *obliged*, by
> ... every two years, to deliberate
> ... keeping a military force on foot; to
> ... the point; and to declare their
> ... by a formal vote in the face of their

The Congress shall have Power . . . To provide and maintain a Navy. Congress can appropriate money to be used in building and equipping battleships and in providing all appliances for the navy, which when thus established is under the control of the President.

The Congress shall have Power . . . To make Rules for the Government and Regulation of the land and naval Forces. This clause gives Congress power to formulate military codes and institute courts-martial by which the President maintains discipline in the army and navy. ⎟

Courts of law may not interfere with courts-martial. In the case of *Dynes vs. Hoover*,[1] an attempt was made to induce the Supreme Court to prevent the execution of the sentence of a naval court-martial on the ground that the Supreme Court has power over all cases arising under the Constitution. Frank Dynes had been convicted at New York under the Act of April 23, 1800, of having attempted to desert from the U. S. Ship *Independence* on September 12, 1854, and sentenced to six months' imprisonment in the penitentiary of the District of Columbia. The President ordered the United States marshal to receive Dynes from a vessel which had brought him from New York to Washington, and commit him to the penitentiary of the District of Columbia. The prisoner tried to regain his liberty by suing the marshal for false imprisonment upon the ground that the President had no constitutional authority to issue such an order. The defendant answered that, as marshal of the District of Columbia, he had imprisoned the plaintiff under the authority of the President and in execution of the sentence of a naval court-martial. Justice Wayne, in the course of the decision of the Supreme Court, took occasion to say that the judiciary has no power to control the action of military and naval courts established by Congress under this constitutional clause. He said in part:

Among the powers conferred upon Congress by the 8th section of the first article of the Constitution, are the following: "to provide and maintain a navy"; "to make rules for the government of the land and naval forces." . . . Congress passed the Act of 23d April, 1800, providing rules for the government of the navy. . . . The 35th article provides for the appointment of courts-martial to try all offenses which may arise in the naval service. . . . In this case, all of us think that the court which tried Dynes had jurisdiction over the subject matter of the charge against him.

The Congress shall have Power . . . . To provide for calling forth the Militia to execute the Laws of the Union, suppress Insurrections and repel Invasions. The framers of the Constitution gave Congress, instead of the President, power to summon the militia for active service, because the law-making bodies were under the control of the People and the States. They limited the power of Congress over the militia by providing that the citizen soldiery should not be called into active service except for three specified objects.

No serious question arose under this clause until, in 1861, it became necessary to use the militia of the loyal States against the States which had attempted to secede from the Union. At the beginning of the Civil

War, President Lincoln, under the authority of certain acts of Congress which dated back to 1795 and 1807, called out the militia, so that the laws should be faithfully executed[1] in those States where the Federal Courts had become ineffective. His proclamation putting the ports of the Confederacy under blockade was challenged in the Supreme Court in *The Prize Cases*,[2] in which the question was whether the citizen soldiers of some States could be used under the authority of acts of Congress to obstruct access to the harbors of other States. Proceedings were brought in the Federal Courts against a number of vessels which had been captured as blockade runners. Some of these were condemned and others released, according to the merits of each case. Justice Grier sustained the war powers of Congress in these words:

By the Constitution, Congress alone has power to declare a national or foreign war. It cannot declare war against a State, or any number of States, by virtue of any clause in the Constitution. The Constitution confers on the President the whole Executive power. He is bound to take care that the laws be faithfully executed. He is Commander-in-chief of the Army and Navy of the United States, and of the militia of the several States when called into the actual service of the United States. He has no power to initiate or declare a war either against a foreign nation or a domestic State. But by the Acts of Congress of February 28, 1795, and 3d of March, 1807, he is authorized to call out the militia and use the military and naval forces of the United States in case of invasion by foreign nations, and to suppress insurrection against the government of a State or of the United States. . . . He does not initiate the war, but is bound to accept the challenge without waiting for any

[1] U. S. Const., Art. II., Sec. 3.   [2] 2 Black's Rep., 635.

special legislative authority. And whether the hostile party be a foreign invader, or States organized in rebellion, it is none the less a war, although the declaration of it be "unilateral."

The Congress shall have Power . . . To provide for organizing, arming, and disciplining the Militia, and for governing such Part of them as may be employed in the Service of the United States, reserving to the States respectively, the Appointment of the Officers, and the Authority of training the Militia according to the discipline prescribed by Congress. The Supreme Court explained the meaning of this clause in the case of *Houston vs. Moore.*[1] A Pennsylvania militiaman named Houston had refused to march with his detachment when called into actual service by the governor in pursuance of an order or requisition made by the President of the United States on July 4, 1814. Houston was tried by court-martial under a Pennsylvania law, which provided that any person who refused to obey when so ordered out should be liable to the penalties prescribed by the Act of Congress of February 28, 1795. A fine was imposed and collected out of his property. He thereupon brought a lawsuit against the deputy marshal who had collected the fine upon the claim that the Pennsylvania law was null and void because the United States alone had power to punish him for disobedience of its orders. Justice Washington said:

Upon the whole, I am of opinion, after the most laborious examination of this delicate question, that the State court-martial had a concurrent jurisdiction with the tribunal pointed out by the acts of Congress to try a militia-man who

[1] 5 Wheaton's Rep., 1.

had disobeyed the call of the President, and to enforce the laws of Congress against such delinquent; and that this authority will remain to be so exercised until it shall please Congress to rest it exclusively elsewhere, or until the State of Pennsylvania shall withdraw from their court-martial the authority to take such jurisdiction.　-

11

CHAPTER XII

Art. I, Sec. 8, Subd. 17. To exercise exclusive Legislation in all Cases whatsoever, over such District not exceeding ten Miles square, as may, by Cession of particular States, and the Acceptance of Congress, become the Seat of the Government of the United States, and to exercise like Authority over all Places purchased by the Consent of the Legislature of the State in which the Same shall be, for the erection of Forts, Magazines, and Arsenals, dock-Yards, and other needful Buildings;—And

The delegates at Philadelphia made provision for a capital city of the United States outside of the boundaries of any of the States, because they remembered that, just at the close of the Revolution, a mutiny of two companies of Continental soldiers had scared the old Congress away from Philadelphia. This unpleasant and disgraceful event showed the necessity of having a place of national business which should not be dependent for protection from disorder or violence upon the good will of the authorities of any State.

It was also necessary to have reservations for forts, arsenals, navy-yards, customs houses, and the other buildings which every government must have for the transaction of its business.

The Supreme Court, in the case of *Fort Leavenworth Railroad Co. vs. Lowe*,' passed upon the constitutionality of laws adopted by Congress for (1) the government of the District of Columbia and other places under national jurisdiction, (2) the acquisition of real estate for public uses by the national government with the consent of the States, and (3) the taking by the United States of land for public uses without the consent of the State in which it is located.

The plaintiff in this case challenged the right of the State authorities to tax a part of its right of way within the national reservation of Fort Leavenworth, Kansas. The government had occupied the reservation before the admission of Kansas to the Union. The Act of 1861 for the admission of that State did not contain any clause giving the United States jurisdiction over the military post. Hence the rights of the United States over the reservation were only those of any land owner. In 1875, however, the State legislature passed an act giving the Federal Government exclusive jurisdiction over all territory within the military reservation, saving to the State its right "to tax railroad, bridge, or other corporations, their franchises or property, on said Reservation." In 1880, the State levied a tax of $394.40 on the right of way and other property of the Fort Leavenworth Railroad Company, situated within the military post. The railroad paid the tax under protest, and at once brought this action to recover the money, upon the ground that a State tax could not lawfully be levied upon property over which the United States had exclusive jurisdiction. The defense was that the tax was lawful because the State of Kansas had expressly reserved its right to assess this particular

' 114 U. S. Rep., 525.

... over the place
... government will
... Unless it were
... ught in time of
... without adequate
... the officers of the
... intimidation, and
... action ....
... cause in question,
... " that is, of ex-
... based by the con-
... which the same shall
... arsenals, dock-
... the necessity of this
... money extended
... property ...
... Not within ...

their acquisition, such consent should carry with it political dominion and legislative authority over them.   Purchase with such consent was the only mode then thought of for the acquisition by the general government of title to lands in the States.   Since the adoption of the Constitution, this view has not generally prevailed.   Such consent has not always been obtained, nor supposed necessary, for the purchase by the general government of lands within the States. . . .   The consent of the States to the purchase of lands within them for the special purposes named is, however, essential under the Constitution to the transfer to the general government, with the title, of political jurisdiction and dominion.   Where lands are acquired without such consent, the possession of the United States, unless some political jurisdiction be ceded to them in some other way, is simply that of an ordinary proprietor.

...ENFORCE THE CON-
STITUTION

...to make all Laws which
shall be necessary and proper for carrying into Execution the foregoing Powers, and all other Powers vested
... Constitution in the Government of the United
States, or in any Department or Officer thereof.

... Justice Marshall's opinion in the case
... clause gives Congress power "to
... which are ... conducive to the
... powers granted by the Constitution. ...
... the ... clause is not to be under-
... Congress is to be allowed
... respect to the means by which the
... are carried into execution,
... to discharge the high duties assigned
... entrusted to the people. If
... within the scope of the Con-
... means which are appropriate, and are
... to ... end, and are not prohibited,
... the letter and spirit of the Constitution,
...

... there has been a great expansion of con-
... power. This expansion has been gained by
... These powers have

been found in this clause of the Constitution. Under this clause, for example, Congress has power to grant corporation charters to national banks, although the Constitution does not say anything at all about corporations and does not mention banks; and it is fully authorized to regulate and limit immigration, although the Constitution makers took it for granted that immigrants had a right to come to the United States.

National banks were not well liked during the first constitutional era. The Act of Congress incorporating the first Bank of the United States was passed in 1791, and was signed by President Washington, who was not at all sure that the Constitution gave Congress power to establish such an institution. Alexander Hamilton, the Secretary of the Treasury, overcame the President's scruples by insisting that a law creating a bank was "necessary and proper for carrying into execution the powers . . . vested by the Constitution in the government of the United States."

The second Bank of the United States was chartered in 1816. The act of incorporation was adopted in spite of much opposition; and the bank, though highly successful, was under fire throughout the twenty years of its existence. For example, in 1818, the legislature of Maryland passed a law imposing stamp taxes upon bank notes issued in that State by banking corporations, elsewhere chartered, thereby furnishing cause for the great action of *McCulloch vs. Maryland*.[1]   This law was aimed at the Bank of the United States, which was the only bank doing business in all the States. The bank refused to pay the tax. McCulloch, its cashier, was sued for the tax on one of its notes, which had been issued at Baltimore. The bank lost in the State courts,

[1] 4 Wheaton's Rep., 316.

but won in the Supreme Court.   Chief Justice Marshall's
decision, by its interpretation of the phrase "necessary
and proper," justified the use by Congress of powers
implied, but not stated, in the Constitution.   He said:

The Constitution of the United States has not left the
right of Congress to employ the necessary means, for the
execution of the powers conferred on the government, to
general reasoning.   To its enumeration of powers is added
that of making "all laws which shall be necessary and
proper for carrying into execution the foregoing powers
and all other powers vested by the Constitution, in the
government of the United States, or in any department
thereof." . . .   We admit, as all must admit, that the
powers of the government are limited, and that its limits
are not to be transcended.   But we think the sound construction of the Constitution must allow to the national
legislature that discretion, with respect to the means by
which the powers it confers are to be carried into execution,
which will enable that body to perform the high duties
assigned to it, in the manner most beneficial to the people.
Let the end be legitimate, let it be within the scope of the
Constitution, and all means which are appropriate, which
are plainly adapted to that end, which are not prohibited,
but consist with the letter and spirit of the Constitution are
constitutional.

That a corporation must be considered as a means not
less usual, not of higher dignity, not more requiring a particular specification than other means, has been sufficiently
proved.   If we look to the origin of corporations, to the
manner in which they have been framed in that government, from which we have derived most of our legal principles and ideas, or to the uses to which they have been
applied, we find no reason to suppose that a Constitution,
omitting, and wisely omitting, to enumerate all the means
for carrying into execution the great powers vested in
government, ought to have specified this.   Had it been

intended to grant this power as one which should be distinct and independent, to be exercised in any case whatever, it would have found a place among the enumerated powers of the government. But being considered merely as a means to be employed only for the purpose of carrying into execution the given powers, there could be no motive for particularly mentioning it. . . . If a corporation may be employed indiscriminately with other means to carry into execution the powers of the government, no particular reason can be assigned for excluding the use of a bank, if required for its fiscal operations.' To use one, must be within the discretion of Congress, if it be an appropriate mode of executing the powers of government. . . . It is the unanimous and decided opinion of this Court, that the act to incorporate the Bank of the United States is a law made in pursuance of the Constitution and is a part of the supreme law of the land."

Justice McLean of the Supreme Court, who, born in 1785, must have known personally many of the members of the Constitutional Convention, could speak with authority on the attitude of the Constitution makers toward the subject of immigration. He said in his opinion in the *Passenger Cases*,' that "to encourage foreign emigration was a cherished policy of this country at the time the Constitution was adopted."

That "cherished policy" certainly did not prevail in 1891, when the *Japanese Immigrant Case* (*Nashimura Ekiu vs. United States*) was decided by the Supreme Court. In May, 1891, a Japanese woman who had come to San Francisco, was excluded and ordered to be deported by the immigration officer at that port on the ground that she was of a class which is prohibited

---

' 7 Howard's Rep., 1.   ' 142 U. S. Rep., 651.

from admission by the immigration laws. She petitioned the United States Circuit Court for release on the ground that she had been unlawfully deprived of her liberty by an administrative decision made under the Immigration Act of 1891, which she claimed was unconstitutional. A hearing was had before a commissioner, who decided that her right to be admitted to the United States had been fully adjudicated by an executive officer whose decision could not be reviewed by the courts. The Circuit Court confirmed this ruling and the case then went to the Supreme Court, where Justice Gray confirmed the ruling of the lower court in these decisive words:

It is an accepted maxim of international law, that every sovereign nation has the power, as inherent in sovereignty, and essential to self-preservation, to forbid the entrance of foreigners within its dominions, or to admit them only in such cases and upon such conditions as it may see fit to prescribe. . . .   In the United States this power is vested in the national government, to which the Constitution has committed the entire control of international relations, in peace as well as in war. It belongs to the political department of the government, and may be exercised either through treaties made by the President and Senate, or through statutes enacted by Congress, upon whom the Constitution has conferred power . . . to make all laws which may be necessary and proper for carrying into effect . . . all powers . . . vested by the Constitution in the government of the United States or in any department or officer thereof. . . .

Thirteenth Amendment.   Section 2.   Congress shall have power to enforce this article by appropriate legislation.

Fourteenth Amendment. Section 5. The Congress shall have power to enforce, by appropriate legislation, the provisions of this article.

Fifteenth Amendment. Section 2. The Congress shall have power to enforce this article by appropriate legislation.

These three clauses give Congress power to provide all the legal machinery which may be needed for the enforcement of the anti-slavery amendments. In the case of *Clyatt vs. United States*[1] the defendant was charged with having unlawfully returned two persons to a condition of peonage, a system of servitude under which persons were compelled to pay their debts in labor. The testimony showed that the defendant had caused the arrest of two persons in Florida, probably in order to take them back to Georgia and make them work out a debt. The Supreme Court let them go because the government had failed to prove a case. Nevertheless, Justice Brewer took advantage of the opportunity to declare the constitutionality of a law which Congress had enacted to enforce the Thirteenth Amendment. Justice Brewer said in part:

This Amendment . . . is undoubtedly self-executing without ancillary legislation, so far as its terms are applicable to any existing state of circumstances. By its own unaided force and effect it abolished slavery, and established universal freedom. Still, legislation may be necessary and proper to meet all the various cases and circumstances to be affected by it, and to prescribe proper modes of redress for its violation in letter or spirit. And such legislation may be primary and direct in its character; for the amendment is

[1] 197 U. S. Rep., 207.

not a mere prohibition of State laws establishing or upholding slavery, but an absolute declaration that slavery and involuntary servitude shall not exist in any part of the United States.

PART V

Limitations upon Legislative Government in the United States—Rights Guaranteed by the Constitution and its Amendments

.

CHAPTER XIV

RIGHTS OF THE STATES AND THEIR CITIZENS AGAINST THE UNITED STATES AS ENUMERATED IN THE ORIGINAL CONSTITUTION

CHIEF JUSTICE MARSHALL, in his opinion in the case of *Barron vs. Baltimore*,[1] said:

The 9th section [of the first Article of the Constitution] . . . [enumerates] in the nature of a *bill of rights*, the limitations intended to be imposed on the powers of the general government. . . .

Art. I., Sec. 9.   The Migration or Importation of such Persons as any of the States now existing shall think proper to admit, shall not be prohibited by the Congress prior to the Year one thousand eight hundred and eight, but a Tax or duty may be imposed for such Importation, not exceeding ten dollars for each Person.

The Constitution makers seem to have believed that the new plan of government would be rejected by the States if it did not contain a compromise concerning the slave trade.   Hence they made this provision which, in effect, is a declaration of the right of citizens of the States to import negro slaves only until 1808.   The words "slave trade" were not used for the sake of appearances.

[1] 7 Peters' Rep., 243.

In 1846, Cyrus Libby, captain of the brig *Porpoise*, was tried for his life in the United States Circuit Court at Portland, Maine, under an indictment which charged that he had taken a negro named Luez on board a ship owned by citizens of the United States for the purpose of making him a slave. In this case, *United States vs. Libby*,[1] Judge Woodbury explained the meaning of the paragraph under discussion:

The whole Union, even before the adoption of the Constitution, had gradually become convinced that the only mode effectually to extirpate what the northern States considered the curse of slavery, was at an early day to stop the addition to the number here from abroad; not only thus cutting off a large and constant reinforcement, but putting an end to the introduction of new ignorance, new superstition, new Paganism, and allowing the arts of civilization gradually to elevate and make more safe the liberation of slaves, long remaining here; and by returning them more civilized, to enlighten and reform slavery at home in Africa; or by releasing them here, when fit subjects for emancipation; thus, in time, to terminate the evil throughout and forever. Seeing and feeling all this, and that slavery might thus in time safely cease, the prudent framers of the Constitution secured a right in it to prohibit the slave trade into the United States after 1808, with an implied power to prohibit it at once from being carried on abroad by American citizens, and left slavery to be abolished here entirely, and as fast as each State should find it expedient and secure to itself.

The Migration or Importation of such Persons as any of the States now existing shall think proper to admit. Justice Miller interpreted this phrase in his opinion in the case of *People vs. Compagnie Gén. Transatlantique*,[2]

---

[1] Woodbury & Minot's Rep., 221.   [2] 107 U. S. Rep., 59.

in which the Supreme Court decided that a State has no right to impose head money taxes on immigrants. He said:

There has never been any doubt that this clause had exclusive reference to persons of the African race. The two words "migration" and "importation" refer to the different conditions of this race as regard freedom and slavery. When the free black man came here, he *migrated;* when the slave came, he was *imported.* The latter was property, and was imported by his owner as other property, and a duty could be imposed on him as an import. We conclude that free human beings are not imports or exports, within the meaning of the Constitution.

Art. I., Sec. 9 (continued). The Privilege of the Writ of Habeas Corpus shall not be suspended, unless when in Cases of Rebellion or Invasion the public Safety may require it.

Art. I., Sec. 9 (continued).   No Bill of Attainder or ex post facto Law shall be passed.

The Privilege of the Writ of Habeas Corpus. The words "habeas corpus" are part of a phrase in law Latin, which freely translated means "we command you to produce the body (of a prisoner) in court"; literally, "that you have the body (of a prisoner) in court." This is the opening sentence of a writ or process at law, which calls for the production of an imprisoned person in open court so that the judge may decide whether or not he is lawfully deprived of his liberty. Any friend of a person confined in a prison, or insane asylum, or any other place where people are kept under lock and key, can present a petition for a writ of habeas corpus. The judge to whom it is presented is under a legal duty to issue the writ. Indeed, under the laws of many States he can be fined heavily, if he refuses. The writ of habeas corpus is an order to the warden or other person in charge of a place of confinement to produce the prisoner in court. If he does not obey, he will be severely punished. When the prisoner is produced in court, the jail keeper makes his "return" or answer, explaining why the man is in custody. Then the judge decides whether the custody is lawful or unlawful. If lawful, the writ is ordered dismissed; if unlawful, the prisoner is ordered released. This procedure is not strictly followed under the laws of the United States, which require judges to issue habeas corpus writs only when constitutional rights have been violated.

Harry K. Thaw, who, when tried in New York for the murder of Stanford White, had been acquitted on the ground of insanity and then confined in the New York State Hospital for the Criminal Insane at Matteawan, made many efforts to obtain his liberty by suing out writs of habeas corpus upon petitions which alleged that, having regained his sanity, he was imprisoned unlawfully. The writs issued by the New York courts were dismissed in every case. When he made an attempt to escape and was arrested in New Hampshire, he again sued out a writ of habeas corpus, and was able to block all attempts to take him back to New York until the Supreme Court at Washington, in its judgment on appeal, ordered the writ dismissed.[1]

The history and nature of the writ of habeas corpus were given in detail by Judge Cobb of the Supreme Court of Georgia in 1903 in the case of *Simmons vs. Georgia Iron and Coal Co.*[1] Simmons, who had been

[1] Drew, Sheriff, vs. Thaw, 235 U. S. Rep., 432.
[1] 119 Georgia Rep., 305.

sentenced for four misdemeanors to what amounted to three years in the chain-gang, asked the Georgia courts to order his release on the ground that the penalty imposed on him was unlawful. In deciding against Simmons, Judge Cobb explained the nature of habeas corpus proceedings as follows:

Many are accustomed to regard the writ as almost obsolete and of little practical value; and doubtless this results from the fact that it is so seldom called into operation. But the writ is as much a palladium of liberty today as it was during the abuses existing in the days of the ancient English sovereigns. . . .

The proceeding by habeas corpus was, strictly speaking, neither a civil nor criminal action. It was not a proceeding in a suit, but was a summary application by the person detained. No party to the proceeding was necessarily before or represented before a judge, except the person detaining, and that person only because he had the custody of the applicant, and was bound to bring him before the judge to explain and justify, if he could, the fact of imprisonment. . . . It . . . is instituted for the sole purpose of having the person restrained of his liberty produced before the judge, in order that the cause of his detention may be inquired into and his status fixed. The person to whom the writ is directed makes response to the *writ*, not to the *petition*. . . . When an answer is made to the writ, the responsibility of the respondent ceases. . . . The court passes upon all questions, both of law and fact, in a summary way. The person restrained is the central figure in the transaction. The proceeding is instituted solely for his benefit. It is not designed to obtain redress against anybody, and no judgment can be entered against anybody. . . . The judgment simply fixes the status of the person for whose benefit the writ was issued; and while anybody disobeying the judgment may be dealt with as for a contempt, the

the Southern
... Lafayette, Warren,
McHenry, ... Within the Capitol Prison, peni-

tentiaries and military camps in the different parts of the country."

An attempt was made to test the validity of the President's action.[1] In 1861, one John Merryman, who had been arrested on a charge of treason upon an order issued by Secretary Seward, was under detention by General George Cadwalader at Fort McHenry. An application was made to Chief Justice Taney of the United States Supreme Court for a writ of habeas corpus. The Chief Justice signed the writ commanding General Cadwalader to produce Merryman before him and show cause for his detention. When the marshal of the United States Court presented the writ, General Cadwalader refused to obey. Chief Justice Taney issued a body attachment against the general, who then shut the marshal out of the fort. Thereupon the Chief Justice wrote an opinion as to the law, in which he said:

The only power . . . which the President possesses where the "life, liberty, or property" of a private citizen is concerned, is the power and duty . . . which requires "that he shall take care that the laws shall be faithfully executed." He is not authorized to execute them himself, or through agents or officers, civil or military, appointed by himself, but he is to take care that they be faithfully carried into execution, as they are expounded and adjudged by the co-ordinate branch of the government to which that duty is assigned by the Constitution. It is thus made his duty to come in aid of the judicial authority, if it shall be resisted by a force too strong to be overcome without the assistance of the executive arm; but in exercising this power he acts in subordination to judicial authority, assisting it to execute its process and enforce its judgments.

[1] *Ex Parte Merryman*, Taney's Rep., 246.

"President Lincoln," continues Mr. Pierce, in his *Federal Usurpation*, "ignored this, but later, in a message to Congress, asserted his right to suspend the writ of habeas corpus without limitation or interference."

"There lies before me as I write," Mr. Pierce says on another page, "a book under the title of *The American Bastile*, written by one John A. Marshall, bearing date of August, 1869, in which he describes the circumstances of the arrest of seventy citizens imprisoned in these fortresses from all the Northern States except New Hampshire, Rhode Island, and Wisconsin. Among them were foreign ministers, United States Senators, Members of Congress, Members of State legislatures, judges, lawyers, ministers, doctors, farmers, editors, merchants, and men from all the other walks of life. The details connected with the arrests of these men, as described by him, are as terrible as those accompanying the state arrests in Russia today, and one draws back from his vivid description with doubt lest perhaps Mr. Marshall's experience caused him to exaggerate the conditions."

The Privilege of the Writ of Habeas Corpus shall not be suspended, unless when in Cases of Rebellion or Invasion the public Safety may require it. On March 3, 1863, Congress passed an act which provided that "During the present Rebellion, the President of the United States, whenever, in his judgment, the public safety may require it, is authorized to suspend the privilege of the writ of habeas corpus in any case throughout the United States, or any part thereof." Subsequently, by public proclamation, the President suspended the privilege of the writ throughout the country, basing the suspension upon the statute. His right so to suspend the writ of habeas corpus was tested in the case of *Ex Parte Milligan*,[1] which grew out of an incident in the Civil War. On August 13, 1864, Lambdin P. Milligan, a lawyer of Huntington, Indiana, delivered a political speech at Fort Wayne, Indiana, in which he attacked the national government on the war issue, and opposed the reëlection of Governor Morton on the ground of his war record. On October 5, he was arrested and taken to Indianapolis by order of the military authorities of the district of Indiana. On October 21, he was tried by court-martial and convicted of conspiracy against the United States, of giving aid and comfort to the rebels, and of disloyal practices; and he was sentenced to death. He petitioned the Federal courts for release by habeas corpus and the petition was denied. He appealed from this decision to the Supreme Court of the United States on the ground that Congress had no constitutional power to enact a law suspending the privilege of the writ of habeas corpus in States where the process of the courts was not obstructed, and that the military court which had convicted and sentenced him to death had no power to deal with criminal charges in States where the civil courts were open. This brought before the Supreme Court all the great questions which are likely to arise under this clause of the Constitutional Bill of Rights. Justice Davis said:

In every war, there are men of previously good character, wicked enough to counsel their fellow-citizens to resist the measures deemed necessary by a good government to sustain its just authority and overthrow its enemies; and their

[1] 4 Wallace's Rep., 2.

influence may lead to dangerous combinations. In the emergency of the times, an immediate public investigation according to law may not be possible; and yet, the peril of the country may be too imminent to suffer such persons to go at large. Unquestionably, there is then an exigency which demands that the government . . . should not be required to produce the persons arrested in answer to a writ of habeas corpus. The Constitution goes no further. It does not say that after a writ of habeas corpus is denied a citizen, he shall be tried otherwise than by the course of the common law; if it had intended that result, it was easy by the use of direct words to have accomplished it. . . . But, it is insisted that the safety of the country in time of war demands that this broad claim for martial law shall be sustained. If this were true, it could be well said that a country, preserved at the sacrifice of all the cardinal principles of liberty, is not worth the cost of preservation. Happily, it is not so. . . . If, in foreign invasion or civil war, the courts are actually closed, and it is then impossible to administer criminal justice according to law, then, on the theatre of active military operations, where war really prevails, there is a necessity to furnish a substitute for the civil authority, thus overthrown, to preserve the safety of the army and society; and as no power is left but the military, it is allowed to govern by martial rule until the laws can have their free course. As necessity creates the rule, so it limits its duration; for if the government is continued after the courts are reinstated, it is a gross usurpation of power. Martial rule can never exist where the courts are open, and in the proper and unobstructed exercise of their jurisdiction. It is also confined to the locality of actual war. Because, during the late Rebellion it could have been enforced in Virginia, where the national authority was overturned and the courts driven out, it does not follow that it should obtain in Indiana, where that authority was never disputed, and justice was always administered.

No Bill of Attainder or ex post facto Law shall be passed.
The methods of procedure known as bills of attainder
and *ex post facto* laws, which had prevailed in England
for centuries, were objectionable because the one inflicted punishment by legislative enactment without
any judicial trial concerning the fact of guilt or inno-
cence, and the other made men liable to punishment for
acts made criminal after the deed had been committed.

When the embers of the Civil War were dying out,
there were serious attempts not only to make treason
odious, but also to make traitors uncomfortable. For
example, the State Constitution of Missouri, adopted in
1865, barred from public office, from being an officer
of any public or private corporation, from acting as a
teacher or professor in any educational establishment,
from holding real estate or other property in trust for
any church or religious society, and from officiating as
a clergyman, any person who did not make oath that
he never had been disloyal to the United States, had
never served against the nation in war nor assisted its
enemies, and had not sought the protection of another
nation in order to avoid military service. Any violation of laws made to carry out this provision was made
a criminal offence. This was a fine dragnet in which
were caught those who had fought for the South, and
the "Copperheads" who had run off to Canada to avoid
the conscription laws.

In the case of *Cummings vs. Missouri,*[1] these facts
appeared: In September, 1865, Rev. Father Cummings,
an estimable Roman Catholic priest, who had not taken
the oath prescribed in the State Constitution, had been
convicted and fined five hundred dollars. He appealed
from the State courts to the Federal Supreme Court

[1] 4 Wallace's Rep., 277.

upon the ground that these provisions of law were *ex post facto*, having been made after the committing of the offences they punished, and also were bills of attainder of the sort known as bills of pains and penalties. The Supreme Court said that the Missouri laws based upon the provisions of the State Constitution cited above were repugnant to the Constitution of the United States in both ways, and so were null and void. In the decision, Justice Field defined bills of attainder and *ex post facto* laws as follows:

A bill of attainder is a legislative act which inflicts punishment without a judicial trial. If the punishment be less than death, the act is termed a bill of pains and penalties. Within the meaning of the Constitution, bills of attainder include bills of pains and penalties. In these cases, the legislative body, in addition to its legitimate functions, exercises the powers and office of a judge; it assumes, in the language of the text books, judicial magistracy; it pronounces upon the guilt of the party, without any of the forms or safeguards of trial; it determines the sufficiency of the proofs produced, whether conformable to the rules of evidence or otherwise; and it fixes the degree of punishment in accordance with its own notions of the enormity of the offence. . . . By an *ex post facto* law is meant one which imposes a punishment for an act which was not punishable at the time it was committed; or imposes additional punishment to that prescribed; or changes the rules of evidence by which less or different testimony is sufficient to convict than was required.

Art. I., Sec. 9 (continued). No Capitation, or other direct, tax shall be laid, unless in Proportion to the Census or Enumeration herein before directed to be taken.

Art. I., Sec. 9 (continued). No Tax or Duty shall be laid on Articles exported from any State.

The clause restricting the levying of capitation or other direct taxes was intended to prevent inequalities of national taxation. Justice Paterson said in the course of his opinion in the case of *Hylton vs. United States*[1] that this declaration was made in favor of the southern States which, if no provisions had been introduced in the Constitution, would have been wholly at the mercy of the other States. "They possessed a large number of slaves; they had extensive tracts of territory, thinly settled, and not very productive. A majority of the States had but few slaves and several of them a limited territory, well settled, and in a high state of cultivation. . . . Congress, in such a case, might tax slaves at discretion, or arbitrarily, and land in every part of the Union after the same rate or measure; so much a head in the first instance and so much an acre in the other."

No Capitation . . . tax. The Supreme Court of North Carolina explained what a "capitation" tax is in the case of *Gardner vs. Hall*,[2] known as the "Deadhead" case. One James L. Gardner had been compelled to pay a State tax imposed upon all persons, other than railroad officials, who travelled on any railroad in that State without paying their fares. He brought an action against the county officers who had collected the tax, claiming that because the law imposed a "capitation" tax contrary to the provisions of the State constitution, he had a right to recover the money paid. Judge Battle said:

A capitation tax is one upon the person simply, without any reference to his property, real or personal, or to any business in which he may be engaged, or to any employment

[1] 3 Dallas' Rep., 171.   [2] 61 North Carolina Rep., 21.

which he may follow. It is rightfully imposed because of
the protection which the government affords to the person,
independently of the connection or relation of the person
to anything else.

*No . . . direct tax shall be laid, unless in Propor-
tion to the Census or Enumeration herein before directed
to be taken.*   Our national bank system was established
in 1864, at the suggestion of Salmon P. Chase, then
Secretary of the Treasury, and afterward Chief Justice
of the United States. His plan was to create a market
for United States government bonds by issuing Federal
corporation charters to as many banks as would agree
to invest a large proportion of their capital in those
bonds. The special inducement offered was the exclusive privilege of issuing for circulation bank notes
to be secured by government bonds deposited with the
Secretary of the Treasury. This privilege of issuing
notes was made exclusive by a section of the National
Bank Law which imposed a prohibitive tax of ten per
cent upon the face value of bank notes issued by banks
which did not take out national charters.

The plan was successful in every way. Everyone was
satisfied, except the bankers who continued to do business under State charters. They protested that the
National Bank Act was unconstitutional because it
levied a "direct" tax not apportioned to the States
in proportion to a national census or enumeration.

The question was brought up in the Supreme Court
in 1869, in the case of *Veazie Bank vs. Fenno.*   The
Veazie Bank, incorporated under the laws of the State
of Maine, paid the tax assessed upon its circulating
notes, and then sued the Federal collector of internal

revenue for the amount, upon the ground that the tax was "direct" and unapportioned, and therefore unconstitutional.

Chief Justice Chase, who as Secretary of the Treasury had originally suggested the law, had an opportunity in this case to pass upon its validity. As might have been expected, he stood up stoutly for what he called the "undisputed constitutional power [of Congress] to provide a currency for the whole country." He said:

Having thus, in the exercise of undisputed constitutional powers, undertaken to provide a currency for the whole country, it cannot be questioned that Congress may, constitutionally, secure the benefit of it to the people by appropriate legislation. To this end, Congress has denied the quality of legal tender to foreign coins, and has provided by law against the imposition of counterfeit and base coin in the community. To the same end, Congress may restrain, by suitable enactments, the circulation as money of any notes not issued under its own authority. Without this power, indeed, its attempts to secure a sound and uniform currency for the country must be futile.

Another taxing measure of the Civil War period provided for an assessment upon incomes, gains, and profits, in the form of an internal revenue tax, not apportioned to the States according to population. The celebrated case of *Springer vs. United States*[1] grew out of an assessment upon William M. Springer of Springfield, Illinois, of $4,799.80, upon his net income, derived partly from real estate, of $50,798. He refused to pay the tax. The collector of internal revenue seized and sold his house to satisfy the levy; and, in

[1] 102 U. S. Rep., 586.

United States, which had bought in the _____ at the sale, commenced an action to obtain _____. Mr. Springer interposed as a defense to the action a claim that the taxing law, under which his property had been sold, was void for unconstitutionality in that, in imposing without apportionment a tax upon his income derived in part from real estate, it imposed what really was a "direct tax" upon land. The question which the Supreme Court had to decide was whether a tax on the income of land is the same thing as a tax on land. The justices answered that a tax on land undoubtedly is a direct tax which must be apportioned, but that a tax on the income of land is an excise duty upon interest and profits, which does not require apportionment in order to be constitutional. Justice Swayne said:

> The tax here in question . . . is not a tax on the "whole . . . personal estate" of the individual, but only on his income, gains, and profits during a year, which may have been but a small part of his personal estate, and in most cases would have been so. . . . Our conclusions are that *direct taxes*, within the meaning of the Constitution, are only capitation taxes, as expressed in that instrument, and taxes on real estate; and that the tax of which the plaintiff . . . . complains, is within the category of an excise or duty.

An income tax measure adopted by Congress in 1894, during President Cleveland's second administration, did not fare so well in the Supreme Court when challenged in the case of *Pollock vs. Farmers' Loan and Trust Company*.[1] Charles Pollock, a citizen of Massachusetts, filed a bill in equity in which he said that he was a

[1] 157 U. S. Rep., 430.

stockholder in the company and that the directors intended to pay the tax of two per cent. on its net income and profits, including its income from its real estate. He urged that the law was unconstitutional because it imposed a direct tax, in the shape of a tax on the income of real estate, without apportioning the amount to the States as required by the Constitution. This brought before the Supreme Court for the second time the whole question of the validity of income taxes not apportioned. In this case, by a vote of five justices against four, the Supreme Court annulled the statute. Chief Justice Fuller said:

The requirement of the Constitution is that no direct tax shall be laid otherwise than by apportionment—the prohibition is not against direct taxes on land, from which the implication is sought to be drawn that indirect taxes on land would be constitutional, but it is against all direct taxes—and it is admitted that a tax on real estate is a direct tax. . . . The name of the tax is unimportant. The real question is, is there any basis upon which to rest the contention that real estate belongs to one of the two great classes of taxes, and the rent or income which is the incident of its ownership belongs to the other? We are unable to perceive any ground for the alleged distinction. An annual tax upon the annual value or annual user of real estate appears to us the same in substance as an annual tax on the real estate, which would be paid out of the rent or income. . . . We are of opinion that the law in question, so far as it levies a tax on the rents or income of real estate, is in violation of the Constitution, and is invalid.

No Tax or Duty shall be laid on Articles exported from any State. "The prohibition of a tax on exports," said

NOTE.—The decision in *Pollock vs. Farmers' Loan and Trust Company* has been reversed by the Sixteenth Constitutional Amendment, which reads as follows:

1874, the United States, which had bought in the property at the sale, commenced an action to obtain possession. Mr. Springer interposed as a defense to this action a claim that the taxing law, under which his property had been sold, was void for unconstitutionality in that, in imposing without apportionment a tax upon his income derived in part from real estate, it imposed what really was a "direct tax" upon land. The question which the Supreme Court had to decide was whether a tax on the income of land is the same thing as a tax on land.   The justices answered that a tax on land undoubtedly is a direct tax which must be apportioned, but that a tax on the income of land is an . excise duty upon interest and profits, which does not require apportionment in order to be constitutional. Justice Swayne said:

> The tax here in question . . . is not a tax on the "whole . . . personal estate" of the individual, but only on his income, gains, and profits during a year, which may have been but a small part of his personal estate, and in most cases would have been so. . . .   Our conclusions are that *direct taxes*, within the meaning of the Constitution, are only capitation taxes, as expressed in that instrument, and taxes on real estate; and that the tax of which the plaintiff. . . . complains, is within the category of an excise or duty.

An income tax measure adopted by Congress in 1894, during President Cleveland's second administration, did not fare so well in the Supreme Court when challenged in the case of *Pollock vs. Farmers' Loan and Trust Company.*[1] Charles Pollock, a citizen of Massachusetts, filed a bill in equity in which he said that he was a

---

[1] 157 U. S. Rep., 430.

stockholder in the company and that the directors intended to pay the tax of two per cent. on its net income and profits, including its income from its real estate. He urged that the law was unconstitutional because it imposed a direct tax, in the shape of a tax on the income of real estate, without apportioning the amount to the States as required by the Constitution. This brought before the Supreme Court for the second time the whole question of the validity of income taxes not apportioned. In this case, by a vote of five justices against four, the Supreme Court annulled the statute. Chief Justice Fuller said:

The requirement of the Constitution is that no direct tax shall be laid otherwise than by apportionment—the prohibition is not against direct taxes on land, from which the implication is sought to be drawn that indirect taxes on land would be constitutional, but it is against all direct taxes—and it is admitted that a tax on real estate is a direct tax. . . . The name of the tax is unimportant. The real question is, is there any basis upon which to rest the contention that real estate belongs to one of the two great classes of taxes, and the rent or income which is the incident of its ownership belongs to the other? We are unable to perceive any ground for the alleged distinction. An annual tax upon the annual value or annual user of real estate appears to us the same in substance as an annual tax on the real estate, which would be paid out of the rent or income. . . . We are of opinion that the law in question, so far as it levies a tax on the rents or income of real estate, is in violation of the Constitution, and is invalid.

No Tax or Duty shall be laid on Articles exported from any State. "The prohibition of a tax on exports," said

NOTE.—The decision in *Pollock vs. Farmers' Loan and Trust Company* has been reversed by the Sixteenth Constitutional Amendment, which reads as follows:

1874, the United States, which had bought in the property at the sale, commenced an action to obtain possession. Mr. Springer interposed as a defense to this action a claim that the taxing law, under which his property had been sold, was void for unconstitutionality in that, in imposing without apportionment a tax upon his income derived in part from real estate, it imposed what really was a "direct tax" upon land. The question which the Supreme Court had to decide was whether a tax on the income of land is the same thing as a tax on land. The justices answered that a tax on land undoubtedly is a direct tax which must be apportioned, but that a tax on the income of land is an excise duty upon interest and profits, which does not require apportionment in order to be constitutional. Justice Swayne said:

The tax here in question . . . is not a tax on the "whole . . . personal estate" of the individual, but only on his income, gains, and profits during a year, which may have been but a small part of his personal estate, and in most cases would have been so. . . . Our conclusions are that *direct taxes*, within the meaning of the Constitution, are only capitation taxes, as expressed in that instrument, and taxes on real estate; and that the tax of which the plaintiff. . . . complains, is within the category of an excise or duty.

An income tax measure adopted by Congress in 1894, during President Cleveland's second administration, did not fare so well in the Supreme Court when challenged in the case of *Pollock vs. Farmers' Loan and Trust Company.*[1] Charles Pollock, a citizen of Massachusetts, filed a bill in equity in which he said that he was a

[1] 157 U. S. Rep., 430.

stockholder in the company and that the directors intended to pay the tax of two per cent. on its net income and profits, including its income from its real estate. He urged that the law was unconstitutional because it imposed a direct tax, in the shape of a tax on the income of real estate, without apportioning the amount to the States as required by the Constitution. This brought before the Supreme Court for the second time the whole question of the validity of income taxes not apportioned. In this case, by a vote of five justices against four, the Supreme Court annulled the statute. Chief Justice Fuller said:

The requirement of the Constitution is that no direct tax shall be laid otherwise than by apportionment—the prohibition is not against direct taxes on land, from which the implication is sought to be drawn that indirect taxes on land would be constitutional, but it is against all direct taxes—and it is admitted that a tax on real estate is a direct tax. . . . The name of the tax is unimportant. The real question is, is there any basis upon which to rest the contention that real estate belongs to one of the two great classes of taxes, and the rent or income which is the incident of its ownership belongs to the other? We are unable to perceive any ground for the alleged distinction. An annual tax upon the annual value or annual user of real estate appears to us the same in substance as an annual tax on the real estate, which would be paid out of the rent or income. . . . We are of opinion that the law in question, so far as it levies a tax on the rents or income of real estate, is in violation of the Constitution, and is invalid.

No Tax or Duty shall be laid on Articles exported from any State. "The prohibition of a tax on exports," said

NOTE.—The decision in *Pollack vs. Farmers' Loan and Trust Company* has been reversed by the Sixteenth Constitutional Amendment, which reads as follows:

1874, the United States, which had bought in the property at the sale, commenced an action to obtain possession. Mr. Springer interposed as a defense to this action a claim that the taxing law, under which his property had been sold, was void for unconstitutionality in that, in imposing without apportionment a tax upon his income derived in part from real estate, it imposed what really was a "direct tax" upon land. The question which the Supreme Court had to decide was whether a tax on the income of land is the same thing as a tax on land. The justices answered that a tax on land undoubtedly is a direct tax which must be apportioned, but that a tax on the income of land is an excise duty upon interest and profits, which does not require apportionment in order to be constitutional. Justice Swayne said:

> The tax here in question . . . is not a tax on the "whole . . . personal estate" of the individual, but only on his income, gains, and profits during a year, which may have been but a small part of his personal estate, and in most cases would have been so. . . . Our conclusions are that *direct taxes*, within the meaning of the Constitution, are only capitation taxes, as expressed in that instrument, and taxes on real estate; and that the tax of which the plaintiff. . . . complains, is within the category of an excise or duty.

An income tax measure adopted by Congress in 1894, during President Cleveland's second administration, did not fare so well in the Supreme Court when challenged in the case of *Pollock vs. Farmers' Loan and Trust Company*.[1] Charles Pollock, a citizen of Massachusetts, filed a bill in equity in which he said that he was a

[1] 157 U. S. Rep., 430.

stockholder in the company and that the directors intended to pay the tax of two per cent. on its net income and profits, including its income from its real estate. He urged that the law was unconstitutional because it imposed a direct tax, in the shape of a tax on the income of real estate, without apportioning the amount to the States as required by the Constitution. This brought before the Supreme Court for the second time the whole question of the validity of income taxes not apportioned. In this case, by a vote of five justices against four, the Supreme Court annulled the statute. Chief Justice Fuller said:

The requirement of the Constitution is that no direct tax shall be laid otherwise than by apportionment—the prohibition is not against direct taxes on land, from which the implication is sought to be drawn that indirect taxes on land would be constitutional, but it is against all direct taxes—and it is admitted that a tax on real estate is a direct tax. . . . The name of the tax is unimportant. The real question is, is there any basis upon which to rest the contention that real estate belongs to one of the two great classes of taxes, and the rent or income which is the incident of its ownership belongs to the other? We are unable to perceive any ground for the alleged distinction. An annual tax upon the annual value or annual user of real estate appears to us the same in substance as an annual tax on the real estate, which would be paid out of the rent or income. . . . We are of opinion that the law in question, so far as it levies a tax on the rents or income of real estate, is in violation of the Constitution, and is invalid.

No Tax or Duty shall be laid on Articles exported from any State. "The prohibition of a tax on exports," said

Note.—The decision in *Pollock vs. Farmers' Loan and Trust Company* has been reversed by the Sixteenth Constitutional Amendment, which reads as follows:

portioned to their ability to pay it; the ability of some being derived in a great measure, not from their exports, but from their fisheries, from their freights, and from commerce at large in some of the branches altogether external to the United States; the profits from all of which, being invisible and intangible, would escape a tax on exports."[1]

Mr. Madison's statement means that taxes on exports were impossible because the whole burden would have fallen on the tobacco, indigo, and rice produced in the South, while the North, which was growing rich out of the ocean transportation of those very products, would have escaped paying export taxes because it had practically nothing to export.

In the case of *Fairbank vs. United States* in which the validity of certain taxes imposed during the Spanish War was questioned,[2] the following facts appeared: A man named Fairbank was found guilty in the Federal District Court of Minnesota of having on March 7, 1900, issued unstamped bills of lading upon a number of carloads of wheat exported from Minnesota to England. He appealed to the Supreme Court at Washington on the ground that the law which required the stamping of bills of lading of merchandise for export was inconsistent with the clause of the Constitution which forbids taxes on exports. Justice Brewer, sustaining this contention, said:

The requirement of the Constitution is that exports should be free from any governmental burden. The language is "no tax or duty." . . . . It is a restriction on the power of Congress; and as in accordance with the rules heretofore noticed the grants of powers should be so con-

---

strued as to give full efficacy to those powers and enable Congress to use such means as it deems necessary to carry them into effect, so in like manner a restriction should be enforced in accordance with its letter and spirit, and no legislation can be tolerated which, although it may not conflict with the letter, destroys the spirit and purpose of the restriction imposed. If, for instance, Congress may place a stamp duty of ten cents on bills of lading on goods to be exported, it is because it has power to do so, and if it has power to impose this amount of stamp duty, it has like power to impose any sum in the way of stamp duty which it sees fit. And it needs but a moment's reflection to show that thereby it can as effectually place a burden upon exports as though it placed a tax directly upon the articles exported.

Art. I, Sec. 9 (continued). No preference shall be given by any Regulation of Commerce or Revenue to the Ports of one State over those of another: nor shall Vessels bound to, or from, one State, be obliged to enter, clear, or pay Duties in another.

Many cities of the old world had flourished greatly by reason of special port privileges which other centers of trade did not enjoy. If Congress had been able to give the ports of one State advantages over those of another by laws providing that vessels should only discharge and take on cargoes in certain harbors, it would have been in the power of a majority of members to ruin the commerce of any State. Justice Nelson, in his decision in the case of *Pennsylvania vs. Wheeling etc. Bridge Co.*,[1] said:

Luther Martin [a delegate to the Constitutional Convention from Maryland] in his letter to the legislature of Mary-

[1] 18 Howard's Rep., 421, 434.

13

land, says that these propositions were introduced into the Convention by the Maryland delegation; and that without them, he observes, it would have been in the power of Congress to compel ships sailing in or out of the Chesapeake to clear or enter at Norfolk, or some port in Virginia—a regulation that would be injurious to the commerce of Maryland. It appears also from the reports of the Convention, that several of the delegates from that State expressed apprehensions that under the power to regulate commerce Congress might favor ports of particular States, by requiring vessels destined to other States to enter and clear at the ports of the favored ones, as a vessel bound for Baltimore to enter and clear at Norfolk.

An act of Congress regulating commerce or revenue which gives incidentally a preference to a port of one State over the ports of another is valid, though the fact of preference might be a good argument against its enactment. It was shown to the court in the *Wheeling Bridge Case*[1] that a bridge across the Ohio River at Wheeling, Virginia (now West Virginia), obstructed the passage of steamboats going up and down the river and thereby gave Wheeling a special advantage as a commercial point over Pittsburg and other Pennsylvania towns north of the bridge. Justice Nelson conceded that this amounted to a port preference. Nevertheless, he said that the act of Congress which declared the bridge a lawful structure was consistent with this clause of the Constitution. He said:

It is urged that the interruption of the navigation of the steamboats engaged in commerce and conveyance of passengers upon the Ohio river at Wheeling from the erection of the bridge, and the delay and expense arising therefrom, virtually operate to give a preference to this port over that

[1] 18 Howard's Rep., 421.

of Pittsburg; that the vessels to and from Pittsburg navigating the Ohio and Mississippi rivers are not only subjected to this delay and expense in the course of the voyage, but that the obstruction will necessarily have the effect to stop the trade and business at Wheeling, or divert the same in some other direction or channel of commerce. Conceding all this to be true, a majority of the court are of opinion that the Act of Congress is not inconsistent with the clause of the Constitution referred to—in other words, that it is not giving a preference to the ports of one State over those of another, within the true meaning of that provision.

Nor shall Vessels bound to, or from, one State, be obliged to enter, clear, or pay Duties in another. Congress may not so use its power to regulate commerce as to impair the commercial equality of the States. At the same time, the States must not take advantage of one another by imposing burdensome harbor charges.

The meaning of this provision was explained by Justice Wayne of the Supreme Court in his opinion in the *Passenger Cases*,[1] in which the statutes of New York and Massachusetts imposing head-money taxes on immigrants were declared unconstitutional. In 1841, George Smith, master of the British ship, *Henry Bliss*, refused to pay the State inspection tax of one dollar a head upon a large number of steerage passengers he had brought to the port of New York. A Mr. Turner, a health commissioner, brought suit in the State courts for the amount of the tax. The defense presented was that the State taxing law was void because inconsistent with the clause in the Constitution of the United States which gives Congress power to regulate commerce with foreign nations. Losing his case in the State courts, the defendant appealed to the

[1] 7 Howard's Rep., 283.

Supreme Court where he won handsomely. Justice Wayne, in giving his decision, referred as follows to this part of the Constitutional Bill of Rights:

The 5th clause of the 9th section of the 1st article of the Constitution, which declares that "no preference shall be given by any regulation of commerce or revenue to the ports of one State over those of another State; nor shall vessels bound to or from one State be obliged to enter, clear, or pay duties in another," is a limitation upon the power of Congress to regulate commerce for the purpose of producing entire commercial equality within the United States, and also a prohibition upon the States to destroy such equality by any legislation prescribing a condition upon which vessels bound from one State shall enter the ports of another.

Art. I., Sec. 9 (continued). No Money shall be drawn from the Treasury, but in Consequence of Appropriations made by Law; and a regular Statement and Account of the Receipts and Expenditures of all public Money shall be published from time to time.

The clause which calls for regular statements and accounts of receipts and disbursements of public money was suggested by Benjamin Franklin,[1] who beyond a doubt was the best business man in the Federal Convention. Once suggested, it seems to have been accepted as a matter of course.

Art. I., Sec. 9 (continued). No Title of Nobility shall be granted by the United States: And no Person holding any Office of Profit or Trust under them, shall without the Consent of the Congress, accept of any present, Emolument, Office, or Title, of any kind whatever, from any King, Prince, or foreign State.

[1] Madison's *Journal*, p. 306.

"Nothing need be said to illustrate the importance of the prohibition of titles of nobility.   This may truly be denominated the corner-stone of republican government; for so long as they are excluded, there can never be serious danger that the government will be any other than that of the people."   *The Federalist*, 84.

CHAPTER XV

Art. I., Sec. 10.   No State shall enter into any Treaty, Alliance, or Confederation; grant Letters of Marque and Reprisal; coin Money; emit Bills of Credit; make any Thing but gold and silver Coin a Tender in Payment of Debts; pass any Bill of Attainder, ex post facto Law, or Law impairing the Obligation of Contracts, or grant any Title of Nobility.

Fourteenth Amendment, Sec. 1 (in part).   No State shall make or enforce any law which shall abridge the privileges or immunities of citizens of the United States; nor shall any State deprive any person of life, liberty, or property, without due process of law; nor deny to any person within its jurisdiction the equal protection of the laws.

Art. I., Sec. 10 (continued).   No State shall, without the Consent of the Congress, lay any Impost or Duties on Imports or Exports, except what may be absolutely necessary for executing it's inspection Laws: and the net Produce of all Duties and Imposts, laid by any State on Imports or Exports, shall be for the Use of the Treasury of the United States; and all such Laws shall be subject to the Revision and Controul of the Congress. No State shall, without the Consent of Congress, lay any Duty of Tonnage, keep Troops, or Ships of War in time of Peace, enter into any Agreement or Compact with another State, or with a foreign Power, or engage in War, unless actually invaded, or in such imminent Danger as will not admit of delay.

Chief Justice Marshall, in his opinion in the great case of *Fletcher vs. Peck*,[1] said:

The restrictions on the legislative power of the States . . . may be deemed a bill of rights for the people of each State.

The question in the case of *Barron vs. Baltimore*[2] was whether the City of Baltimore was liable for damages for injuries suffered by a man whose wharf property had been made valueless as a result of certain street improvements made by the city under the authority of its charter from the State of Maryland. In the course of these improvements, the city had diverted the waters of certain brooks in such a way that the new water courses had made deposits of sand near the wharf and rendered it inaccessible to ships. Mr. Barron had brought an action against the City of Baltimore in the Maryland courts, which had decided against him. Then he had taken the case to the Supreme Court at Washington upon the ground that the State courts had not decided the case justly. Chief Justice Marshall said:

It is worthy of remark, too, that these inhibitions generally restrain State legislation on subjects intrusted to the general government, or in which the people of all the States feel an interest. A State is forbidden to enter into any treaty, alliance, or confederation. If these compacts are with foreign nations they interfere with the treaty making

[1] 6 Cranch's Rep., 87, 138. [2] 7 Peters' Rep., 243.

power, which is conferred entirely on the general government; if with each other, for political purposes, they can scarcely fail to interfere with the general purpose and intent of the Constitution. To grant letters of marque and reprisal, would lead directly to war, the power of declaring which is expressly given to Congress. To coin money is also the exercise of a power conferred on Congress. It would be tedious to recapitulate the several limitations on the powers of the States which are contained in this section. They will be found, generally, to restrain State legislation on subjects intrusted to the government of the Union, in which the citizens of all the States are interested.

No State shall enter into any Treaty, Alliance, or Confederation. Any State law which is inconsistent with a treaty of the United States is void for unconstitutionality. In 1880, in the early days of anti-Chinese agitation in California, before the Chinese Exclusion Law was enacted by Congress, the California legislature forbade under penalty of law the employment by any corporation of any Chinaman or Mongolian. Tiburcio Parrott, president of the Sulphur Bank Mining Company, arrested for employing Chinamen, claimed that he was unlawfully imprisoned under a State law which conflicted with the treaty between the United States and China. This was the case of *In re Parrott,*[1] in which the constitutional question was decided in his favor by Circuit Judge Sawyer, who said:

The States have surrendered the treaty making power to the general government, and vested it in the President and Senate; and when duly exercised by the President and Senate, the treaty resulting is the supreme law of the land, to which not only State laws but State constitutions are in express terms subordinated.

[1] 1 Federal Reporter, 481.

No State shall . . . grant Letters of Marque and Reprisal.   The United States would not be able to make a lasting peace, if the States retained any of the powers incidental to offensive warfare.

No State shall . . . coin Money; emit Bills of Credit; make any Thing but gold and silver Coin a Tender in Payment of Debts.   The Constitution makers wisely prohibited the States from attempting to exercise governmental functions inconsistent with the sovereignty of the nation.   In 1827, Justice Washington, in his opinion in the case of *Ogden vs. Saunders*,[1] said:

These prohibitions, associated with the powers granted to Congress "to coin money, and to regulate the value thereof and of foreign coin," most obviously constitute members of the same family, being upon the same subject and governed by the same policy.   This policy was to provide a fixed and uniform standard of value throughout the United States, by which the commercial and other dealings between the citizens thereof, or between them and foreigners, as well as the moneyed transactions of the government should be regulated.

In the early days of western settlement, the States were eager to evade this provision of the Constitution because they wanted money to help build up the country.   In 1821, Missouri enacted a law which authorized the issue of certificates for sums of not less than thirty cents nor more than ten dollars, which were loaned out to individuals in amounts of less than $200, and were intended to be used as money.   On October 1, 1821, Hiram Craig borrowed from the State $199.99 in certificates and gave his note for that sum.   In due course of time he was sued on the note.   This case, *Craig vs.*

[1] 12 Wheaton's Rep., 213.

Missouri,[1] turned upon the question whether these loan certificates were bills of credit which under the Constitution of the United States, the State of Missouri had no right to emit.   The Supreme Court thus had to decide whether a State could evade the clause forbidding it to emit bills of credit, by calling its paper money loan certificates or some other name.   Chief Justice Marshall answered the question as follows:

The term "bills of credit" signify a paper medium intended to circulate between individuals, and between government and individuals, for the ordinary purposes of society.   Such a medium always has been liable to considerable fluctuation.   Its value is continually changing; and these changes, often great and sudden, expose individuals to immense loss, are the sources of ruinous speculations, and destroy all confidence between man and man.   To cut up this mischief by the roots, a mischief which was felt throughout the United States, and which deeply affected the interest and prosperity of all, the people declared in their Constitution that no State should emit bills of credit.   If the prohibition means anything, if the words are not empty sounds, it must comprehend the emission of any paper medium, by a State government, for the purpose of common circulation.

No State shall . . . pass any Bill of Attainder, ex post facto Law, . . . or grant any Title of Nobility. This is a balancing clause.   The Constitution makers had declared that Congress must not pass bills of attainder or *ex post facto* laws, or grant titles of nobility.[2] For the sake of consistency, the States had to be laid under the same prohibition.

No State shall . . . pass any . . . Law impairing

[1] 4 Peters' Rep., 410.   [2] U. S. Const., Art. I., Sec. 9, Subds. 3, 8.

the Obligation of Contracts.   This provision forbidding State laws impairing the obligation of contracts adds to the force and effect of the clause in the eighth section of the first article of the Constitution, giving Congress power to regulate commerce.   Indeed, the power of Congress to regulate commerce among the States would not have amounted to much if the States had been left free to pass laws preventing the enforcement in their courts of commercial contracts.

The meaning of the phrase "obligation of contracts" was explained by Justice Swayne in his opinion in the case of *Edwards vs. Kearzey*,[1] as follows:

The Constitution of the United States declares that "No State shall pass . . . any law impairing the obligation of contracts."

A contract is an agreement of minds, upon a sufficient consideration, that something specified shall be done, or shall not be done.

The lexical definition of "impair" is "to make worse; to diminish in quantity, value, excellence, or strength; to lessen in power; to weaken; to enfeeble; to deteriorate."— Webster's Dict.

"Obligation" is defined to be "the act of obliging or binding; that which obligates; the binding power of a vow, promise, oath, or contract," etc.—Id.

The word is derived from the Latin word *obligatio*, tying up; and that from the word *obligo*, to bind up or tie up; to engage by the ties of a promise or oath, or form of law; and *obligo* is compounded of the verb *ligo*, to tie or bind fast, and the preposition *ob*, which is prefixed to increase its meaning.

In 1809, twenty years after the establishment of government under the Constitution, the Supreme Court

[1] 96 U. S. Rep., 595.

was called upon, in the case of *Fletcher vs. Peck*, to explain this right of the nation against the States. In 1795, the legislature of Georgia had been corruptly influenced to pass a law for the sale of certain public lands. In course of time, the lands had been bought by people who had had nothing to do with the bribery. A succeeding State legislature, however, had passed another act annulling the original sale for fraud. This had left the innocent holders of deeds, some of whom had not taken actual possession of lands, nothing except **title deeds to show their right of ownership**. One of the purchasers, Robert Fletcher, brought in the United States Circuit Court in Massachusetts a suit for damages against John Peck, who had made a deed in which there was a guarantee of title. This case was carried to the Supreme Court upon the claim that the Georgia law annulling the original sale had impaired the obligation of a contract and therefore was a law which that State had no right to enact. In his opinion, Chief Justice Marshall said:

When . . . a law is in the nature of a contract, when absolute rights have vested under that contract, a repeal of the law cannot divest those rights. . . . Georgia cannot be viewed as a single, unconnected, sovereign power, on whose legislature no other restrictions are imposed than may be found in its own Constitution. She is a part of a large empire; she is a member of the American Union; and that Union has a Constitution, the supremacy of which all acknowledge, and which imposes limits to the legislatures of the several States, which none claim a right to pass. The Constitution of the United States declares that no State shall pass any bill of attainder, ex post facto law, or law impairing the obligation of contracts. Does the case

¹ 6 Cranch's Rep., 87.

now under consideration come within this prohibitory section of the Constitution?

In considering this very interesting question, we immediately ask ourselves what is a contract? Is a grant a contract? A contract is a compact between two or more parties, and is either executory or executed. An executory contract is one in which a party binds himself to do, or not to do a particular thing; such was the law under which the [original] conveyance was made by the governor. A contract executed is one in which the object of contract is performed; and this, says Blackstone, differs in nothing from a grant. The contract between Georgia and the purchaser was executed by the grant. A contract executed, as well as one which is executory, contains obligations binding on the parties. A grant, in its own nature, amounts to an extinguishment of the right of the grantor, and implies a contract not to reassert that right. A party is, therefore, always estopped [prevented from trying to dispute] by his own grant.

Since, then, in fact, a grant is a contract executed, the obligation of which still continues, and since the Constitution used the general term contract, without distinguishing between those which are executory and those which are executed, it must be construed to comprehend the latter as well as the former. . . . If, under a fair construction of the Constitution, grants are comprehended under the term contracts, is a grant from the State excluded from the operation of the provision? Is the clause to be considered as inhibiting the State from impairing the obligation of contracts between two individuals, but as excluding from that inhibition contracts made with itself? . . .

It is . . . the unanimous opinion of the Court, that, in this case, the estate having passed into the hands of a purchaser for a valuable consideration, without notice, the State of Georgia was restrained, either by general principles which are common to our free institutions, or by the particular provisions of the Constitution of the United States, from passing a law whereby the estate of the plaintiff in the premises so purchased could be constitutionally and legally impaired and rendered null and void.

The property right of the people in their contracts was explained again, in 1812, by Chief Justice Marshall in the case of *New Jersey vs. Wilson*. In 1758 the colonial legislature of New Jersey, in settling a disputed claim, had conveyed certain lands to the remnant of the tribe of Delaware Indians by an Act which said "that the lands to be purchased for the Indians aforesaid shall not hereafter be subject to any tax, any law, usage, or custom to the contrary thereof in any wise notwithstanding.' The Indians had held the lands until 1801, when wishing to join their brethren at Stockbridge, N. Y., they had applied for and obtained an act of the legislature authorizing them to sell their New Jersey land. In 1802, commissioners appointed for the purpose had sold the lands to Wilson and others. In 1804, the legislature had repealed the part of the act which exempted the lands from taxation. The lands had then been assessed for taxes, which the owners had refused to pay. Chief Justice Marshall said:

Every requisite to the formation of a contract is found in the proceedings between the then colony of New Jersey and the Indians. The subject was a purchase on the part of the government of extensive claims of the Indians, the extinguishment of which would quiet the title to a large portion of the province. A proposition to this effect is made, the terms stipulated, the consideration agreed upon, which is a tract of land with the privilege of exemption from taxation, and then, in consideration of the arrangements previously made, one of which this act of assembly is stated

* 7 Cranch's Rep., 164.

to be, the Indians executed their deed of cession.   This is certainly a contract clothed in forms of unusual solemnity. The privilege, though for the benefit of the Indians, is annexed, by the terms which create it, to the land itself, not to their persons.   It is for their advantage that it should be annexed to the land, because, in the event of a sale, on which alone the question could become material, the value would be enhanced by it.   It is not doubted but that the State of New Jersey might have insisted on a surrender of this privilege as the sole condition on which a sale of the property should be allowed.   But this condition has not been insisted on.   The land has been sold, with the assent of the State, with all its privileges and immunities.   The purchaser succeeds, with the assent of the State, to all the rights of the Indians.   He stands, with respect to this land, in their place, and claims the benefit of their contract.   *The contract* is certainly impaired by a law which would *annul* this essential part of it.

In the case of *Sturgis vs. Crowninshield*,[1] the question before the Supreme Court was whether or not a State law for the relief of insolvent debtors was void under this clause of the Constitution.   Chief Justice Marshall, who delivered the opinion of the court, admitted that, until Congress had exercised its power "to establish uniform laws on the subject of bankruptcies throughout the United States,"[2] a State could pass any bankruptcy law which did not impair the obligation of a contract. He said, however, that a State could not by such a law, impair the obligation of a contract in a promissory note made before the law was enacted.   The opinion is as follows:

Does the law of New York, which is pleaded in this case, impair the obligation of contracts, within the meaning of

[1] 4 Wheaton's Rep., 122.   [2] U. S. Const., Art. 1, Sec. 8, Subd. 4.

the Constitution of the United States? This act liberates the person of the debtor, and discharges him from all liability for any debt previously contracted, on his surrendering his property in the manner it prescribes. In discussing the question whether a State is prohibited from passing such a law as this, our first inquiry is into the meaning of words in common use. What is the obligation of a contract? and what will impair it? . . . A contract is an agreement in which a party undertakes to do, or not to do, a particular thing. The law binds him to perform his undertaking; and this is, of course, the obligation of his contract. In the case at bar, the defendant has given his promissory note to pay the plaintiff a sum of money on or before a certain day. The contract binds him to pay that sum on that day, and this is its obligation. Any law which releases a part of this obligation, must, in the literal sense of the word, impair it. Much more must a law impair it which makes it totally invalid, and entirely discharges it. . . . .

Although . . . the States may, until that power shall be exercised by Congress, pass laws concerning bankrupts, yet they cannot constitutionally introduce into such laws a clause which discharges the obligations the bankrupt has entered into.

In the great case of *Dartmouth College v. Woodward*,[1] the Supreme Court decided that a corporation charter is a contract, the obligation of which cannot be impaired even by the State which creates and protects it. If this ruling still governed, corporations would be dangerously powerful.

The Dartmouth College case originated in an attempt in 1816 by the New Hampshire legislature to amend the charter which King George the Third had granted, in 1769, to Rev. Eleazer Wheelock for an Indian mission school. Gifts of land and other property had been

[1] 4 Wheaton's Rep., 518, 642.

made by many good people, including the Earl of Dartmouth, whose name was adopted when the school became a college. Under its royal charter, the institution had been governed by a board of trustees who had power to fill all vacancies in their number. In June and December, 1816, the New Hampshire legislature enacted laws "enlarging and improving the corporation and amending the charter" in such a way as to give the State full control over the corporation. William H. Woodward, the defendant in the case, had been secretary and treasurer of the original corporation known as the "Trustees of Dartmouth College." On August 27, 1816, he had been removed from both offices. On February 4, 1817, the college corporation had been organized according to the provisions of the new acts, and the new trustees appointed Woodward secretary and treasurer of the college. He had accepted the offices and thereby obtained custody of the books and some other property of the corporation.

The trustees under the old royal charter brought this case of *Trustees of Dartmouth College vs. Woodward* in order to obtain possession of the college books and other property. The case was heard first in the Court of Common Pleas of Grafton County, N. H., where the jury reported to the court that, if the New Hampshire laws changing the college charter did not impair the obligations of a contract under the provisions of the Constitution of the United States, judgment ought to be in favor of Woodward; but that, if those acts were void for unconstitutionality, the judgment should be for the old trustees. Chief Justice Marshall carried the Supreme Court with him in a far-reaching decision in which he said:

Dr. Wheelock, acting for himself and for those who, at his solicitation, had made contributions to his school, applied for this charter, as the instrument which should enable him and them to perpetuate their beneficent intention. It was granted. An artificial, immortal being was created by the crown, capable of receiving and distributing forever, according to the will of the donors, the donations which should be made to it. On this being, the contributions which had been collected were immediately bestowed. These gifts were made, not indeed to make a profit for the donors or their posterity, but for something in their opinion of inestimable value; for something which they deemed a full equivalent for the money with which it was purchased. The consideration for which they stipulated, is the perpetual application of the fund to its object, in the mode prescribed by themselves. Their descendants may take no interest in the preservation of this consideration. But in this respect their descendants are not their representatives. They are represented by the corporation. The corporation is the assignee of their rights, stands in their place, and distributes their bounty as they would themselves have distributed it, had they been immortal. So with respect to the students who are to derive learning from this source. The corporation is a trustee for them also. Their potential rights, which, taken distributively, are imperceptible, amount, collectively, to a most important interest. These are in the aggregate, to be exercised, asserted, and protected, by the corporation. . . .

Had parliament, immediately after the emanation of this charter, and the execution of those conveyances which followed it, annulled the instrument, so that the living donors would have witnessed the disappointment of their hopes, the perfidy of the transaction would have been universally acknowledged. Yet, then, as now, the donors would have had no interest in the property; then, as now, those who might be students would have had no rights to be violated; then, as now, it might be said, that the trustees, in whom the rights of all were combined, possessed no private, individual, beneficial interest in the property confided to their protection. Yet the contract would at that time have been deemed sacred by all. What has since occurred to strip it of its inviolability? Circumstances have not changed it. In reason, in justice, and in law, it is now what it was in 1769.

This is plainly a contract to which the donors, the trustees, and the crown, (to whose rights and obligations New Hampshire succeeds,) were the original parties. It is a contract made on a valuable consideration. It is a contract for the security and disposition of property. It is a contract on the faith of which, real and personal estate has been conveyed to the corporation. It is a contract within the letter of the Constitution, and within its spirit also, unless the fact that the property is invested by the donors in trustees, for the promotion of religion and education, for the benefit of persons who are perpetually changing, though the objects remain the same, shall create a particular exception, taking this case out of the prohibition contained in the Constitution.

It is more than possible that the preservation of rights of this description was not particularly in the view of the framers of the Constitution, when the clause under consideration was introduced into that instrument. It is probable that interferences of more frequent recurrence, to which the temptation was stronger, and of which the mischief was more extensive, constituted the great motive for imposing this restriction on the State legislatures. But although a particular and a rare case may not, in itself, be of sufficient magnitude to induce a rule, yet it must be governed by the rule, when established, unless some plain and strong reason for excluding it can be given. It is not enough to say, that this particular case was not in the mind of the convention, when the article was framed, nor of the American people when it was adopted. . . . The case being within the words of the rule, must be within its operation likewise, unless there be something in the literal construction so obviously absurd or mischievous, or repugnant to the general spirit of the instrument, as to justify those who expound the Constitution in making it an exception.

The founders of the college contracted, not merely for the perpetual application of the funds which they gave, to the objects for which those funds were given; they contracted also, to secure that application by the constitution of the corporation.   They contracted for a system, which should, as far as human foresight can provide, retain forever the government of the literary institution they had formed, in the hands of persons approved by themselves.   This system is totally changed.   The charter of 1769 exists no longer.   It is reorganized; and reorganized in such a manner, as to convert a literary institution, moulded according to the will of its founders, and placed under the control of private literary men, into a machine entirely subservient to this will of government.   This may be for the advantage of the college in particular, and may be to the advantage of literature in general; but it is not according to the will of the donors, and is subversive of that contract, on the faith of which the property was given. . . .

It results from this opinion, that the acts of the legislature of New Hampshire . . . are repugnant to the Constitution of the United States.

During the era of railroad building, the rule in the Dartmouth College case became "obviously absurd, mischievous, [and] repugnant to the general spirit of" the Constitution.   The building of railroads along lines of travel parallel with turnpikes and canals had diminished the value of the franchises of many turnpike and canal companies operating under charters granted by States.   If the turnpike and canal charters, like the Dartmouth College charter, were contracts, the obligation of which could not lawfully be impaired by any subsequent laws of the same States, the charters of the railroad companies were not valid.

The case of *Proprietors of Charles River Bridge vs. Proprietors of Warren Bridge*[1] came before the Supreme Court in 1837. In 1650, the colonial legislature of Massachusetts had given Harvard College a right to operate for profit a ferry across Charles River between Boston and Charlestown. The college had conducted the enterprise successfully until 1785, when the State legislature had incorporated a company under the name of "The Proprietors of the Charles River Bridge" to build a bridge in the place where the ferry ran, and incidentally to pay Harvard College £200 a year to replace the income it had derived from ferry charges. This charter was limited to forty years. The bridge had been built and opened to the public on June 17, 1786. In 1792, the charter had been extended seventy years from the opening of the bridge. In 1828, the Massachusetts legislature had incorporated a company under the name of "The Proprietors of the Warren Bridge" to erect another bridge over Charles River, from Charlestown to Boston. This bridge had been built only a few rods from the old structure. Before its completion the Charles River Bridge Company had filed a petition praying for an injunction. The case had been heard by the Supreme Judicial Court of Massachusetts in 1829. This court, deciding that the charter to the Warren Bridge did not impair the obligation of the contract contained in the charter of the Charles River Bridge, had dismissed the suit. The case had then been taken to the Supreme Court at Washington. In the meantime, the Warren Bridge had been built and turned over to the State of Massachusetts in accordance

[1] 11 Peters' Rep., 421, 547.

with a charter provision that it should belong to the State as soon as the proprietors had received in tolls the full cost of the structure. This made the Warren Bridge free, thereby destroying the value of the old bridge because no one would pay for going over a toll bridge when a free bridge was just as convenient. Harvard College lost at the same time the £200 a year for which it had surrendered its property rights in the old ferry. The Supreme Court at Washington would not agree that there had been any impairment of the obligations of any contracts in any part of the whole affair. Chief Justice Taney said:

The object and end of all government is to promote the happiness and prosperity of the community by which it is established; and it can never be assumed, that the government intended to diminish its power of accomplishing the end for which it was created. . . . A State ought never to be presumed to surrender this power, because, like the taxing power, the whole community have an interest in preserving it undiminished. And when a corporation alleges, that a State has surrendered for seventy years, its power of improvement and public accommodation, in a great and important line of travel, along which a vast number of citizens must daily pass; the community have a right to insist in the language of this court . . . "that its abandonment ought not to be presumed, in a case, in which the deliberate purpose of the State to abandon it does not appear." . . . It [the Warren Bridge] does not interrupt the passage over the Charles River Bridge, nor make the way to it or from it less convenient. None of the facilities or franchises granted to that corporation have been revoked by the legislature, and its right to take the tolls granted by the charter remains unaltered. In short, all the franchises and rights of property enumerated in the charter, and there mentioned to have been granted to it, remain un-impaired. But its income is destroyed by the Warren Bridge; which, being free, draws off the passengers and property which would have gone over it, and renders their franchise of no value. This is the gist of the complaint. . . . In order then to entitle themselves to relief, it is necessary to show that the legislature contracted [in the charter of the Charles River Bridge] not to do the act of which they complain, and that they impaired, or, in other words, violated that contract by the erection of the Warren Bridge. . . .

And what would be the fruits of this doctrine . . . of property in a line of travel by a corporation, if it should now be sanctioned by this court? . . . If this court should establish the principle now contended for, what is to become of the numerous railroads established on the same line of travel with turnpike companies; and which have rendered the franchises of the turnpike corporations of no value? Let it once be understood that such charters carry with them these implied contracts, and give this unknown and undefined property in a line of travelling, and you will soon find the old turnpike corporations awakening from their sleep, and calling upon this court to put down the improvements which have taken their place. The millions of property which have been invested in railroads and canals, upon lines of travel which had been before occupied by turn-pike corporations, will be put in jeopardy. We shall be thrown back to the improvements of the last century, and obliged to stand still, until the claims of the old turnpike corporations shall be satisfied, and they shall consent to permit these States to avail themselves of the lights of modern science, and partake of the benefit of those im-provements, which are now adding to the wealth and prosperity, and the convenience and comfort of every other part of the civilized world. . . . This court are not prepared to sanction principles which must lead to such results.

No State shall make or enforce any law which shall abridge the privileges or immunities of citizens of the United States. Justice Miller, in his opinion in the *Slaughter House Cases*,[1] enumerated the privileges and immunities of citizens of the United States as follows:

We may hold ourselves excused from defining the privileges and immunities of citizens of the United States which no State can abridge, until some case involving those privileges may make it necessary to do so. But lest it should be said that no such privileges and immunities are to be found if those we are considering are excluded, we venture to suggest some which owe their existence to the Federal government, its national character, its Constitution, or its laws.

One of these is well described in the case of *Crandall vs. Nevada.* It is said to be the right of the citizen of this great country, protected by implied guarantees of its Constitution, "to come to the seat of government, to assert any claim he may have upon that government, to transact any business he may have with it, to seek its protection, to share its offices, to engage in administering its functions. He has a right to free access to its seaports, through which all operations of foreign commerce are conducted, to the sub-treasuries, land offices, and courts of justice in the several States." And quoting from the language of Chief Justice Taney in another case, it is said "that for all the great purposes for which the Federal government was established, we are one people, with one common country, we are all citizens of the United States"; . . .

Another privilege of a citizen of the United States is to demand the care and protection of the Federal government over his life, liberty, and property when on the high seas or within the jurisdiction of a foreign government. Of this there can be no doubt, nor that the right depends upon his

[1] 16 Wallace's Rep., 36.

character as a citizen of the United States. The right to
peaceably assemble and petition for redress of grievances,
the privilege of the writ of habeas corpus, are rights of the
citizen guaranteed by the Federal Constitution.   The right
to use the navigable waters of the United States, however
they may penetrate the territory of the several States, all
rights secured to our citizens by treaties with foreign nations, are dependent upon citizenship of the United States,
and not citizenship of a State.   One of these privileges is
conferred by the very article under consideration.   It is
that a citizen of the United States can, of his own volition,
become a citizen of any State of the Union by a *bona fide*
residence therein, with the same rights as other citizens of
that State.

*No State shall . . . deprive any person of life, liberty,
or property, without due process of law.*   It is not easy
to realize that, as late as 1885, the power of a State to
regulate railroad charges within its own borders was
seriously challenged as a taking of property without
due process of law.   What seems to us a matter of
course was then contested strenuously in the *Railroad
Commission Cases*,[1] in which the Farmers' Loan and
Trust Company of New York City asked the Federal
courts to restrain the Railroad Commission of Mississippi from regulating local freight and passenger charges.
The duty of the commission under the law creating it
was to prevent the railroads from exacting unreasonable
or discriminating rates upon transportation within the
limits of that State.   Chief Justice Waite decided that
such regulation does not necessarily deprive persons of
property without due process of law.   He said:

It is now settled in this court that a State has power to
limit the amount of charges by railroad companies for the

[1] 116 U. S. Rep., 307.

... Chicago, Milwau-
... to compel that ... railroad, which was
... corporation, had ... by the Terri-
... that charter pro-
... corporation should have
... regulations and by-
... the manner of ...
... Minnesota was bound by the
... charter granted by the Terri-
... had the same
... regulating ... rates of
... late in ... State bringing upon
... in the ... in the contract
... Court of Minnesota decided in favor of
... the judgment was reversed by the Su-
... Court in Minnesota, ... U.S. Rep., 410, 456.

preme Court.   Justice Blatchford, in the opinion rendered by the national tribunal, said:

The construction put upon the statute [giving a commission power to fix rates] by the Supreme Court of Minnesota must be accepted by this court, for the purposes of the present case, as conclusive and not to be re-examined here as to its propriety and accuracy.   The Supreme Court [of Minnesota] authoritatively declares that it is the expressed intention of the legislature of Minnesota, by the statute, that the rates recommended and published by the commission, if it proceeds in the manner pointed out by the act, are not simply advisory, nor merely *prima facie* equal and reasonable, but final and conclusive as to what are equal and reasonable charges; that the law neither contemplates nor allows any issue to be made or inquiry to be had as to their equality or reasonableness in fact; that, under the statute, the rates published by the commission are the only ones that are lawful, and, therefore, in contemplation of law the only ones that are equal and reasonable. . . .   In other words, though the railroad is forbidden to establish rates that are not equal and reasonable, there is no power in the courts to stay the hands of the commission, if it chooses to establish rates that are unequal and unreasonable.

This being the construction of the statute by which we are bound in considering the present case, we are of opinion that, so construed, it conflicts with the Constitution of the United States in the particulars complained of by the railroad company.   It deprives the company of its rights to a judicial investigation, by due process of law, under the forms and with the machinery provided by the wisdom of successive ages for the investigation judicially of the truth of a matter in controversy, and substitutes therefor, as an absolute finality, the action of a railroad commission which, in view of the power conceded to it by the State court, cannot be regarded as clothed with judicial functions or possessing the machinery of a court of justice.

Nor shall any State . . . deny to any person within its jurisdiction the equal protection of the laws. "The Fourteenth Amendment," said Justice Field in his opinion in the case of *Barbier v. Connolly*,[1] "in declaring that no State 'shall deprive any person of life, liberty, or property without due process of law, nor deny to any person within its jurisdiction the equal protection of the laws,' undoubtedly intended not only that there should be no arbitrary deprivation of life or liberty, or arbitrary spoliation of property, but that equal protection and security should be given to all under like circumstances in the enjoyment of their personal and civil rights; that all persons should be equally entitled to pursue their happiness and acquire and enjoy property; that they should have like access to the courts of the country for the protection of their persons and property, the prevention and redress of their wrongs, and the enforcement of contracts; that no impediment should be interposed to the pursuits of any one except as applied to the same pursuits by others under like circumstances; that no greater burdens should be laid upon one than are laid upon others in the same calling and condition, and that in the administration of criminal justice no different or higher punishment should be imposed upon one than such as is prescribed to all for like offences."

The limitations upon the powers of the States imposed by the constitutional bill of rights in the tenth section of the first article and by the provisions of the Fourteenth Amendment are controlled to some extent by the police powers of the local governments. Each State has an undoubted right to enforce many laws which apparently violate these constitutional prohi-

---

[1] 113 U. S. Rep. 27.

bitions, if it appears that such laws are necessary for the safety, health, and morals of their citizens. This doctrine of the police powers of the States dates back to the case of *Coates vs. Mayor and Aldermen of New York City*,[1] in which the New York courts asserted that, in preserving the health of its citizens, a State does not impair the obligation of a contract. The question in this case was whether the city of New York could compel the sexton of Trinity Church to pay a penalty of $250 for burying a body in Trinity churchyard in violation of a city ordinance. Coates defended himself by claiming that the rectors, church-wardens, and vestrymen of Trinity Church had a property right to inter the bodies of deceased persons in this churchyard, and received fees, perquisites, and profits for so doing. He claimed that this property right amounted to a contract, the obligation of which could not be impaired by the State of New York. The court denied this contention upon the ground that a by-law of a city, made pursuant to a State law, enacted to preserve the health of the inhabitants, was a *policing regulation* and not a law impairing the obligation of a contract. The court said in part:

It was conceded, on the argument, that the corporation [City of New York] have, in general, power so to order the use of private property in the city, as to prevent its proving pernicious to the citizens generally. A contrary doctrine would strike at the root of all police regulations. . . . A lot is granted as a place of deposit for gunpowder, or other purpose, innocent, in itself, at the time; it is devoted to that purpose, till, in the progress of population, it becomes dangerous to the property, the safety, or the lives of hundreds; it cannot be, that the mere form of the grant, because

[1] 7 Cowen's [N. Y.] Rep., 585, 604.

present period in the constitutional history of this country, always conceded to belong to the States, however it may now be questioned in some of its details. "Unwholesome trades, slaughter-houses, operations offensive to the senses, the deposit of powder, the application of steam power to propel cars, the building with combustible materials, and the burial of the dead, may all," says Chancellor Kent [2 *Commentaries*, 340], "be interdicted by law, in the midst of dense masses of population, on the general and rational principle, that every person ought so to use his property as not to injure his neighbors; and that private interests must be made subservient to the general interests of the community." . . . The power is, and must be from its very nature, incapable of any very exact definition or limitation. Upon it depends the security of social order, the life and health of the citizen, the comfort of an existence in a thickly populated community, the enjoyment of private and social life, and the beneficial use of property. . . . The regulation of the place and manner of conducting the slaughtering of animals, and the business of butchering within a city, and the inspection of the animals to be killed for meat, and of the meat afterwards, are among the most necessary and frequent exercises of this power. . . . It cannot be denied that the statute under consideration is aptly framed to remove from the more densely populated part of the city, the noxious slaughter-houses, and large and offensive collections of animals necessarily incident to the slaughtering business of a large city, and to locate them where the convenience, health, and comfort of the people require they shall be located.

In the case of *Fertilizing Company vs. Hyde Park*,[1] the Supreme Court decided that a State could compel the removal of a malodorous·business away from the place where it had been located under the authority of a cor-

[1] 97 U. S. Rep., 659.

poration charter.   The ruling made was that, by virtue
of its power to enact laws to preserve the health of citizens, a State legislature, if necessary to put an end to
a public nuisance, has an absolute right to modify a
charter previously granted.   Justice Swayne said in
this case:

That a nuisance of a flagrant character existed . . . is
not controverted.   We cannot doubt that the police power
of the State was applicable and adequate to give an effectual
remedy.   That power belonged to the States when the
Federal Constitution was adopted.   They did not surrender
it, and they all have it now.   It extends to the entire property and business within their local jurisdiction.   Both
are subject to it in all proper cases.   It rests upon the fundamental principle that every one shall so use his own as
not to wrong and injure another.   To regulate and abate
nuisances is one of its ordinary functions. . . .

The charter [of the Fertilizing Company] was a sufficient
license until revoked; but we cannot regard it as a contract,
guaranteeing, in the locality originally selected, exemption
for fifty years from the exercise of the police power of the
State, however serious the nuisance might become in the
future, by reason of the growth of population around it.
The owners had no such exemption when they were incorporated, and we think the charter did not give it to them.

The police power of the States is a limitation upon
the powers of the United States.   It is a right upon a
right.   It is, for example, the legal justification of State
prohibitory liquor laws, which often impair the obligations of a contract and always lessen without compensation to the owners the value of property employed in
brewing and distilling.   In the case of *Mugler vs. Kansas*,[1] in which the owners of a brewery located in Kansas

[1] 123 U. S. Rep., 623, 664.

complained of the operation of the Kansas prohibitory amendment, Justice Harlan, giving the opinion of the Supreme Court, said:

It is contended [by the brewers] that as the primary and principal use of beer is as a beverage; as their respective breweries were erected when it was lawful to engage in the manufacture of beer for every purpose; as such establishments will become of no value as property, or, at least, will be materially diminished in value, if not employed in the manufacture of beer for every purpose; the prohibition upon their being so employed is, in effect, a taking of property for public use without compensation, and depriving the citizen of his property without due process of law.   In other words, although the State, in the exercise of her police powers, may lawfully prohibit the manufacture and sale, within her limits, of intoxicating liquors to be used as a beverage, legislation having that object in view cannot be enforced against those who, at the time, happen to own property, the chief value of which consists of its fitness for such manufacturing purposes, unless compensation is first made for the diminution in the value of their property, resulting from such prohibitory amendments. . . .

The Supreme Court in the case of *Barbier vs. Connolly*,[1] ruled that State policing measures which in effect deny to some persons the equal protection of the laws, are not void under the provisions of the Fourteenth Amendment.   For example, on April 8, 1884, the City of San Francisco, California, enacted a municipal ordinance, making it unlawful to carry on a laundry business in certain parts of the city without first obtaining one certificate from the city health officer that the sanitary arrangements of the laundry were good, and another from the Board of Fire Wardens that

[1] 113 U. S. Rep., 27.

the stoves and appliances for heating smoothing irons were so managed as not to be a source of danger from fire to surrounding property. A Mr. Barbier, who had a laundry within the city limits, was sentenced to imprisonment for five days for violation of this ordinance. He petitioned the United States Court for release on the ground that his constitutional right to the equal protection of the laws had been violated. Justice Field, in giving the opinion of the Court, said that Mr. Barbier had no just cause for complaint because he had received the same protection of the laws as all the other laundrymen of San Francisco, and, therefore, had been punished under a law which did not violate this clause of the Fourteenth Amendment. The decision is in part as follows:

A prohibition simply upon the use of property for purposes that are declared, by valid legislation, to be injurious to the health, morals, or safety of the community, cannot, in any just sense, be deemed a taking or an appropriation of property for the public benefit. Such legislation does not disturb the owner in the control or use of his property for lawful purposes, nor restrict his right to dispose of it, but is only a declaration by the State that its use by any one, for certain forbidden purposes, is prejudicial to the public interests. Nor can legislation of that character come within the Fourteenth Amendment, in any case, unless it is apparent that its real object is not to protect the community, or to promote the general well-being, but, under the guise of police regulation, to deprive the owner of his liberty, or property without due process of law. The power which the States have of prohibiting such use by individuals of their property as will be prejudicial to the health, the morals, or the safety of the public, is not—and, consistently with the existence and safety of organized society, cannot be —burdened with the condition that the State must compensate such individual owners for pecuniary losses they may sustain, by reason of their not being permitted, by a noxious use of their property, to inflict injury upon the community. The exercise of the police power by the destruction of property which is itself a public nuisance, or the prohibition of its use in a particular way, whereby the property becomes depreciated, is very different from taking property for public use, or from depriving a person of his property without due process of law. In the one case, a nuisance only is abated; in the other, unoffending property is taken away from an innocent owner.

Neither the [Fourteenth] amendment—broad and comprehensive as it is—nor any other amendment, was designed to interfere with the power of the State, sometimes termed its police power, to prescribe regulations to promote the health, peace, morals, education, and good order of the people, and to legislate so as to increase the industries of the State, develop its resources, and add to its wealth and prosperity. . . . Regulations for these purposes may press with more or less weight upon one than upon another, but they are designed, not to impose unequal or unnecessary restrictions upon any one, but to promote, with as little individual inconvenience as possible, the general good. Though, in many respects, necessarily special in their character, they do not furnish just ground for complaint if they operate alike upon all persons and property under the same circumstances and conditions. Class legislation, discriminating against some and favoring others, is prohibited, but legislation which, in carrying out a public purpose, is limited in its application, if within the sphere of its operation it affects alike all persons similarly situated, is not within the amendment.

A State even may take private property for private uses without compensation, if the taking serves a public use. The Oklahoma Depositor's Guaranty Fund Act, for example, was sustained by the Supreme Court in the case of *Noble State Bank v. Haskell.*[1] This was an action to restrain the State Banking Board from levying and collecting an assessment upon the Noble State Bank upon the ground that the Guaranty Fund Act was unconstitutional. To compel a bank to pay an assessment of one per cent upon its average deposits in order to create a depositors' guaranty fund was claimed to be a taking of private property without compensation. The Supreme Court, however, ruled that a State has a right to regulate banking by such laws. Justice Holmes said:

It may be said in a general way that the police power extends to all the great public needs. . . . It may be put forth in aid of what is sanctioned by usage, or held by the prevailing morality or strong and preponderant opinion to be greatly and immediately necessary to the public welfare. Among matters of that sort probably few would doubt that both usage and preponderant opinion give their sanction to enforcing the primary conditions of successful commerce. One of those conditions at the present time is the possibility of payment by checks drawn against bank deposits, to such an extent do checks replace currency in daily business. If then the legislature of the State thinks that the public welfare requires the measure under consideration, analogy and principle are in favor of the power to enact it. . . . In short, when the Oklahoma legislature declares by implication that free banking is a public danger and that incorporation, inspection, and the above described co-operation are necessary safeguards, this court certainly cannot say it is wrong.

The police powers of the States shrink into nothingness when they conflict with the power of Congress to regulate commerce among the States. Under no cir-

[1] 219 U. S. Rep., 104.

cumstances can a State so use its right to legislate concerning public safety, health, and morals, as to interfere
directly or indirectly with the national authority over
interstate commerce.   For example, it was shown to
the Supreme Court in the case of *Minnesota vs. Barber*,[1]
that, in 1889, the State of Minnesota had enacted a law
forbidding the selling or offering for sale for human food
of any fresh beef, veal, mutton, lamb, or pork, not taken
from an animal which had been inspected and certified
before slaughter to be healthy and in suitable condition
to be slaughtered for human food.   One Henry E.
Barber, who had been convicted of selling in Minnesota one hundred pounds of beef which had been killed
in Illinois without inspection or certification, took his
case into the United States Courts.   The Federal
Circuit Court ruled that the Minnesota law infringed
the Constitution of the United States by restricting
commerce among the States.   The State of Minnesota
appealed to the Supreme Court of the United States,
which affirmed the decision of the Circuit Court in an
opinion in which Justice Harlan said:

> The enactment of a similar statute by each one of the
> States composing the Union would result in the destruction
> of commerce among the several States, so far as such com-
> merce is involved in the transportation from one part of
> the country to another of animal meats designed for human
> food and entirely free from disease. . . .   As the inspec-
> tion must take place within the twenty-four hours im-
> mediately before the slaughtering, the act, by its necessary
> operation, excludes from the Minnesota market, practically,
> all fresh beef, veal, mutton, lamb, or pork—in whatever
> form, and although entirely sound, healthy, and fit for
> human food—taken from animals slaughtered in other

[1] 136 U. S. Rep., 313.

... the slaughtering of
... Minnesota for human
... use in that State. This
... ... and labor of sending
... Minnesota to points in that
... bringing them back after
... ... place from where they
... take place within twenty-
... the certificate of inspection
... ... great as ... amount ... at
... ... Minnesota, if meat was
... its limits. When ... this is
... by its necessary operation
... of fresh beef, veal, mutton,
... that may have been inspected
... the State where they were
... remain as to its effect upon
... States. . . . If this legis-
... discrimination against the pro-
... States in favor of the products
... interferes with and burdens
... States, it would be difficult
... ... have that result.

... the Consent of the Congress, lay
... Imports or Exports. The clause
... laws imposing customs duties
... taxing powers. In the case of
... holders of New York licenses
... the navigable waters of that
... State have all powers over com-
... been taken from them by this
... ... In answering this conten-
... showed that it refers only

We must . . . determine whether the act of laying "duties or imposts on imports or exports," is considered in the Constitution as a branch of the taxing power, or of the power to regulate commerce. We think it very clear, that it is considered as a branch of the taxing power. It is so treated in the first clause of the 8th section: "Congress shall have power to lay and collect taxes, duties, imposts, and excises"; and before commerce is mentioned, the rule by which the exercise of this power must be governed is declared. It is, that all duties, imposts, and excises shall be uniform. In a separate clause of the enumeration, the power to regulate commerce is given, as being entirely distinct from the right to levy taxes and imposts, and as being a new power not before conferred. The Constitution, then, considers these powers as substantive and distinct from each other; and so places them in the enumeration it contains. The power of imposing duties on imports is classed with the power to levy taxes, and that seems to be its natural place. But the power to levy taxes never could be considered as abridging the right of the States on that subject; and they might, consequently, have exercised it by levying duties on imports or exports, had the Constitution contained no prohibition on this subject. The prohibition, then, is an exception from the acknowledged power of the States to levy taxes, not from the questionable power to regulate commerce.

No State shall . . . lay any Impost or Duties . . . except what may be absolutely necessary for executing it's inspection Laws. The States never have surrendered their power to protect the health and well-being of their citizens by all sorts of quarantine regulations and other inspection laws. Undesirable articles of commerce, including diseased cattle, foods unfit for use, and merchandise which contains the germs of contagious disease, may be stopped at the border line of any State.

As the article of the Constitution which prescribes the limit goes on to provide that "all such laws shall be subject to the revision and control of Congress," it seems to me that Congress is the proper tribunal to decide the question, whether a charge or duty is or is not excessive.

No State shall, without the Consent of Congress, lay any Duty of Tonnage. Chief Justice Marshall, in his opinion in the case of *Gibbons vs. Ogden,*[1] defined the phrase "duty of tonnage" as follows:

"A duty of tonnage" is as much a tax as a duty on imports or exports; and the reason which induced the prohibition of those taxes extends to this also. This tax may be imposed by a State with the consent of Congress; and it may be admitted that Congress cannot give a right to a State in virtue of its own powers. But a duty of tonnage being a part of the power of imposing taxes, its prohibition may certainly be made to depend on Congress, without affording any implication respecting a power to regulate commerce.

No State shall . . . keep Troops, or Ships of War in time of Peace. Judge Scott of Illinois, in his opinion in the case of *Dunn vs. The People,*[2] held that the active militia of a State does not come within the prohibition of the second clause, section 10, art. 1, of the Constitution of the United States. "Our understanding," he said, "is, the organization of the active militia of the State conforms exactly to the definitions usually given to militia. Lexicographers and others define militia, and so the common understanding is, to be 'a body of armed citizens trained to military duty, who may be called out in certain cases, but may not be kept on service like standing armies, in time of peace.' That

---

[1] *Vide supra.*   [2] 94 Illinois Rep., 121, 138.

is the case as to the active militia of this State. The
men comprising it come from the body of the militia,
and when not engaged at stated periods in drilling and
other exercises, they return to their usual avocations as
is usual with militia, and are subject to call when the
public exigencies demand it. Such an organization,
no matter by what name it may be designated, comes
within no definition of 'troops' as that word is used in
the Constitution."

*No State shall . . . enter into an Agreement or Com-
pact with another State.* The purpose of this clause was
to make the new central government the referee in such
disputes over boundaries as those between Virginia,
Connecticut, and Massachusetts over a part of the
territory northwest of the Ohio River, between Connecticut and Pennsylvania over the strip along the
northerly boundary of the latter, and between New
York and New Hampshire about the territorial area
which soon after the Constitution was in operation
was admitted as the State of Vermont. In the notable
case of *Rhode Island vs. Massachusetts*,[1] decided in 1838,
the important question was not whether the power to
decide these controversies had been given to the central
government, but whether the judicial department had
sole power to pass upon them. This action had been
brought to settle an old boundary line dispute between
the two States. Rhode Island under a survey made in
1642 had claimed all the territory up to a line three miles
south of the Charles River. Massachusetts had insisted that the surveyors had been mistaken about the
location of Charles River. In support of this argument,
Massachusetts had referred to the reports of boundary
commissioners who had fixed the State line in 1709 and

[1] 12 Peters' Rep., 723.

in 1718.   Rhode Island had refused to be bound by these reports on the ground that her colonial government never had accepted them.   Justice Baldwin, an able Pennsylvania jurist, who gave the decision of the Court, said:

There can be but two tribunals under the Constitution who can act on the boundaries of States, the legislative or the judicial power; the former is limited in express terms to assent or dissent, where a compact or agreement is referred to them by the States; and as the latter can be exercised only by this Court when a State is a party, the power is here, or it cannot exist.   For these reasons we cannot be persuaded that it could have been intended to provide only for the settlement of boundaries when States could agree, and to altogether withhold the power to decide controversies on which the States could not agree, and presented the most imperious call for speedy settlement.

No State shall . . . engage in War, unless actually invaded, or in such imminent Danger as will not admit of delay.   "The prohibition against the States engaging in war," according to *Watson on the Constitution*,[1] "was established upon old colonial precedents.   In the New England Union of 1643, it was provided that neither Massachusetts, Plymouth, Connecticut, nor New Haven, should engage in any war without the consent of the commissioners [who represented each colony at annual meetings] (but they might do so in case of sudden exigencies).   So Franklin's plan of a Confederation provided that no colony should engage in an offensive war with any nation of Indians without the consent of the Congress, or Grand Council.   This prohibition was continued in the Articles of Confederation, which

[1] i, 848.

forbade any State engaging in war without the consent
of the United States, unless it were actually invaded by
enemies.   The exception which is found in all the prohibitions is substantially the same, viz.: 'in case of
actual invasion or such imminent danger as would not
admit of delay.' In such case, it would of course be necessary to take such action as would best protect life and
property.   In such cases the probabilities are that war
would be resorted to by any of the States, whether
here was a provision in the Constitution authorizing it
or not. '

CHAPTER XVI

RIGHTS OF THE STATES AND THEIR CITIZENS AGAINST THE UNITED STATES AS ENUMERATED IN AMENDMENTS I-X

"AN American bill of rights," said Chief Justice Doe of New Hampshire in the decision of *Orr vs. Quimby*,[1] "is a declaration of private rights reserved in a grant of public powers, — a reservation of a limited individual sovereignty, annexed to and made part of a limited form of government established by the independent, individual action of the voting class of the people. The general purpose of such a bill of rights is to declare those fundamental principles of the common law, generally called the principles of English constitutional liberty, which the American people always claimed as their English inheritance, and the defense of which was the justification of the war of 1776."

The people of the United States were nearly all English by birth and inheritance, the sons and grandsons of Englishmen who had dared all things and suffered all things for the sake of rights and liberties worth fighting for and, if need be, dying for. . Englishmen in America in the closing years of the eighteenth century were proudly mindful of the Great Charter of Rights and Liberties which Englishmen in England had wrested from King John nearly six centuries before. The Pe-

[1] 54 N. H. Rep., 590.

tition of Right, which English Puritans had forced upon Charles the First in 1628, was like a family heirloom to the descendants of New England Puritans. The English Bill of Rights adopted by a convention parliament in 1689, which declared the rights and liberties of English subjects, was one of the models that Thomas Jefferson followed in drafting the Declaration of Independence. The Instrument of Government of 1653, which established the Commonwealth of England under the great Lord Protector, Oliver Cromwell, was the prototype of the Massachusetts Constitution of 1780, and in part of the Constitution of the United States.

The first charter of Virginia, granted by King James the First in 1606, shows that Englishmen in America had English rights from the beginning. Its fifteenth section says:

Also we do . . . Declare . . . that all and every the Persons, being our Subjects, which shall dwell and inhabit within every or any of the said several Colonies and Plantations, and every of their children, which shall happen to be born within any of the Limits and Precincts of the said several Colonies and Plantations, shall Have and enjoy all Liberties, Franchises, and Immunities, within any of our other Dominions, to all Intents and Purposes, as if they had been abiding and born, within this our realm of *England*, or any other of our said Dominions.

The Stamp Act Congress of 1765 declared "that trial by jury is the inherent and invaluable right of every British subject in the Colonies."

The Declaration of Rights adopted by the First Continental Congress began with a broad statement "that the inhabitants of the English colonies in

people in the legislature, and of judicial proceedings according to the course of common law. All persons shall be bailable, unless for capital offences, where the proof shall be evident, or the presumption great. All fines shall be moderate; and no cruel or unusual punishments shall be inflicted. No man shall be deprived of his liberty or property, but by the judgment of his peers, or the law of the land, and should the public exigencies make it necessary, for the common preservation, to take any person's property, or to demand his particular services, full compensation shall be made for the same. And, in the just preservation of rights and property, it is understood and declared, that no law ought ever to be made or have force in the said territory, that shall, in any manner whatever, interfere with or affect private contracts, or engagements, *bona fide*, and without fraud previously formed.

The people of the different States had incorporated bills of rights in their constitutions. The declaration in the first Constitution of the State of New York adopted in 1777, for example, reads as follows:

That the free exercise and enjoyment of religious profession and worship, without discrimination or preference, shall forever hereafter be allowed within this State to all mankind: Provided, however, that the liberty of conscience hereby granted shall not be so construed as to excuse acts of licentiousness, or justify practises inconsistent with the peace and safety of this State. . . . That trial by jury, in all cases, in which it hath heretofore been used in the Colony of New York, shall be established and remain inviolate forever: And that no acts of attainder shall be passed by the legislature of this State, for crimes other than those committed before the termination of the present war [the Revolution]; and that such acts shall not work corruption of blood. And further, that the legislature of this State shall, at no time hereafter, institute any new court or courts, but such as shall proceed according to the course of the common law.

The history of the adoption of the Bill of Rights as embodied in Amendments I-X was summed up by Justice Harlan in his dissenting opinion in the case of *Maxwell v. Dow*,[1] as follows:

When the Constitution was adopted by the Convention of 1787 and placed before the people for their acceptance or rejection, many wise statesmen whose patriotism no one then questioned or now questions earnestly objected to its acceptance upon the ground that it did not contain a Bill of Rights guarding the fundamental guaranties of life, liberty, and property against the unwarranted exercise of power by the National Government. But the friends of the Constitution, believing that the failure to accept it would destroy all hope for permanent union among the people of the original States, and following the advice of Washington who was the leader of the constitutional forces, met this objection by showing that when the Constitution had been

[1] 176 U. S. Rep., 581, 606.

accepted by the requisite number of States and thereby became the supreme law of the land, such amendments could be adopted as would relieve the apprehensions of those who deemed it necessary, by express provisions, to guard against the infringement by the agencies of the General Government of any of the essential rights of American freemen. This view prevailed, and the implied pledge thus given was carried out by the first Congress, which promptly adopted and submitted to the people of the several States the first ten amendments. These amendments have ever since been regarded as the National Bill of Rights.

What confuses most people is that these provisos do not limit the powers of the States. The average man who has been told that the authority of the United States is supreme, cannot understand why a positive prohibition should bar the general government only and have nothing to do with the subordinate governments. Chief Justice Marshall in his opinion in the case of *Barron vs. Baltimore*[1] said:

Had the framers of these [the first ten] amendments intended them to be limitations on the powers of the State governments, they would have imitated the framers of the original Constitution, and have expressed that intention. Had Congress engaged in the extraordinary occupation of improving the constitutions of the several States by affording the people additional protection from the exercise of power by their own governments in matters which concerned themselves alone, they would have declared this purpose in plain and intelligible language.

First Amendment. Congress shall make no law respecting an establishment of religion, or prohibiting the free exercise thereof; or abridging the freedom of

[1] 7 Peters' Rep., 243.

speech, or of the press; or the right of the people peaceably to assemble, and to petition the Government for a redress of grievances.

These are the priceless personal rights for the sake of which in every age man has associated in tribes, clans, nations, or other social organizations. It is not easy to realize the value of these rights—to believe in and follow any form of religious worship; to have a mind of one's own and speak it anywhere and everywhere, no matter whether others like it or not; to join with others in telling those who have power just what the speaker thinks of them and their doings, especially those doings which are injurious. Infinitely valuable as these rights are, they are not unlimited. The limit is this: that he who asserts his rights must not make them a means of destroying the equal rights of others. And with this limitation imposed in the fullest proper measure, these personal liberties are so much worth while that, if a choice had to be made, every man in his senses would keep them, if he had to lose every other right which the most perfect government could give to the governed.

Congress shall make no law respecting an establishment of religion. It is generally believed that this part of the amendment was suggested by Mr. Madison and other Virginia members of the First Congress, whose attention had been called to the subject by a controversy which had been settled in their own State a few years before. The Church established by law in England had few followers in Colonial America, which was peopled mostly by Puritans, Presbyterians, Quakers, and a few Catholics. Virginia had been colonized for the most part by adherents of the English Church. The

Episcopal clergyman had a parish which was under a legal obligation to support him by payments of money or its equivalent in tobacco, which then served the purposes of money in the colony. This plan worked well enough except when tobacco fluctuated in price; then the clergy got their pay in the less valuable currency. Lawsuits followed, in which the clergymen again got the worst of it. Patrick Henry represented the planters. One burst of his matchless eloquence made him famous, and helped to deprive the Church of England in Virginia of its legal rights. The dispute, however, did not come to an end until 1784, when the Virginia legislature passed the famous "Act for establishing religious Freedom," which Thomas Jefferson drafted. This law, declaring "that no man shall be compelled to frequent or support any religious worship," was rather hard on the poor parsons who, up to that time, had had a legal right to compel the planters to support them. This right had always been held to be a tithe claim on land, and its value always had been deducted from the purchase prices when sales were made. By this law, the land owners, who had paid less because of the incumbrance, received a free present of its cash value and the clergy were the losers. The Virginia Representatives had this clause put in this amendment in order to keep the advantage in that quarrel.

Congress shall make no law . . . prohibiting the free exercise thereof [of religion]. The right to the free exercise of religion so long as no act injurious to others is committed, was explained by the Supreme Court in 1871, in the case of *Watson vs. Jones*.[1] This was a quarrel in the Walnut Street Presbyterian Church of

[1] 13 Wallace, Rep., 679.

Louisville, Kentucky, about the rights and wrongs of slavery. One party tried to withdraw the church from the General Presbyterian Church in the United States of America, and turn it over to the General Presbyterian Church in the United States, commonly known as the Southern Presbyterian Church. The others, who were actually in possession of the church edifice, wished to keep it in association with the Northern churches. The court refused to make such an order on the ground that religious freedom includes the right of a church to govern itself. Justice Miller said:

In this country the full and free right to entertain any religious belief, to practise any religious principle, and to teach any religious doctrine which does not violate the laws of morality and property, and which does not infringe personal rights, is conceded to all. The law knows no heresy and is committed to the support of no dogma, the establishment of no sect. The right to organize voluntary religious associations to assist in the expression and dissemination of any religious doctrine, and to create tribunals for the decision of controverted questions of faith within the association, and for the ecclesiastical government of all the individual members, congregations, and officers within the general association, is unquestioned.

Freedom of religion may not be made a cloak for immorality, vice, or crime, under the guise of conscientious belief. The Mormon Church, insisting upon the contention that the plural wife system was a part of its religion, fought to the last ditch every national statute for the suppression of polygamy. The justices of the Supreme Court have been against them on every occasion, and with especial vehemence of argument in the case of *Mormon Church vs. United States*,[1] in which Justice Bradley delivered an opinion covering that point as follows:

It is distinctly stated in the pleadings and findings of fact that the property of the said corporation was held for the purpose of religious and charitable uses. But it is also stated in the findings of fact, and is a matter of public notoriety, that the religious and charitable uses intended to be subserved and promoted are the inculcation and spread of the doctrines and usages of the Mormon Church, or Church of Latter Day Saints, one of the distinguishing features of which is the practise of polygamy—a crime against the laws, and abhorrent to the sentiments and feelings of the civilized world. Notwithstanding the stringent laws which have been passed by Congress—notwithstanding all the efforts made to suppress this barbarous practise—the sect or community composing the Church of Jesus Christ of Latter Day Saints perseveres, in defiance of law, in preaching, upholding, promoting, and defending it. . . . One pretence for this obstinate course is, that their belief in the practise of polygamy, or in the right to indulge in it, is a religious belief, and, therefore, under the protection of the constitutional guaranty of religious freedom. This is altogether a sophistical plea. No doubt the Thugs of India imagined that their belief in the right of assassination was a religious belief; but their thinking so did not make it so. The practise of suttee by the Hindu widows may have sprung from a supposed religious conviction. The offering of human sacrifices by our own ancestors in Britain was no doubt sanctioned by an equally conscientious impulse. But no one, on that account, would hesitate to brand those practises, now, as crimes against society, and obnoxious to condemnation and punishment by the civil authority. The State has a perfect right to prohibit polygamy, and all

[1] 136 U. S. Rep., 1.

other open offences against the enlightened sentiment of mankind, notwithstanding the pretence of religious conviction by which they may be advocated and practised.

Congress shall make no law . . . . abridging the freedom of speech, or of the press. As now enforced, liberty of speech and of the press goes farther perhaps than the founders of the republic would have approved. What they wanted was a rule which would prevent the federal authorities from meddling with the right of citizens to say or print what they chose. What was to be permitted in the way of free speech and a free press in each State, they were willing to leave to the authorities of each locality. Speeches and pamphlets had helped the cause of American independence almost as much as gunpowder and cold steel. Madison, Hamilton, and Pinckney had used the power of the press in *The Federalist* to present the reasons why the Constitution ought to be adopted.

Freedom of speech is the same thing as freedom of the press to this extent that the rights refer to different ways of giving information to other people. The right to speak freely is the same as the right to print and publish freely, and each has the same limitation: it must not be used to the injury of others. This point was explained by Judge Bennett of Kentucky in his opinion in the case of *Riley vs. Lee.*[1] A Dr. Thelkeld had published in the Owenton (Ky.) *News* a card saying that O. V. Riley had said that the doctor's sister, Bettie Thelkeld, could not secure a position as school teacher in the Cedar Hill district, and that this statement had driven her to despair, undermined her constitution, and assisted the ravages of disease. Dr. Thelkeld added that, before Mr. Riley said this, his own sister had applied for the position. "Therefore," he said, "I regard this conduct in him as uncalled for, ungentlemanly, and detestable, as his statement was fallacious." Mr. Riley took his part in this pretty quarrel by bringing an action against the publishers of the Owenton *News*, who set up as a defense that they were protected by the provision in the Kentucky Constitution concerning freedom of the press. The Court decided otherwise. Judge Bennett said in the course of the decision:

By the provisions of the United States and State constitutions guaranteeing the "freedom of the press," it was simply intended to secure to the conductors of the press the same rights and immunities that are enjoyed by the public at large. The citizen has the right to speak the truth in reference to the acts of government, public officials, or individuals. The press is guaranteed the same right, but no greater right. The citizen has the right to criticise the acts of government, provided it is with the good motive of correcting what he believes to be existing evils or defects and of bringing about a more efficient or honest administration of government. For like purpose and with like motive he may criticise the acts of public officials, and for the honest purpose of better subserving the public interest he may criticise the fitness and qualifications of candidates for office, not only in respect to their ability, fidelity, and experience, but in respect to their honesty and personal habits. The press has precisely the same rights, but no more. An individual may, in what he honestly believes to be in the interest of good morals and good order and the suppression of immorality and disorder, criticise the acts of other individuals. So may the press. But in no case has the citizen the right to injure the rights of others—among the most sacred of which is the right to good name and fame—

their rights are as absolute as his, and neither can injure the rights of the other. This negation extends to the denial of the citizen's right to speak, write, or print that which tends to injure the character or reputation of another unless it is in fact true. The press is under the same restraints.

Congress shall make no law . . . . abridging . . . . the right of the people peaceably to assemble, and to petition the Government for a redress of grievances. Broad as this right is, it is limited by the rule that the people, in assembling peaceably to petition the government, may not make their assembling a pretext for violating the rights of others. The anarchist may be silenced by the police because his freedom of speech may cause others to lose their right to life, liberty, or property. Any other public speaker who attracts a disorderly crowd, may be suppressed because other people have a right to the undisturbed use of the public streets.

The United States declares by this amendment that it will not infringe this ancient prerogative of the free man. This limitation of power binds the nation, not the States; yet, if the State authorities should venture to interfere with their own citizens assembled to petition Congress for a redress of their grievances against the United States, then the national courts could interfere. During the first years after the Civil War, there was much trouble in the Southern States because the white people were unwilling to recognize the rights of those who had been their slaves. The Ku Klux Klan and other lawless organizations, in order to make the negroes afraid to vote, went about the country districts in disguise, threatening and in some cases assaulting the colored people. In 1870, Congress enacted a law for the express purpose of suppressing crimes of this kind. In 1875, the Supreme Court was asked to decide, under this statute, the case of *United States vs. Cruikshank*,[1] in which a number of citizens of Louisiana had been found guilty of having banded together to intimidate colored citizens from voting. One question before the Supreme Court was whether, under the First Amendment, the United States could punish men who had been guilty of a crime which usually would be punished under the laws of the State where it had been committed. This amendment had been understood to be a limitation upon the law-making power of the nation. The Court now had to decide whether it also gave to Congress another power—the power to guard the right of the people to assemble. Chief Justice Waite said:

The right of the people peaceably to assemble for the purpose of petitioning Congress for a redress of grievances, or for anything else connected with the powers or the duties of the national government, is an attribute of national citizenship, and, as such, under the protection of, and guaranteed by, the United States. The very idea of a government, republican in form, implies a right on the part of its citizens to meet peaceably for consultation in respect to public affairs and to petition for redress of grievances.

Second Amendment. A well regulated Militia, being necessary to the security of a free State, the right of the people to keep and bear Arms, shall not be infringed.

The meaning and the purpose of the Second Amendment were discussed in the case of *Presser vs. Illinois*.[2]

[1] 92 U. S. Rep., 542.   [2] 116 U. S. Rep., 252.

... Presser, a citizen of the United States and of the State of Illinois, and been tried in the state court ... charge that, in violation of state law, he had ... and drilled in the streets ... ... called the *Lehr und Wehr Verin*. ... ... on the ground that his company was not ... the state militia which alone had ... ... arms. Presser took his case to the National ... ... Court and lost his claim. Justice Woods ...

... thinks it clear that the actions of the Military ... ... under consideration, that ... only certain classes of ... associate together as military organizations, or to ... or parade with arms ... does not ... unless authorized by law, do not infringe the right of the people to keep and bear arms. But a delusive answer to the intention of the amendment ... the ... in question ... ... the amendment ... limitation only upon the power of Congress and the National Government and not of ... ... of the states ... The second amendment ... that ... held ... ...

Third Amendment. No Soldier shall in time of peace be quartered in any house, without the consent of the owner nor in time of war, but in a manner to be prescribed by law.

... The ... Third Amendment ... ...

The poorest man may in his cottage bid defiance to all the force of the crown. It may fall, its roof may shake; the wind may blow through it; the storms may enter, the rain may enter—but the King of England cannot enter. All his forces dare not cross the threshold of the ruined tenement.

Fourth Amendment. The right of the people to be secure in their persons, houses, papers, and effects, against unreasonable searches and seizures, shall not be violated, and no Warrants shall issue, but upon probable cause, supported by Oath or affirmation, and particularly describing the place to be searched, and the persons or things to be seized.

This noble amendment declares that the Federal Government must not misuse the weapons and processes of the law. Our ancestors knew by bitter experience that the law, which ought to protect liberty and right, can be used to oppress and destroy. Many of those who, in 1790, framed this amendment, could remember how writs of assistance, or general warrants in which no persons were charged with crime, had been used by royal revenue officers to enable them to go into any person's house and search for articles that might have been smuggled.

So oppressive had become the practice that here, as in England, it caused great alarm among the people, and here, as there, resistance was made to such writs on the ground of their illegality. These warrants were principally issued and the seizures made in the colony of Massachusetts. The trial which tested their legality occurred in Boston in February, 1761. It proved to be more than a mere trial, as we shall see, for the greatest question which could affect the interests of the colonists was involved. James Otis, a native of Massachusetts, was Advocate-General of the Crown at Boston, a legal position of great responsibility and honor; but he was so wrought up at the outrage which had been committed by the arrests under these warrants that he resigned his office, and, though offered a most remunerative fee if he would take charge of the defense, he said: "In such a cause as this I despise a fee." He then acted as one of the counsel in resisting the arrests. He spoke for five hours, and it is doubtful if any legal argument ever made on this continent produced a more profound or lasting impression. He set fire to a torch which is still burning, and which will continue to burn, for in that masterful effort he impressed upon the American heart the great lesson of resistance to tyranny and outrage. As the result of the trial the writs were never afterwards served by judicial sanction. This trial occurred thirty years before the [Fourth] amendment . . . was adopted, but its adoption was largely due to the opposition to the Writs of Assistance, and the powerful influence of the speech of Otis.—*Watson on the Constitution*, ii, 1415.

The right of the people to be secure . . . against unreasonable searches and seizures, shall not be violated.

Fifth Amendment Part of).   No person shall be . . . compelled in any Criminal Case to be a witness against himself.

The meaning of the immunities stated in these extracts was explained at length by Justice Bradley in his opinion in the great case of *Boyd vs. United States,*[1] a proceeding under the revenue laws of the United States for the forfeiture of thirty-five cases of plate glass which some one or, probably, the claimant Boyd, had tried to smuggle through the New York Custom House. The United States Attorney had occasion to prove, as a part of his case, the value of the glass, and, therefore, had obtained an order of court requiring the persons who claimed that it belonged to them to produce the invoice. They obeyed under protest, and, having lost the case, took an appeal upon the claim that the order of court had authorized an unreasonable search and seizure and had compelled them to be witnesses against themselves. Justice Bradley's opinion is especially important in that it is based upon a decision of Lord Camden, who in his time was the greatest of English judges. He said:

In order to ascertain the nature of the proceedings intended by the Fourth Amendment to the Constitution under the terms "unreasonable searches and seizures," it is only necessary to recall the contemporary or then recent history of the controversies on the subject, both in this country and in England. The practise had obtained in the colonies of issuing writs of assistance to the revenue officers, empowering them, in their discretion, to search suspected places for smuggled goods, which James Otis pronounced "the worst instrument of arbitrary power, the most destructive of English liberty, and the fundamental principles of law, that ever was found in an English law book"; since they placed "the liberty of every man in the hands of every petty officer." This was in February, 1761, in Boston, and the famous debate in which it occurred was perhaps the most prominent event which inaugurated the resistance of the colonies to the oppressions of the mother country. "Then and there," said John Adams, "then and there was the first scene of the first act of opposition to the arbitrary claims of Great Britain. Then and there the child Independence was born."

These things, and the events which took place in England immediately following the argument about writs of assistance in Boston, were fresh in the memories of those who achieved our independence and established our form of government. In the period from 1762, when the *North Briton* was started by John Wilkes, to April, 1766, when the House of Commons passed resolutions condemnatory of general warrants, whether for the seizure of persons or papers, occurred the bitter controversy between the English government and Wilkes, in which the latter appeared as the champion of popular rights, and was, indeed, the pioneer in the contest which resulted in the abolition of some grievous abuses which had gradually crept into the administration of public affairs. Prominent and principal among these was the practice of issuing general warrants by the Secretary of State, for searching private houses for the discovery and seizure of books and papers that might be used to convict their owner of the charge of libel. Certain numbers of the *North Briton*, particularly No. 45, had been very bold in denunciation of the government, and were esteemed heinously libellous. By authority of the secretary's warrant, Wilkes' house was searched, and his papers were indiscriminately seized. For this outrage he sued the perpetrators and obtained a verdict of £1,000 against Wood, one of the parties who made the search, and £4,000 against Lord Halifax, the Secretary of State, who issued the warrant.

The case, however, which will always be celebrated as being the occasion of Lord Camden's memorable discussion of the subject, was that of *Entick vs. Carrington and Three Other King's Messengers*. . . . This action was trespass for entering the plaintiff's dwelling-house in November, 1762, and breaking open his desks, boxes, etc., and searching and examining his papers. The jury rendered a special verdict, and the case was twice solemnly argued at the bar. Lord Camden pronounced the judgment of the court in Michaelmas Term, 1765, and the law as expounded by him has been regarded as settled from that time to this, and his great judgment on that occasion is considered as one of the landmarks of English liberty. It was welcomed and applauded by the lovers of liberty in the colonies as well as in the mother country. It is regarded as one of the permanent monuments of the British Constitution, and is quoted as such by the English authorities on that subject down to the present time.

As every American statesman, during our revolutionary and formative period as a nation, was undoubtedly familiar with this monument of English freedom, and considered it as the true and ultimate expression of constitutional law, it may be confidently asserted that its propositions were in the minds of those who framed the Fourth Amendment to the Constitution, and were considered as sufficiently explanatory of what was meant by unreasonable searches and seizures. . . . Lord Camden says:

"By the laws of England, every invasion of private property, be it ever so minute, is a trespass. No man can set his foot upon my ground without my license, but be is liable to an action though the damage be nothing; which is proved by every declaration in trespass where the defendant is called upon to answer for bruising the grass and even treading upon the soil. If he admits the fact, he is bound to show, by way of justification, that some positive law has justified or excused him. . . . If no such excuse can be found or produced, the silence of the books is an authority against the defendant, and the plaintiff must have judgment. According to this reasoning, it is now incumbent upon the defendants to show the law upon which this seizure is warranted. If that cannot be done, it is a trespass. .

"Papers are the owner's goods and chattels; they are his dearest property; and are so far from enduring a seizure, that they will hardly bear an inspection; and though the eye cannot by the laws of England be guilty of a trespass, yet where private papers are removed and carried away the secret nature of those goods will be an aggravation of the trespass, and demand more considerable damages in that respect. Where is the written law that gives any magistrate such a power? I can safely answer, there is none;

case to be a witness against himself," which is condemned in the Fifth Amendment, throws light on the question as to what is an "unreasonable search and seizure" within the meaning of the Fourth Amendment. And we have been unable to perceive that the seizure of a man's private books and papers to be used in evidence against him is substantially different from compelling him to be a witness against himself. We think it is within the clear intent and meaning of those terms.

In the case of *Counselman vs. Hitchcock*,[1] it was shown to the court that, in 1890, Charles Counselman, a Chicago commission merchant, had refused to testify before a grand jury which was investigating violations of the Interstate Commerce Act. He had been asked whether he had received rates on grain shipments on any railroads coming to Chicago less than the tariff or open rate, and had declined to answer on the ground that it might tend to incriminate him. The grand jury had reported his refusal to the United States District Judge who had ordered him to answer the questions. He again had refused on the same grounds. Then be had been fined $500 and ordered imprisoned until he should answer these and similar questions, and pay the fine and costs. He had at once petitioned the Federal Circuit Court to order his release on the ground that to compel him to be a witness against himself had been a violation of his constitutional rights. The case finally reached the Supreme Court, which ordered him to be discharged from custody. Justice Blatchford, in giving the opinion of the court, said:

The relations of Counselman to the subject of inquiry before the grand jury, as shown by the questions put to

[1] 142 U. S. Rep., 547.

him, in connection with the provisions of the Interstate Commerce Act, entitled him to invoke the protection of the Constitution. . . . It remains to be considered whether Sec. 860 of the Revised Statutes removes the protection of the constitutional privilege of Counselman. That section must be construed as declaring that no evidence obtained from a witness by means of a judicial proceeding shall be given in evidence, or in any manner used against him or his property or estate, in any court of the United States, in any criminal proceeding or for the enforcement of any penalty or forfeiture. It follows, that any evidence which might have been obtained from Counselman by means of his examination before the grand jury could not be given in evidence or used against him or his property in any court of the United States, in any criminal proceeding, or for the enforcement of any penalty or forfeiture. This, of course, protected him against the use of his testimony against him or his property, in any criminal proceeding, in a court of the United States. But it had only that effect. It could not, and would not, prevent the use of his testimony to search out other testimony to be used in evidence against him or his property, in a criminal proceeding in such court. It could not prevent the obtaining and the use of witnesses and evidence which should be attributable directly to the testimony he might give under compulsion, and on which he might be convicted, when otherwise, and if he had refused to answer, he could not possibly have been convicted.

The constitutional provision distinctly declares that a person shall not be "compelled in any criminal case to be a witness against himself"; and the protection of Sec. 860 is not coextensive with the constitutional provision. Legislation cannot detract from the privilege afforded by the Constitution. It would be quite another thing if the Constitution had provided that no person shall be compelled in any criminal case to be a witness against himself, unless it should be provided by statute that criminating evidence extracted from a witness against his will should not be used against him.   But a mere act of Congress cannot amend the Constitution, even if it should engraft thereon such a proviso.

The Federal immunity statute referred to in the Counselman case, while protecting a person from testifying against himself under compulsion, also gives him a chance to save himself from punishment by giving testimony under compulsion against himself and guilty associates.   In such cases, a witness refuses to answer the questions of the prosecutor upon the ground that by answering he will incriminate himself.   If the judge commands him to answer and he refuses, and cannot show that his answers would lead to obtaining testimony against himself upon another charge, he will be punished for contempt of court.   If, on the other hand, his answers would not tend to incriminate him, except in the case on trial, and he complies, he will automatically put himself out of danger, and will have taken what is called the "immunity bath."

No Warrants shall issue, but upon probable cause, supported by Oath or affirmation, and particularly describing the place to be searched, and the persons or things to be seized.   Under this provision of the fundamental law, whoever wishes to start a prosecution for crime against any person, must begin by proving to a magistrate that there is "probable cause" to believe that the crime was committed by the person against whom a warrant or order of arrest is asked.

Chief Judge Cranch of the Federal Circuit Court of the District of Columbia explained the meaning of the words "probable cause" in the course of an opinion in the case of *United States vs. Bollman,*[1] in which the

---

[1] 1 Cranch's C. C. Rep., 373, or 24 Fed. Cases, 1189, Case No. 14,622.

Nor shall any

alliance to be twice

submit the competency of his defence to the decision of a jury of his peers. He is in their hands, exposed to the danger of conviction with all its consequences; or in the language of the bill of rights, he is 'in jeopardy.'"

When is a person in jeopardy? This question was answered, in 1889, by the Supreme Court in the case of *United States vs. Ball.*[1] It was shown to the court in this case that Millard Fillmore Ball and two others had been tried in a Federal Circuit Court in Texas for the murder of one William T. Box. Ball had been acquitted and the others found guilty and sentenced to death. The convicted men had taken the case to the Supreme Court on the ground that the indictment did not state when and where Box had died. The Supreme Court had sustained this appeal and ordered a new trial. Thereupon a second indictment on the same charge was found against the three men. To this indictment Millard Fillmore Ball made answer that he had already been in "jeopardy of his life" on a charge of murdering the man Box, and, under this clause of the Fifth Amendment, did not have to defend himself a second time. Justice Gray sustained Ball's contention, saying:

> The question being now for the first time presented to this court, we are unable to resist the conclusion that a general verdict of acquittal upon the issue of not guilty to an indictment undertaking to charge murder, and not objected to before the verdict as insufficient in that respect, is a bar to a second indictment for the same killing. The Constitution of the United States, in the Fifth Amendment, declares "nor shall any person be subject to be twice put in jeopardy of life or limb." The prohibition is not against being twice punished, but against being twice put in jeop-

[1] 163 U. S. Rep., 662.

erly, and the accused, whether convicted or acquitted, would put in jeopardy at the first trial. The verdict of the jury, after a trial upon the issue of guilty or not guilty, acquitted Gillard, Hall of the whole charge, or murder, as well as of one less offence included therein. Gillard, Hall's acquittal by the verdict of the jury, could not be deprived of its legitimate effect by the subsequent action of his court of the judgment against the other defendants. For these reasons, the verdict of acquittal is conclusive in favor of Gillard, Hall, and as to him the judgment must be rendered, or him now is tea of owner acquittal.

Fifth Amendment. Part 4.. No person shall be deprived of life, liberty, or property, without due process of law.

Fourteenth Amendment. Part 4.. Nor shall any State deprive any person of life, liberty, or property, without due process of law.

"... "due process of law," without which no person may be deprived of life, liberty, or property, begins ... and if arrest has been issued upon the ... required in the fourth amendment. ... is arrested under a lawful warrant, accused of ... an offence by an "information," or ... indictment or a "presentment" of a grand ... which ... the accused person committed the ... and a judge, who decides whether that ... charged of the petit jury say the ... not guilty is released. If the ... finds ... is guilty the judge ... sentence which the State has prescribed ... The guilty person is then put in charge of the executive branch of the government, — in the case of a Federal crime, the President; in the case of a local crime, the governor of the State — which inflicts the penalty.

Under due process of law are included many terms that require definition.

A "misdemeanor" is any act which is prohibited and punished by law, the penalty of which is less than death or imprisonment in a State prison.

The old word "felony," which originally signified an act of madness or insanity, was defined as follows by District Judge Hammond in the case of *United States vs. Coppersmith*[1]:

Felonies by common law are such as either concern the taking away of life, or concern the taking away of goods, or concern the habitation, or concern the obstruction of justice in criminal and capital causes, as escapes, rescues, etc. . . . These crimes were of such enormity that the common law punished them by forfeiture: (1) the offender's wife lost her dower; (2) his children became base and ignoble and his blood corrupted; (3) he forfeited his goods and chattels, lands and tenements. The superadded punishment was either capital or otherwise, according to the degree of guilt. . . .

In American law, forfeiture as a consequence of crime being generally abolished, the word "felony" has lost its original and characteristic meaning, and is rather used to denote any high crime punishable by death or imprisonment. . . . The term is so interwoven with our criminal law that it should have a definition applicable to its present use; and this notion of moral degradation by confinement in the penitentiary has grown into a general understanding that it constitutes any offence a felony, just as, at common law,

Justice Matthews of the Supreme Court in his opinion in the case of *Hurtado vs. California,*[1] defined the "due process of law," without which no man may be deprived of life, liberty, or property. On May 7, 1882, one Hurtado had been convicted in California of the murder of a man named José Antonio Stuardo upon an "information" filed in court, in accordance with a State law, by the district attorney of Sacramento County. He had appealed to the Supreme Court of the State, which affirmed the judgment of conviction. When asked in court why sentence of death should not be pronounced upon him, he had answered that he "had been tried and illegally found guilty of said crime without any presentment or indictment of any grand or other jury, and that the judgment, rendered upon the alleged verdict of the jury in such case, was and is void, and if executed would deprive him of his life or liberty without due process of law." In other words, he claimed that a charge of murder made by an "information," was not sufficient to support a conviction; that, in such cases, an "indictment" by a grand jury was the only "due process of law." His objection was overruled by the State Supreme Court. He then took the question to the Federal Supreme Court, which also decided against him. Justice Matthews said:

Arbitrary power, enforcing its edicts to the injury of the persons and property of its subjects, is not law, whether manifested as the decree of a personal monarch or of an impersonal multitude. And the limitations imposed by our constitutional law upon the action of the governments, both State and National, are essential to the preservation of public and private rights, notwithstanding the representa-

[1] 110 U. S. Rep., 516.

... character of our political institutions. The enforcement of these limitations by judicial process is the device of self-governing communities to protect the rights of individuals and minorities, as well against the power of numbers, as against the violence of public agents transcending the limits of lawful authority, even when acting in the name and wielding the force of the government . . .

It follows that any legal proceeding enforced by public authority, whether sanctioned by age and custom, or newly devised in the discretion of the legislative power in furtherance of the general public good, which regards and preserves these principles of liberty and justice, must be held to be due process of law.

No person shall be . . . deprived of life . . . without due process of law. It was claimed in behalf of Leo M. Frank,¹ whose sentence to death for murder in Georgia was afterward commuted to life imprisonment, that, if he had been executed, he would have been deprived of life without due process of law, because he had not been present in court when the jury announced their verdict of guilty . . . He had asked the Supreme Court of Georgia to set aside the judgment of conviction and give him a new trial. This request had been denied. He had petitioned the same court to set aside the judgment on the ground that, not being present when the verdict was rendered, the trial had not been the due process of law to which he was entitled under the Constitution of Georgia and of the United States. This . . . request was denied on the ground that he had already made a second plea for a new trial. He thereupon petitioned the United States District Court for the District of Georgia for a writ of habeas corpus directed to the person having him in custody to

¹ . . . Frank v. Mangum, 237 U.S. Rep., 309

produce him in court, so that the lawfulness of the judgment that he had been guilty of murder could be tested.   The Federal District Judge ~~refused to issue this~~ writ and an appeal was taken to the Supreme Court at Washington, which decided that the State of Georgia had retained jurisdiction over him [Frank], and had "accorded to him the fullest right and opportunity to be heard, according to established modes of procedure." Hence, said Justice Pitney, "in our opinion, he is not shown to have been deprived of any right guaranteed to him by the Fourteenth Amendment or any other provision of the Constitution or laws of the United States; on the contrary, he has been convicted, and is now held in custody, under 'due process of law' within the meaning of the Constitution."

In the case of *Hopt vs. Utah*,[1] which involved some of the questions decided in the case of Leo M. Frank, the Supreme Court ruled that, under the laws of the Territory of Utah, a prisoner on trial for murder had a constitutional right to be present even when it was being decided whether proposed jurors to whom he had objected on the ground of bias, really were prejudiced against him.   Justice Harlan held that this right could not be waived, saying:

We are of opinion that it was not within the power of the accused or his counsel to dispense with the statutory requirement [of Utah] as to his personal presence at the trial. . . . The public has an interest in his life and liberty. Neither can be lawfully taken except in the mode prescribed by law. That which the law makes essential in proceedings involving the deprivation of life or liberty cannot be dispensed with or affected by the consent of the accused, much less by his mere failure, when on trial and

[1] 110 U. S. Rep., 574.

in custody, to object to unauthorized methods. . . .
Such being the relation which the citizen holds to the public,
and the object of punishment for public wrongs, the legislature has deemed it essential to the protection of one whose
life or liberty is involved in a prosecution for felony, that
he shall be personally present at the trial, that is, at every
stage of the trial when his substantial rights may be affected
by the proceedings against him. If he be deprived of
life or liberty without being so present, such deprivation
would be without that due process of law required by the
Constitution.

*No person shall be . . . deprived of . . . liberty
. . . without due process of law.* "It is undoubtedly
true," said Justice Field in his opinion in the case of
Crowley vs. Christensen,[1] "that it is the right of every
citizen of the United States to pursue any lawful trade
or business, under such restrictions as are imposed upon
all persons of the same age, sex, and condition. But the
possession and enjoyment of all rights are subject
to such reasonable conditions as may be deemed by
the governing authority of the country essential to the
safety, health, peace, good order, and morals of the
community. Even liberty itself, the greatest of all
rights, is not unrestricted license to act according to
one's own will. It is only freedom from restraint under
conditions essential to the equal enjoyment of the same
right by others."

*No person shall be . . . deprived of . . . property
without due process of law.* The notable case of *Public
Clearing House vs. Coyne,*[2] decided by the Supreme
Court in 1904, hinged upon the question whether the
postmaster of Chicago, acting under the orders of the
Postmaster General, had or had not deprived a highly

speculative concern of its property without due process of law, by stopping its letters, stamping them "fraudulent," and returning them to the senders. The decision of the Supreme Court in this case established the validity of those "fraud orders" by which thousands of people, who ought to know better, are protected from the consequences of their own foolishness and credulity. Justice Brown delivered the opinion of the Supreme Court which decided that these orders are due process of law, saying in part:

It is too late to argue that due process of law is denied whenever the disposition of property is affected by the order of an executive department. . . . Inasmuch as the action of the postmaster in seizing letters and returning them to the writers is subject to revision by the judicial department of the government in cases where the Postmaster General has exceeded his authority under the statute, . . . we think it within the power of Congress to entrust him with the power of seizing and detaining letters upon evidence satisfactory to himself, and that his action will not be reviewed by the court in doubtful cases.

Fifth Amendment. (Concluded.) Nor shall private property be taken for public use, without just compensation.

What constitutes a taking of private property for public use? This question was answered by the Supreme Court in the case of *Pumpelly vs. Green Bay Company*,[1] in which the plaintiff asked the courts to award him compensation for damages to his land caused by a canal company which had built a dam across Fox River, Wisconsin. The water had overflowed his land,

[1] 13 Wallace's Rep., 166.

taken for public use?   The Supreme Court stood firmly for the rights of property owners in the case of *The Monongahela Navigation Company vs. United States*,[1] in which a Secretary of War backed by Congress had tried to take over a lock and dam, belonging to the Monongahela Company, without just compensation for the income derived from tolls levied by that Company upon vessels passing through the locks.   The case was tried in the United States Circuit Court for the Western District of Pennsylvania, which awarded the Company $209,000 for its property, "not considering or estimating in this decree the franchise of the company to collect tolls."   The Navigation Company won the case in the Supreme Court, where Justice Brewer delivered an opinion in which he explained the meaning of "just compensation" as follows:

The noun "compensation," standing by itself, carries the idea of an equivalent.   Thus we speak of damages by way of compensation, or compensatory damages, as distinguished from punitive or exemplary damages, the former being the equivalent for the injury done, and the latter imposed by way of punishment.   So that if the adjective "just" had been omitted, and the provision was simply that property should not be taken without compensation, the natural import of the language would be that the compensation should be the equivalent of the property.   And this is made emphatic by the adjective "just."   There can, in view of the combination of those two words, be no doubt that the compensation must be a full and perfect equivalent for the property taken.   And this just compensation, it will be noticed, is for the property and not to the owner.   Every other clause in this Fifth Amendment is personal.   "No person shall be held to answer for a capital, or otherwise

[1] 148 U. S. Rep., 312, 325.

infamous crime." etc.   Instead of continuing the formula
statement, and saying that no person shall be deprived of
his property without just compensation, the personal statement is left out, and the "just compensation" is to be a full
equivalent for the property taken.   This excludes the
taking into account, as an element in the compensation,
any supposed benefit that the owner may receive in common
with all from the public uses to which his property is appropriated, and leaves it to stand as a declaration; that no
private property shall be appropriated for public uses unless
a full and exact equivalent for it be returned to the owner.

Sixth Amendment. (In part.)   In all criminal prosecutions, the accused shall enjoy the right . . .   to be
informed of all nature and cause of the accusation; to
be confronted with the witnesses against him; to have
compulsory process for obtaining witnesses in his favor,
and to have the assistance of counsel for his defense.

The most helpless creature in the world is a prisoner
held upon a charge of crime.   The whole body of the
community is arrayed against him.   The government
has its skilled prosecuting lawyers and has means to
compel witnesses to come to the court to testify against
him.   His situation is of all men most miserable, unless
some way be given him an equal chance to defend himself.
If then the courts could hear privately the
witnesses against the prisoner and then call him into
court on charges which he never had heard of,
against him the testimony of witnesses he never had
seen, without any legal means of compelling his own
witnesses to come to court to testify for him, and without any lawyer to speak for him against the trained
lawyers for the government.   Many of these abuses had
been weeded out before the Constitution was adopted.

Almost all the reforms needed to make criminal procedure humane and just, had been incorporated into the constitutions and laws of the States during the first era of independence; but the People of the United States had no such safeguards.

In all criminal prosecutions, the accused shall enjoy the right . . . to be informed of the nature and cause of the accusation. The charge to be answered by a defendant on trial in a criminal court must be clear, explicit, and definite. The prosecution has no right to compel any man to show that he is a good member of society. In the case of *United States vs. Mills,*[1] the defendant had to answer an indictment charging him with "advising, procuring, and assisting Joseph I. Shaughan, a mail carrier, to rob the mail." Having been found guilty by a jury, the defendant asked the court to set aside the verdict upon the ground that the indictment on which he had been tried did not set forth that the mail carrier actually had robbed the mail. In other words, he claimed that he had been found guilty of taking part in a robbery upon an indictment which did not say that there had been any robbery. In delivering the decision of the court, sustaining the conviction on the ground that in the case of a misdemeanor, it was not necessary to specify the act charged so definitely as in the case of a crime, Justice Thompson explained what information a defendant has a right to have of the nature and cause of an accusation. He said:

The general rule is that in indictments for misdemeanors created by statute, it is sufficient to charge the offence in the words of the statute. There is not that technical nicety required as to form, which seems to have been adopted and

[1] 7 Peters' Rep., 138.

18

sanctioned by long practice in cases of felony and with respect to some crimes, where particular words must be used, and no other words, however synonymous they may seem, can be substituted. But in all cases the offence must be set forth with clearness, and all necessary certainty, to apprise the accused of the crime with which he stands charged.

In all criminal prosecutions, the accused shall enjoy the right . . . to be confronted with the witnesses against him. Evidence of what some one else has said against a person on trial on a charge of crime cannot be heard in a Federal court. For example, in the case of *United States vs. Angell,* [1] a number of New Hampshire farmers once had clubbed together to buy a barrel of rum "to get through the haying season." The man who had divided it up among the purchasers was indicted in the United States Court for selling liquor without a Federal license. In the course of his trial, the defendant offered to prove statements which had been made by a witness at the preliminary hearing before the magistrate. Then he asked that this evidence be received instead of the oral testimony of the witness himself, because the latter had left the State and could not be brought to court. The judge refused to allow testimony of this kind to be heard by the jury, which found the defendant guilty. The convicted man then made a motion that the verdict be set aside on the ground that his offer of testimony had been improperly rejected. District Judge Clark, in denying this motion, explained the right of an accused person to be confronted with the witnesses against him:

I think that the law must be held to be that when the witness is living he must be produced, or his testimony cannot be received in criminal cases, even if he be beyond the jurisdiction of the court or of all the United States. The Constitution of the United States provides . . . that in all criminal prosecutions the accused shall enjoy the right to be confronted with the witnesses against him; and this without exception. Not if they can be produced, nor if they be within the jurisdiction, but absolutely and on all occasions. And, if the accused have this right it must be mutual, and exist on the part of the government. The trial would not be a fair one otherwise.

In all criminal prosecutions, the accused shall enjoy the right . . . to have compulsory process for obtaining witnesses in his favor. A defendant in a criminal case in a Federal court can have his witnesses summoned by the same process as the government uses in summoning its witnesses. The subpœna, an ancient court order which commands a person to attend the court *sub pœna* (under the penalty stated in the order), is at the service of prosecutor and prosecuted alike. Some judges have insisted upon an almost unlimited use, at the request of accused person, of this process for summoning witnesses. In the case of *United States vs. Aaron Burr,*[1] Chief Justice Marshall issued a *subpœna duces tecum* (a subpœna commanding a witness to bring something, usually written documents, to court) to President Jefferson, who paid no attention to it. The Chief Justice did not try to punish him for contempt of court, because the President of the United States is not so easily dealt with as other persons who disobey a court order. The right of an accused person to this process was sustained, however, in an opinion in which Judge Marshall said in substance:

In the provisions of the Constitution, and of the statute

[1] 4 Cranch's C. C. Rep., 469; 25 Fed. Cases, 30.

which give to the accused a right to the compulsory process
of the court, there is no exception whatever. The obligation, therefore, of those provisions is general; and it would
seem that no person could claim an exemption from them,
but one who would not be a witness. . . . If then, as is
admitted by counsel for the United States, a *subpœna* may
issue to the President, the accused is entitled to it of course;
and whatever difference may exist with respect to the power
to compel the same obedience to the process as if it had been
directed to a private citizen, there exists no difference with
respect to the right to obtain it.

*In all criminal prosecutions, the accused shall enjoy
the right . . . to have the assistance of counsel for his
defence.* The old common law did not allow an accused
person to have a lawyer except to advise him what to
say and do during the trial. The judge was supposed
to guard the rights of prisoners. Ordinarily the man
on trial for his life did not have much chance unless
the public prosecutor was unusually fair. Since the
adoption of the Sixth Amendment, however, every
defendant in a criminal case in the Federal Courts has
had the assistance of counsel as a matter of constitutional right.

Some persons believe that this constitutional provision does not sufficiently protect the rights of accused
persons. They urge that the defendant ought to have
every advantage which the State gives to the prosecutor. Hence the demand for public defenders as well
as public prosecutors.

**Seventh Amendment. In suits at common law,
where the value in controversy shall exceed twenty
dollars, the right of trial by jury shall be preserved, and
no fact tried by a jury shall be otherwise re-examined**

in any Court of the United States, than according to the rules of the common law.

The People of the United States, whose ideas of right and justice are grounded in the common law of England, believe implicitly that, with all its imperfections and shortcomings, a trial by a jury is still the best way to sift out the facts of any dispute. In the Federal courts, suits at common law in which the subject matter in dispute is valued at more than twenty dollars, always are tried by juries. This is not the rule in State courts. Some of them have jury trials only when one party or the other so demands. In others, like New York, the parties do not have to have jury trials if they do not wish to.

In suits at common law. "The common law consists of those principles and maxims, usages and rules of action which observation and experience of the nature of man, the constitution of society and the affairs of life have commended for the government and security of persons and property. Its principles are developed by judicial decision as necessities arise from time to time demanding the application of those principles to particular cases in the administration of justice. The authority of its rules does not depend upon positive legislative enactment, but upon the principles which they are designed to enforce, the nature of the subject to which they are to be applied and their tendency to accomplish the ends of justice. It follows that these rules are not arbitrary in their nature nor invariable in their application, but from their nature as well as the necessities in which they originate, they are and must be susceptible of a modified application suited to the circumstances under which that application is to be made. The

charge) to set aside their verdict if in his opinion it is against the law or evidence. . . .

No fact tried by a jury shall be otherwise re-examined in any Court of the United States, than according to the rules of the common law. In the case of *Parsons vs. Bedford,*[1] the plaintiffs had sued at common law for the value of a quantity of tobacco which they had sold to the Louisiana agent of a Boston mercantile firm. The case had been tried before a jury in the United States Court of Louisiana. The defendants had asked the court to order the testimony given at the trial to be taken down in writing and made part of the record of the case. This request had been denied. The case then had been taken to the Federal Supreme Court, which was asked to rule that the lower court ought to have submitted the testimony in the case to be reviewed by the higher court. The Supreme Court decided that, in a suit at common law, it had no right to weigh the testimony upon which the jury had found their verdict, and perhaps set that verdict aside if that testimony had been insufficient. If the justices of the Supreme Court, in deciding the case, had examined the testimony to see whether the verdict was justified, they would, contrary to the provisions of this amendment, have reëxamined a "fact" tried by a jury, "otherwise . . . than according to the rules of the common law." Justice Story said:

The phrase "common law," found in this clause, is used in contradistinction to equity, and admiralty and maritime jurisdiction. . . . It is well known that in civil causes, in courts of equity and admiralty, jurors do not intervene, and that courts of equity use the trial by jury only in ex-

[1] 3 Peters' Rep., 433.

abiding people favor mildness and humanity, but there are exceptions. Hence it is well to have this constitutional check upon those who judge the people.

Excessive bail shall not be required. The word "bail," as commonly used, refers to the bond or obligation given by those who undertake to produce in the court, when required, a person charged with crime. The sureties or persons that furnish the bail sometimes are called "bailers." This is a corruption of the correct name, which is "bail." In the case of *Worthen v. Prescott,*[1] the word "bail" was defined as follows:

Lord Coke says that "in truth *baily* is an old Saxon word, and signifieth a safe keeper or protector, and *baile* or *ballium* is safe keeping or protection; and thereupon we say, when a man upon surety is delivered out of prison, *traditur in ballium*, he is delivered into bayle—that is, into their safe keeping, or protection from prison." Blackstone derives the word *bail* from the French *bailler*, to deliver. Some derive it from the Greek *ballein*, to deliver into hands. Hence, a defendant who is delivered to special bail is looked upon in the eye of the law as being constantly in their custody. They are regarded as his jailers, and have him always as it were upon a string and they may pull at pleasure and surrender him in their own discharge.

At one time, the judges of the Federal Courts seem to have thought that this provision of the Constitution made it necessary to inquire into the financial condition of the defendant when fixing the amount of security to be given. The facts in the case of *U. S. vs. Lawrence,*[2] heard in the U. S. Circuit Court at Washington in 1835, were as follows: On January 30, 1835, a man named

[1] 160 Vermont Rep., 66.
[2] 4 Cranch's Circuit Court Rep., 518; 26 Federal Cases, 887.

Richard Lawrence tried to kill President Jackson as he came out of the rotunda of the Capitol after attending the funeral of a member of the House of Representatives. The pistols missed fire; and the man, who was demented, was taken into custody upon a charge of attempted murder. He was brought before Chief Judge Cranch of the Federal Circuit Court of the District of Columbia, who after inquiring into his property fixed bail at $1,000. The United States Attorney, who was no other than Francis Scott Key, author of *The Star Spangled Banner*, asked to have the amount increased because he feared that others who might be concerned in the crime would bail the man out and induce him to make a second attempt. "The Chief Judge then said that there was no evidence before him to induce a suspicion that any other person was concerned in the act; that the Constitution forbade him to require excessive bail; and that to require larger bail than the prisoner could give would be to require excessive bail, and to deny bail in a case clearly bailable by law."

Magistrates now fix bail with the one idea of making sure of the prisoner's appearance in court when wanted. The accused man is presumed to be innocent for all purposes except bail. In the case of *Ex Parte Ryan*,[1] a man under $15,000 bail upon a charge of having attempted to murder a San Francisco policeman, applied to Chief Justice Wallace of the Supreme Court of California for a reduction of the amount. The chief justice refused, saying in part:

Assuming then that the defendant is guilty of the offense charged, is the sum of fifteen thousand dollars excessive as

[1] 44 California Rep., 555.

being the amount in which he is to be let to bail? . . .   In order to constitute it "excessive" it must be *per se* [in itself] unreasonably great, and clearly disproportionate to the offense involved, or the peculiar circumstances appearing must show it to be so in the particular case. . . .   I cannot undertake to say that, as a matter of law, fifteen thousand dollars is excessive bail to be demanded of one assumed to be guilty of the offense of assault with intent to kill.

Nor excessive fines imposed. "A fine is a sum of money exacted of a person guilty of a misdemeanor or crime, the amount of which may be fixed by law or left in the discretion of the court."—*Lancaster vs. Richardson.*[1]

According to the decision of the Supreme Court of Michigan in the case of *Robison vs. Minor,*[2] a fine which seriously impairs the capacity of the convicted person to earn a livelihood is excessive.   This case involved the constitutionality of a State law which imposed severe penalties for unlawful liquor selling.   A druggist, allowed to sell liquors only for chemical, scientific, medicinal, mechanical, and sacramental purposes, if convicted of unlawful liquor selling, was liable to be fined from $100 to $500, and imprisoned for not less than ninety days nor more than a year; and if convicted a second time, was to be debarred from that business for five years.   Other persons in the liquor business were, if convicted under this law, barred from doing in Michigan any business subject to a license tax.   Judge Campbell, who delivered the opinion of the court, said that these penalties were in violation of the State constitution for the following reasons:

Our State Constitution declares that—"excessive bail

shall not be required; excessive fines shall not be imposed; cruel and unusual punishment shall not be inflicted." . . . A druggist, cut off for five years from his business, may suffer a loss of immense sums, and so may any large manufacturer or large dealer by having his store shut up and his business barred. It not only must usually bring about bankruptcy, but it also includes what is meant to be an infamous disability,—to receive credit as a surety. . . . The great fines imposed during the times of the Stuarts, especially by the Star Chamber, were among the worst abuses of that period of tyranny. . . . The forfeiture of indefinite interests or sums only occurred in felonies when the penalty was death as well as forfeiture. . . . These punishments have always been regarded as incompatible with our institutions, and there can be no doubt that the cruel and unusual punishments forbidden by the United States Constitution had special reference to the barbarities of the old law of felony. It is equally clear that any fine or penalty is excessive which seriously impairs the capacity of gaining a business livelihood.

Nor cruel and unusual punishments inflicted. Our State and national courts have put it on record that the punishments for crime which are customary in this country are neither cruel nor unusual. The Supreme Court of New Mexico, in the case of *Garcia vs. Territory*,[1] said that "thirty lashes on the bare back, well laid on," was neither cruel nor unusual. In 1861, the Supreme Court of New York, in the case of *Done vs. People*,[2] decided that death by hanging is not a cruel punishment. Death by shooting, the penalty for murder in some Western States, was declared constitutional in the case of *Wilkerson vs. Utah*.[3]

[1] 1 New Mexico Rep., 415.
[2] 5 Parker's [N. Y.], Crim. Rep., 364.
[3] 99 U. S. Rep., 130.

Electrocution or the infliction of the death penalty "by causing to pass through the body of the convict, a current of electricity of sufficient intensity to cause death" was adopted by the State of New York in 1888, and has since been imposed by the laws of many other States.   The New York courts held in the case of *People vs. Kemmler*[1] that this was not a cruel or unusual penalty within the meaning of the State constitution.   The national Supreme Court, when asked in the case of *In Re Kemmler*[2] to interfere with the sentence in that case, refused on the ground that the privileges and immunities of a citizen of the United States who has been found guilty of murder in the first degree, are not denied or abridged by a State law inflicting the punishment of death by electrocution.   Chief Justice Fuller said:

Punishments are cruel when they involve torture or a lingering death; but the punishment of death is not cruel within the meaning of that word as used in the Constitution. It implies there something inhuman and barbarous, something more than the mere extinguishment of life. The courts of New York held that the mode adopted in this instance might be said to be unusual because it was new, but that it could not be assumed to be cruel in the light of that common knowledge which has stamped certain punishments as such; that it was for the legislature to say in what manner sentence of death should be executed; that this act was passed in the effort to devise a more humane method of reaching the result; that the courts were bound to presume that the legislature was possessed of the facts upon which it took action; and that by evidence taken *aliunde* [outside of] the statute that presumption could not be overthrown. They went further, and expressed the

[1] 119 New York Rep., 580.   [2] 136 U. S., Rep., 436.

opinion that upon the evidence the legislature had intended by the act the object had in view in its issue. The decision of the State courts sustaining the validity of an act under the State constitution is not reexamined here.

In the case of *Jackson vs. United States*, it was held that any sentence which is not greater than the maximum provided by law is not "cruel." Jackson was convicted in the Federal District Court of Alaska of assault with a dangerous weapon, and was sentenced to ten years' imprisonment at hard labor in the penitentiary at McNeil's Island, State of Washington. The Circuit Court of Appeals struck out the "hard labor" part of the sentence because the law did not authorize it, but on the ground that the judge had authority to impose the total imprisonment, and was merely in error in part, held that the prisoner had no right to be discharged, but must serve the term of imprisonment.

... that the sentence ...

Ninth Amendment. The enumeration in the Constitution, of certain rights, shall not be construed to deny or disparage others retained by the people.

The First Congress was called upon to deal with thirty-five amendments proposed to it by the ratifying conventions of the States.   These amendments passed successively through the hands of a Committee of Eleven and of a Special Committee of Three before reaching their present form.   The Ninth Amendment, for example, probably suggested by Madison, originally ran as follows:

The exceptions here or elsewhere in the Constitution made in favor of particular rights, shall not be construed as to diminish the just importance of other rights retained by the people, or to enlarge the powers delegated by the Constitution; but either as actual limitations of such powers, or as inserted merely for greater caution."

It emerged from the Committee of Eleven in the following form:

The enumeration in this Constitution of certain rights, shall not be construed to disparage others retained by the people.

The Special Committee of Three gave it its present form.[1]

Tenth Amendment.   The powers not delegated to the United States by the Constitution, nor prohibited by it to the States, are reserved to the States respectively, or to the people.

Chief Justice Marshall, in his opinion in the case of *McCulloch vs. Maryland*,[2] explained the origin and purpose of the Tenth Amendment as follows:

\
[1] Thorpe's *Constitutional History of the U. S.*, vol. ii., pp. 226, 258.
[2] 4 Wheaton's Rep., 316, 406.

The 10th amendment ... formed for the purpose of ... the ... jealousies which had been excited ... and that "the powers ' not delegated to the United States, nor prohibited to the States, are reserved to the ... ... the people ... thus leaving the question, whether his any particular power which may become the subject of contest, has been delegated to the one government or prohibited to the other, to depend on a fair construction of the whole instrument.

CHAPTER XVII

RIGHTS OF CITIZENS OF THE UNITED STATES AGAINST THE STATES AND THE NATION

Thirteenth Amendment, Sec. 1. Neither slavery nor involuntary servitude, except as a punishment for crime whereof the party shall have been duly convicted, shall exist within the United States, or any place subject to their jurisdiction.

This noble pronouncement of the People of the United States was published to the world on December 18, 1865. Mountains of treasure had been spent and rivers of blood had been shed in order to place on the statute books of this nation a permanent law abolishing slavery in every form throughout the United States and every place under its control. They did not die in vain who gave their lives to vindicate the greatest of human rights, the right to freedom.

It seems to have been taken for granted at first by almost every one that the amendment which made all men free, also made all men equal and with equal rights and privileges everywhere in the United States. The Senators and Representatives who voted for the once famous Civil Rights Bill of 1875, apparently believed that a negro, being a freeman, had as much right as a white man in any hotel, theater, or special car of a railroad train, and that to deny him such rights was to impose an "involuntary servitude." Accordingly, they declared that to deny any such privileges to any citizen of the United States, should be a misdemeanor, punishable by fine or imprisonment, or by forfeiture of the sum of $500, to be sued for by the person aggrieved. The *Civil Rights Cases*,[1] decided in 1883, brought squarely before the Supreme Court the question whether the general government of the United States has any power under this amendment to regulate the conduct and morals of citizens of the States.   Two of these cases were indictments against hotel-keepers who had refused to accommodate persons of color.   A third was based upon the refusal of a theatrical manager to allow negroes to occupy seats in certain parts of a theater. Another was an action to recover the statutory penalty from a railroad company that had prevented a colored woman from riding in a "Ladies" Car, a special kind of accommodation reserved for women traveling alone or with their families.   The Court decided that the regulation of the conduct and behavior of citizens of the States was not a matter upon which Congress could make a law under the authority of the Thirteenth Amendment, and therefore that the Civil Rights Bill was unconstitutional.   Justice Bradley said:

It [the Civil Rights Bill] proceeds *ex directo* [directly] to declare that certain acts committed by individuals shall be deemed offences, and shall be prosecuted and punished by proceedings in the courts of the United States.   It does not profess to be corrective of any constitutional wrong committed by the States; it does not make its operation to depend upon any such wrong committed.   It applies equally to cases arising in States which have the justest laws respecting the personal rights of citizens, and whose authorities are ever ready to enforce such laws, as to those which

[1] 109 U. S. Rep., 3.

arise in States that may have violated the provisions of the amendment. In other words, it steps into the domain of local jurisprudence, and lays down rules for the conduct of individuals in society towards each other, and imposes sanctions for the enforcement of those rules, without referring in any manner to any supposed action of the State or its authorities. . . . The only question under the present head, therefore, is, whether the refusal to any persons of the accommodations of an inn, or a public conveyance, or a place of public amusement, by an individual, and without any sanction or support from any State law or regulation, does inflict upon such persons any manner of servitude, or form of slavery as those terms are understood in this country? . . . After giving to these questions all the consideration which their importance demands, we are forced to the conclusion that such an act of refusal has nothing to do with slavery or involuntary servitude.

Involuntary servitude . . . shall [not] exist within the United States, or any place subject to their jurisdiction. Although the Thirteenth Amendment abolished negro slavery throughout the United States, the "Peonage" system, under which men sold their services or were compelled to work out debts, continued to exist in New Mexico until prohibited by the Peonage Law of 1867. A similar plan of forced labor, under the guise of imprisonment for debt, was afterward introduced in some of the Southern States. The prisons for such debtors were stockades in which unlucky men, mostly negroes, were compelled to work for the benefit of their creditors. According to a charge delivered by District Judge Jones to a grand jury in the United States District Court of Alabama on June 16, 1903, in the *Peonage Cases,*[1] such forced labor was involuntary servitude. He said:

[1] 123 Federal Rep., 671, 679.

What is meant by ... ...
... turning thereto, ...
... statute [Peonage Law] ... ...
... New Mexico, when ... ...
... der the abolished system, ...
... old sell his own services, ...
... the exercise of dominion ... ...
... ty, so that he could be held ... ...
... to the performance of his obligation ... ...
... or transfer his interest in ... ...
... vice due, or claimed to be the ... ...
... thus cause them to be ... ...
... rased over person and ... ...
... formance of contract ... ...
... ers alike, ...

purpose of compelling him to work out a real or alleged
obligation. This, if done, created a condition of peonage.
A peon is defined as "a debtor held by his creditor in a
qualified servitude to work out the debt.". . . The involuntary servitude prohibited by the Constitution is a personal servitude, and this "consists in the subjection of one
person to another. If it consists in the right of property
which a person exercises over another, it is slavery. When
the subjection of one person to another is not slavery, it
consists simply in the right of requiring of another what he is
bound to do or not to do. This right arises from all kinds
of contracts or quasi contracts.". . . It follows, then,
that an unwilling servitude enforced by the stronger to
collect a debt is to reduce the victim to the condition of a
peon, and logically to a condition of peonage.

**Fourteenth Amendment, Sec. 4. (Part of.) Neither
the United States nor any State shall assume or pay any
debt or obligation incurred in aid of insurrection or
rebellion against the United States, or any claim for the
loss or emancipation of any slave; but all such debts,
obligations and claims shall be held illegal and void.**

The Fourteenth Amendment was adopted in 1868,
when the great issues which had caused the Civil War
were fresh in the public mind. The men who had waged
the battle for freedom in that great struggle had no
intention of permitting any future legislation for the
settlement in money of claims which they had settled
on the battlefield. Particularly they meant to make
sure that those who had aided the rebellion should not
recover money which had been used to prolong the
conflict.

*Neither the United States nor any State shall assume or
pay . . . any claim for the loss or emancipation of any*

United States, however, from giving preference, in this particular, to one citizen of the United States over another on account of race, color, or previous condition of servitude. Before its adoption, this could be done. It was as much within the power of a State to exclude citizens of the United States from voting on account of race, etc., as it was on account of age, property, or education. Now it is not. If citizens of one race having certain qualifications are permitted by law to vote, those of another having the same qualifications must be. Previous to this amendment, there was no constitutional guaranty against this discrimination; now there is. It follows that the amendment has invested the citizens of the United States with a new constitutional right which is within the protecting power of Congress. That right is exemption from discrimination in the exercise of the elective franchise on account of race, color, or previous condition of servitude.

One of the odd things about the Constitution is that the "People of the United States" who ordained and established it, did not make any provision for their own right to vote. The phrase in the Preamble, "We, the People of the United States," did not mean much to the framers of the Constitution or to the statesmen of the era before the Civil War. The States had ruled the general government during the Revolutionary War and under the Confederation. The people of the States had elected the members of the State legislatures, who in turn elected the delegates to the old Congress. Thus the citizens of the States which formed the United States of the Constitution-making era, had been the supreme body politic. The makers of the Constitution and their successors who ruled the destinies of the republic before the Civil War took it for granted the phrase "People of the United States" meant "People of the

States of the United States." The Fifteenth Amendment by giving the "People of the United States" political rights, which may not be denied or abridged by the United States or by any State, practically created a new supreme political body under the Constitution.

The Fifteenth Amendment was adopted in 1870 to prevent the Southern States from enacting laws which would have barred from the privileges of citizenship the colored "People of the United States" who had been slaves. "It does not confer the right of suffrage on any one. It merely invests citizens of the United States with the constitutional right to exemption from discrimination in the enjoyment of the electoral franchise on account of race, color, or previous condition of servitude."

Neither the Constitution nor any of the amendments prevent many restrictions which the States may impose upon the right of citizens of the United States to vote. In the first era of constitutional government nearly all the States had laws which declared that only those should vote who had a certain amount of property. In Massachusetts, until long after this amendment was adopted, the payment of a poll tax of two dollars was a condition of the right of the citizen to cast his ballot. Paupers, insane persons, and criminals are barred from the ballot box, even if they are citizens. In nearly all the States, only those citizens who have been registered as voters before the election have a right to vote. This is only a way of preventing election frauds.

What is called the "grandfather" clause has been adopted in some States in order to prevent illiterate colored people from voting, without at the same time barring illiterate white citizens. For example, in 1908, the legislature of the State of Maryland enacted a law providing that no persons should be allowed to vote at municipal elections in the city of Annapolis, except, (1) male citizens over twenty-one years of age, who have not been convicted of crime, have resided more than one year in the State, and are tax-payers assessed upon more than $500 worth of property, (2) naturalized aliens and their male children, over twenty-one years of age, (3) *male descendants of voting age, of persons who before January 1, 1868, were entitled to vote in Maryland or any other State of the Union.* The Constitution of Maryland in force on January 1, 1868, had limited the right to vote to white persons, and this provision had been valid until the adoption on July 21, 1868, of the Fourteenth Amendment, which declared that all persons born or naturalized in the United States are citizens of the United States and of the State in which they reside. The members of the Maryland legislature seem to have thought that the law of 1908, without depriving any white man of the right to vote, would bar from the polls negroes who had not had the right to vote on January 1, 1868, and their descendants. Test cases were brought against two election officers who had refused to register the names of three colored men, one of whom, named Anderson, plaintiff in the case of *Anderson vs. Myers,* said in his complaint that he was a citizen of the United States, born in Maryland in 1834, and that he would have been entitled to vote in Maryland on January 1, 1868, if the right to vote had not then, by the State Constitution, been restricted to white persons. In this action, brought in the United States court of Maryland, the plaintiff asked for damages on the ground that the defendants, by refusing to place his name on the voting list, had deprived him of his constitutional right to vote. The defendants answered by referring to the Maryland laws. The plaintiff replied that this law was void because it denied the right of the citizen of the United States to vote on account of his race and color. District Judge Morris sustained the plaintiff's contention that the "grandfather" clause was void upon the ground that "the Fifteenth Amendment had the effect of eliminating the qualifying adjective 'white' from all State constitutions and laws . . . . . fixing the qualifications of voters."

In the case of *Guinn vs. United States*, Frank J. Guinn and J. J. Beal, Oklahoma election officers, had been convicted in the United States District Court of Oklahoma of having prevented negroes from voting at an election of members of Congress held in 1910. They had defended themselves by calling the attention of the court to an amendment of the Constitution of Oklahoma which reads as follows:

No person shall be registered as an elector of this State or be allowed to vote in any election herein, unless he be able to read and write any section of the Constitution of the State of Oklahoma; but no person who was, on Jan. 1, 1866, or at any time prior thereto, entitled to vote under any form of government, or who at that time resided in some foreign nation, and no lineal descendant of such person, shall be denied the right to register and vote because of his inability to to read and write sections of such constitution.

These cases, *Anderson vs. Myers* and *Guinn vs. United States*, were taken to the Supreme Court, which, on June 21, 1915, handed down decisions holding that the "grandfather" clauses were void because inconsistent with the Fifteenth Amendment. Chief Justice

White, in delivering the opinion of the Court in the Maryland case, said that the "election officials could not ignore the potency of the Fifteenth Amendment in striking out the word 'white' as a qualification for voting, and that this Amendment applies to municipal as well as to Federal elections." In the decision of the Oklahoma case, he said:

There seems no escape from the conclusion that to hold that there was even possibility for dispute on the subject would be but to declare that the Fifteenth Amendment not only had not the self-executing power which it has been recognized to have from the beginning, but that its provisions were wholly inoperative because susceptible of being rendered inapplicable by mere forms of expression embodying no exercise of judgment and resting upon no discernible reason other than the purpose to disregard the prohibitions of the amendment by creating a standard of voting which on its face was in substance but a revitalization of the conditions which, when they prevailed in the past, had been destroyed by the self-operative force of the amendment. . . .

We are unable to discover how, unless the prohibitions of the Fifteenth Amendment were considered, the slightest reason was afforded for basing the classification upon a period of time prior to the Fifteenth Amendment. Certainly it cannot be said that there was any peculiar necromancy in the time named which engendered attributes affecting the qualification to vote which would not exist at another and different period unless the Fifteenth Amendment was in view.

PART VI

Executive Government in the United States

CHAPTER XVIII

THE Americans of the first era of independence had learned by bitter experience that government by Congress through executive committees was good for nothing. A Committee on Foreign affairs had been appointed by Congress to manage our diplomatic relations; but Franklin, in his negotiations with France, was hampered rather than helped by that committee. There had been a Committee on Military Affairs to which General Washington was theoretically responsible; but, luckily for the cause, our great captain had carried on the war without the help of congressional advisers, who had annoyed him sometimes, but certainly never had controlled him. Hence our ancestors were quite ready to have a reasonably powerful chief executive. They knew that no man can do good work with his hands tied; but they knew also that it would not be wise to make the man important because his work was important. They provided for the appointment of a national business manager who should have all the powers he ought to have in order to execute efficiently the objects and purposes for which the people of the United States were forming the "more perfect Union." They did not see fit to grant titles, honors, or privileges which sometimes interfere with equality before the law.

Art. II., Sec. 1. The executive Power shall be vested in a President of the United States of America. He shall hold his Office during the Term of four years, and, together with the Vice President, chosen for the same Term, be elected, as follows.

Most of us know that there is a central government at Washington only through the activities of the President of the United States and his officers. The citizen who votes at Federal elections cannot avoid learning that, once in four years, one man is taken from the body of the people and made the chief executive magistrate of the nation. The letter carrier is the President's officer, hired and paid to deliver the mail. It is the President who in the person of a custom-house officer takes a look at the trunks full of presents which the traveling American brings home from foreign parts. His consuls keep us out of trouble when we are abroad. His attorneys prosecute those who send forbidden articles through the mails or form combinations in restraint of trade. His collectors of internal revenue receive the income taxes of the well-to-do, and put the revenue stamp on the poor man's bag of tobacco. The people may not know what Congress and the courts are doing; but when the President acts, every one knows because every one is affected by his acts. The executive power is everywhere.

Art. II., Sec. 1 (continued). Each State shall appoint, in such Manner as the Legislature thereof may direct, a Number of Electors, equal to the whole Number of Senators and Representatives to which the State may be entitled in the Congress; but no Senator or Representative, or Person holding an Office of Trust

or Profit under the United States, shall be appointed an Elector.

"The sole function of the presidential electors," said Justice Gray in the case of *In re Green*,[1] "is to cast, certify, and transmit the vote of the State for President and Vice President of the nation. Although the electors are appointed and act under and pursuant to the Constitution of the United States, they are no more officers and agents of the United States than are members of the State legislatures when acting as electors of federal senators, or the people of the States when acting as electors of representatives in Congress."

Senators, representatives, and other national officials were made ineligible for the office of electors in order to prevent scandalous political deals for the presidency; national officers, living most of the time at the seat of the government, could have devised and carried out all sorts of schemes for continuance in power, if they could have served as electors of Presidents with whom they were to have close relations.

Art. II., Sec. 1 (continued). The electors shall meet in their respective States, and vote by ballot for two Persons, of whom one at least shall not be an Inhabitant of the same State with themselves. And they shall make a List of all the Persons voted for, and of the Number of Votes for each; which List they shall sign and certify, and transmit sealed to the Seat of the Government of the United States, directed to the President of the Senate. The President of the Senate shall, in the Presence of the Senate and House of Representatives,

[1] 134 U. S. Rep., 377.

... such ... then be
... ... Number of
... ... such Number be a
... Government Electors appointed;
... ... such Majority,
... ... Number of Votes, then the House of
... immediately chuse by Ballot one
... ... have a Majority,
... ... the List the said House
... ... chuse the President. But in
... ... the Votes shall be taken by
... ... from each State having one
... ... this Purpose shall consist of a
... ... from two-thirds of the States,
... ... States shall be necessary to a
... ... after the Choice of the Presi-
... ... having the greatest Number of Votes
... ... be the Vice President. But if
... ... two or more who have equal Votes,
... ... chuse from them by ballot the Vice
... ...

... ... Convention, the choice of the
... given to the national legislature.
... appointment, however, does not seem to
... satisfactory, for, a short time afterwards,
... consideration of the subject, it was voted by
... ... states, one being divided, that the
... be chosen by Electors appointed for
... The motive which induced a
... the choice of the President from the national
... unquestionably was, to have the sense of the
... ... in the choice of the person to whom so
... a trust was confided. This would be accom-

plished much more perfectly by committing the right of choice to persons selected for that sole purpose at the particular conjuncture, instead of persons selected for the general purposes of legislation."—*Story on the Constitution.*[1]

"The process of election affords a moral certâinty that the office of President will never fall to the lot of any man who is not in an eminent degree endowed with the requisite qualifications. Talents for low intrigue, and the little arts of popularity, may alone suffice to elevate a man to the first honors of a single State; but it will require other talents, and a different kind of merit, to establish him in the esteem and confidence of the whole Union, or of so considerable a portion of it as will be necessary to make him a successful candidate for the distinguished office of President of the United States."—*The Federalist*, No. 68.

The original plan of choosing Presidents and Vice Presidents was the result of an effort to satisfy the members of the Constitutional Convention from the smaller States. They were afraid that Virginia, Massachusetts, and Pennsylvania would combine to control the election of the national executive officer. If the presidential electors voted for two persons without naming the person voted for as President and the person voted for as Vice President, the smaller States, which might not be able to elect a President, might still be able to prevent any candidate from getting a "majority of the whole number of electors appointed." This would throw the choice of President into the House of Representatives in Congress, where the vote would be taken by States, the representatives of each State having one vote between them. In other words, the

[1] Secs. 1455, 1456.

open all the ... ...
counted. The ... ...
Vote, ... be ... ...
Majority of the ... ...
and ... ... Washington
and has ... ... Adams, ...
R... ... ...
of the ... ... At the ...
the ... ...
... ... who ... ...
... ... 1800, there were
... ... and ... ...
Vote, ... received seventy-
... ... the electors. There
... ... the choice had to
... ... Representatives. At that
... ... but eight of these
... ... two were divided.
... ... being necessary, the
... thirty-sixth ballot,

... method of choosing
... ... in the elec-
... ... the Twelfth
... ...
... ...

... ... The Electors shall ... ...
... ... by death or President
... ... shall not be
... ... Senators. They
... ... as ... voted for as
President, and ... ... of person voted for as

Vice-President, and they shall make distinct lists of all persons voted for as President, and of all persons voted for as Vice-President, and of the number of votes for each, which lists they shall sign and certify, and transmit sealed to the seat of the government of the United States, directed to the President of the Senate; —The President of the Senate shall, in presence of the Senate and House of Representatives, open all the certificates and the votes shall then be counted;—The person having the greatest number of votes for President, shall be the President, if such number be a majority of the whole number of Electors appointed; and if no person have such majority, then from the persons having the highest numbers not exceeding three on the list of those voted for as President, the House of Representatives shall choose immediately, by ballot, the President. But in choosing the President, the votes shall be taken by states, the representation from each state having one vote; a quorum for this purpose shall consist of a member or members from two-thirds of the states, and a majority of all the states shall be necessary to a choice. And if the House of Representatives shall not choose a President whenever the right of choice shall devolve upon them, before the fourth day of March next following, then the Vice-President shall act as President, as in the case of the death or other constitutional disability of the President. The person having the greatest number of votes as Vice-President, shall be the Vice-President, if such number be a majority of the whole number of Electors appointed, and if no person have a majority, then from the two highest numbers on the list, the Senate shall choose the Vice-President; a quorum for the purpose shall consist of two-thirds of the whole number of Senators, and a majority of the whole number shall be necessary to a choice. But no person constitutionally ineligible to the office of President shall be eligible to that of Vice-President of the United States.

Since the adoption of the Twelfth Amendment, only one disputed presidential election has occurred, the Hayes–Tilden election of 1876. The point then in dispute involved, not the method laid down in this amendment, but the way in which the popular vote had been counted in certain States. At some future election there may be more than three candidates none of whom have a majority of electoral votes, though each have an equal number of votes, that number being the highest number cast. Only a prophet can tell us how, in such a case, the House of Representatives will be able "from the persons having the highest numbers not exceeding three on the list of those voted for as President" to "choose immediately, by ballot, the President." Thomas Jefferson, in a letter written in 1823, said: "I have no hesitation in saying that I have ever considered the constitutional mode of election ultimately by the legislature voting by States as the most dangerous blot in our Constitution, and which some unlucky chance will some day hit. . . . Another general convention can alone relieve us." .

Art. II., Sec. 1 (continued). The Congress may determine the Time of chusing the Electors, and the Day on which they shall give their Votes; which Day shall be the same throughout the United States.

An Act of Congress of February 3, 1887, provides "That the electors of each State shall meet and give their votes on the second Monday in January next following their appointment, at such place in each State as the legislature of such State shall direct." This reads nicely, but it does not provide against the chance that the electors may not be able to reach the appointed place on time. For example, in the election of 1856, the Wisconsin electors were detained by a blizzard and did not reach the State capital until the day after their votes ought to have been cast. As it happened, it made no difference in the result whether those votes were counted or not.

Art. II., Sec. 1 (continued.) No Person except a natural born Citizen, or a Citizen of the United States, at the time of the Adoption of this Constitution, shall be eligible to the Office of President; neither shall any Person be eligible to that Office who shall not have attained to the Age of thirty five Years, and been fourteen Years a Resident within the United States.

"Limiting the Presidency to one who is a natural born citizen of the United States was a wise provision which has been appreciated and justified by the sentiment of the country. It prevents wealthy and ambitious foreigners from scheming for the position after having been citizens a short time, and secures our country from machinations which might cause serious embarrassment."—*Watson on the Constitution.*[1]

The exception in favor of those who might be citizens when the Constitution should be adopted has been explained as a compliment to a number of distinguished foreigners who had served in the Continental army

[1] I., 889.

Officer shall act accordingly, until the Disability be removed, or a President shall be elected.

Thus far no serious complication over a presidential succession has occurred; five Presidents of the United States have died in office, and under the provisions of this section have been succeeded by Vice Presidents. Suppose, however, the President chosen by the electors, whose election has been announced at the joint meeting of the two Houses of Congress, on the second Wednesday of February next after a national election, should die before the fourth day of the following March, upon whom would the office of President "devolve"? The Constitution answers that it would devolve upon the Vice President. But what Vice President is meant? Obviously the incoming Vice President could not take the office in that contingency, because he was not Vice President when the President-elect died. It is hardly supposable that the outgoing Vice President is meant. Our people will win out of the muddle some way if ever they have to, but it is a pity that a proper "stitch in time" is not taken.

In Case of the . . . Inability [of the President] to discharge the Powers and Duties of the said Office, the same shall devolve on the Vice President. Who is to decide what constitutes an "inability" to discharge the powers and duties of the President? The People of the United States certainly would not have allowed any tribunal to declare that President Garfield, during the months when he was dying from the assassin's wound, was under such an "inability" that Vice President Arthur ought to have taken his place. A President might be a drunkard or a moral degenerate or anything else on the safe side of impeachment, without incurring any serious risk of losing his office on account of "inability" to perform its duties. He might even suffer from some forms of insanity and still hold his position. One so highly placed always will have enough friends to pull him through everything except an actual conviction upon an impeachment trial, which naturally would settle the case with satisfactory finality.

The Congress may by Law provide for the Case of Removal, Death, Resignation or Inability, both of the President and Vice President, declaring what Officer shall then act as President. The Presidential Succession Act of 1886 provides that in case of removal, death, resignation, or inability of both the President and Vice President, the office of President shall devolve upon the Secretary of State, the Secretary of War, the Attorney General, the Postmaster General, the Secretary of the Navy, or the Secretary of the Interior, in the order named, until the disability of the President or Vice President is removed or a President shall be elected.

According to the case of *Attorney General vs. Taggart,*[1] however, the existence of a vacancy is a question of law and fact for a court to decide. In 1890, Governor Goodell of New Hampshire, being ill, instructed the attorney general of the State to take the necessary legal steps under a similar clause in the New Hampshire constitution, to declare a vacancy in the office of governor and to compel the president of the State senate to assume the office. David A. Taggart, then president of the senate, refused to take over the governorship without a court decision that such was his duty. Thereupon a petition for an order requiring him to do so was filed in the Supreme Court of New Hampshire. Upon this, Chief Justice Doe said:

[1] 66 New Hampshire Rep., 362.

While a determination of the question of vacancy, on a petition of this kind, is not legally requisite to call the president of the senate to the executive chair, it may be a convenient mode of avoiding embarrassment that might sometimes arise from doubt and controversy in regard to his authority and the validity of his acts. The existence of an executive vacancy is a question of law and fact within the judicial jurisdiction. If the defendant exercised executive power without a previous judgment on that question, the legality of his acts could be contested and determined in subsequent litigation; and the judicial character of the question does not depend upon the time when it is brought into court. With adequate legal process, the consideration and decision may be prospective as well as retrospective.

Art. II., Sec. 1 (continued). The President shall, at stated Times, receive for his Services, a Compensation, which shall neither be encreased nor diminished during the Period for which he shall have been elected, and he shall not receive within that Period any other Emolument from the United States, or any of them.

"The wisdom of this clause can scarcely be too highly commended. The legislature, on the appointment of a President, is once for all to declare what shall be the compensation for his services during the time for which he shall have been elected. This done, they will have no power to alter it, either by increase or diminution, till a new period of service by a new election commences. They can neither weaken his fortitude by operating upon his necessities, nor corrupt his integrity by appealing to his avarice. Neither the Union, nor any of its members will be at liberty to give, nor will he be at liberty to receive any other emolument."—*Story on the Constitution.*[1]

Art. II., Sec. 1 (continued). Before he enter on the Execution of his Office, he shall take the following Oath or Affirmation:—"I do solemnly swear (or affirm) that I will faithfully execute the Office of President of the United States, and will to the best of my Ability, preserve, protect and defend the Constitution of the United States."

"There is little need of commentary upon this clause. No man can well doubt the propriety of placing a President of the United States under the most solemn obligations to preserve, protect, and defend the Constitution. It is a suitable pledge of his fidelity and responsibility to his country; and creates upon his conscience a deep sense of duty, by an appeal, at once in the presence of God and man, to the most sacred and solemn sanctions which can operate upon the human mind."—*Story on the Constitution.*[2]

[1] Sec. 1486.   [2] Sec. 1488.

CHAPTER XIX

Art. II., Sec. 2. The President shall be Commander in Chief of the Army and Navy of the United States, and of the Militia of the several States, when called into the actual Service of the United States; he may require the Opinion, in writing, of the principal Officer in each of the executive Departments, upon any Subject relating to the Duties of their respective Offices, and he shall have power to grant Reprieves and Pardons for Offences against the United States, except in Cases of Impeachment.

"It is somewhat singular that the Constitution of a Republic whose President—it could have reasonably been presumed—would be selected from the peaceful vocations of life—without military or naval training—should make its President Commander in Chief of the military and naval force of the country. But there was no opposition to this provision in the Convention which framed the Constitution. The action of the Convention was probably due to some particular cause, and none seems more reasonable than the fact that, during the Revolution, Washington experienced great trouble and embarrassment from the failure of Congress to support him with firmness and despatch. There was a want of directness in the management of affairs during that period which was attributable to the absence of centralized authority to command. The members of the Convention knew this and probably thought they could prevent its recurrence by making the President Commander in Chief of the Army and Navy."—*Watson on the Constitution.*[1]

The President shall be Commander in Chief of the Army and Navy of the United States, and of the Militia of the several States, when called into the actual Service of the United States. Congress has power "to raise and support armies . . . to provide and maintain a navy . . . to provide for calling forth the militia, and to make rules for the government of the land and naval forces." Nevertheless, the President disposes of the army and navy as he pleases. Congress lays down the rules for managing the forces, but the President controls their activities. "Congress," said Chief Justice Chase in *Ex Parte Milligan*,[2] "has the power not only to raise and support armies but to declare war. It has, therefore, the power to provide by law for carrying on war. This power necessarily extends to all legislation essential to the prosecution of war with vigor and success, except such as interferes with the command of the forces and the conduct of campaigns. That power and duty belong to the President as commander-in-chief."

The dividing line between the war powers of Congress and the war powers of the President is drawn in the decision of the case of *Fleming vs. Page*,[3] in which the broad rule was laid down that under the war powers granted him the President cannot extend the boundaries of the United States. In 1847, during the Mexican War, our troops occupied the City of Tampico, Mexico. Fleming and Marshall of Philadelphia paid under pro-

[1] Ib., 912.   [2] 4 Wallace's Rep., 2.   [3] 9 Howard's Rep., 603.

test customs duties levied on goods which they had imported from Tampico. If Tampico, while occupied by our troops, were a part of the United States, the levying of duties was unlawful, because duties are not collected on merchandise shipped from one part of the country to another. The Supreme Court therefore had to decide whether the President enlarges the national domain whenever the armies under his command hold places outside the boundary lines. Chief Justice Taney answered the question involved as follows:

A war . . . declared by Congress, can never be presumed to be waged for the purpose of conquest or the acquisition of territory; nor does the law declaring the war, imply an authority to the President to enlarge the limits of the United States by subjugating the enemy's country. The United States . . . may extend its boundaries by conquest or treaty, and may demand the cession of territory as the condition of peace, in order to indemnify its citizens for the injuries they have suffered, or to reimburse the government for the expenses of the war. But this can be done only by the treaty-making power or the legislative authority, and is not a part of the power conferred upon the President by the declaration of war. His duty and his power are purely military. As commander-in-chief he is authorized to direct the movements of the naval and military forces placed by law at his command, and to employ them in the manner he may deem most effectual to harass and conquer and subdue the enemy. He may invade the hostile country, and subject it to the sovereignty and authority of the United States. But his conquests do not enlarge the boundaries of this Union, nor extend the operation of our institutions and laws beyond the limits before assigned to them by the legislative power.

The President's power, as defined above by Chief Justice Taney, "to direct the movements of the naval

and military forces placed by law at his command, and
to employ them in the manner he may deem most
effectual to harass and conquer and subdue the enemy"
is as unlimited as any power granted to Congress by the
Constitution.   President Lincoln used this absolute
power in the early days of the Civil War by proclaiming
and enforcing a blockade of the ports of the States which
had attempted to secede from the Union.   In the *Prize
Cases*,[1] decided in 1862, the owners of a number of
captured blockade runners challenged the validity of
the seizures on the ground that no war existed at the
time of seizure, and that they had a right to send their
vessels to the blockaded ports.   Justice Grier, who gave
the opinion of the Supreme Court in these cases, said:

Whether the President in fulfilling his duties as commander-in-chief in suppressing an insurrection, has met
with such armed hostile resistance, and a civil war of such
alarming proportions as will compel him to accord to them
[the states in rebellion] the character of belligerents, is a
question to be decided *by him*, and this court must be
governed by the decisions and acts of the political department of the government to which this power was entrusted.
"He must determine what degree of force the crisis demands."   The proclamation of blockade is itself official and
conclusive evidence to the court that a state of war existed
which demanded and authorized a recourse to such a
measure, under the circumstance peculiar to the case.

In the case of *The Springbok*,[2] decided in 1866, the
Supreme Court, sustaining the power of the President
to enforce a blockade, inflicted, says Moore's *International Digest*, "a more serious blow on neutral rights
than did all the orders in council [made by the British

[1] 2 Black's Rep., 635.   [2] 5 Wallace's Rep., 1.

just before the war of 1812] put together. . . . **The decision can not be accepted without discarding those rules** as to neutral rights for which the United States made war in 1812, and which, except in the *Springbok* and cognate cases, the executive department of the United States Government, when stating the law, has since then consistently vindicated. The first of these is that blockades must be of specific ports. The second is that there can be no confiscation of non-contraband goods owned by neutrals and in neutral ships, on the ground that it is probable that such goods may be, at one or more intermediate points, transshipped or re-transshipped, and then find their way to a port blockaded by the party seizing."

The British bark, *The Springbok*, chartered by a London mercantile house, had sailed on December 8, 1862, from London with clearance papers declaring the "destination of the voyage, Nassau, New Providence," a British possession. On February 3, 1863, she was captured at sea by the United States gunboat *Sonoma*, and brought to the port of New York as a prize. Her cargo consisted in part of gray army blankets marked "C. S. N.," cavalry sabres, army boots, and similar articles. "The port [Nassau] which lay not very far from a part of the southern coast of the United States, it was common knowledge, had been largely used as one for call and transshipment of cargoes intended for the ports of the insurrectionary States of the Union then under blockade by the Federal Government. The vessel when captured made no resistance and all her papers were given up without attempt at concealment or spoliation." *The Springbok* was libelled as a prize on February 12, 1863, in the United States Court at New York. On March 9, 1863, her owners, who were

. . . .

. . . . essel, which
. . . . . . British port
. . . . . . owners, but that
. . . . to be trans-
. . . . band of war and
. . . . to the United
. . . . . of its highest
. . . . by its citizens
. . . . . another, are liable
. . . . similar circum-
. . . . . . in this decision:

. . . . . . doubt that the cargo
. . . . violate the blockade;
. . . . that it should be
. . . . vessel more likely to
. . . . port than the
. . . . to the blockaded
. . . . the intent of the
. . . . to condemnation,
. . . . attached to the

. . . .

. . . .
. . . . against the United
. . . .
. . . . the Prize
. . . . prescribed . .
. . . . when the
. . . .
. . . .
. . . .

offender is as innocent as if he had never committed the offence. If granted before conviction, it prevents any of the penalties and disabilities consequent upon conviction from attaching; if granted after conviction, it removes the penalties and disabilities, and restores him to all his civil rights; it makes him, as it were, a new man, and gives him a new credit and capacity."

What is a "pardon" which makes a man as innocent as if he had never committed the offence? The Supreme Court has answered the question in the case of *Osborn vs. United States.*[1] A Southern man, who had received a pardon for treasonable acts as a Confederate soldier, petitioned the United States District Court of Kansas for the restoration of certain bonds and mortgages which had been confiscated during the Civil War. The bonds and mortgages had been collected or foreclosed, and the proceeds paid into court, where the clerk, judge, and court officers seem to have divided the money among themselves. At all events none of it ever got into the national treasury. The District Court denied the application on the ground that one of the conditions of his pardon was that he should not claim any property which had been sold by order of court under confiscation laws. The case was taken to the Supreme Court, where Justice Field sustained the petitioner in an opinion which is alive with the just indignation of an honest man. He said:

The pardon, as is seen, embraces all offences arising from participation of the petitioner, direct or indirect, in the rebellion. It covers, therefore, the offences for which the forfeiture of his property was decreed. . . . The pardon of the offence necessarily carried with it the release of the

[1] 91 U. S. Rep., 474.

penalty attached to its commission, so far as such release was in the power of the government, unless specially restrained by exceptions embraced in the instrument itself. It is of the very essence of a pardon that it releases the offender from the consequences of his offence.

The President has power to grant reprieves and pardons except in cases of impeachment.   This exception was made in order to keep the control of administrative officers in the hands of the Congress.   The founders of our republic did not propose to let the President, by exercising the prerogative of mercy in impeachment cases, keep undesirable favorites in office.

Art. II., Sec. 2 (continued).   He [the President] shall have Power, by and with the Advice and Consent of the Senate, to make Treaties, provided two-thirds of the Senators present concur; and he shall nominate, and by and with the Advice and Consent of the Senate, shall appoint Ambassadors, other public Ministers and Consuls, Judges of the supreme Court, and all other Officers of the United States, whose Appointments are not herein otherwise provided for, and which shall be established by Law: but the Congress may by Law vest the Appointment of such inferior Officers, as they think proper, in the President alone, in the Courts of Law, or in the Heads of Departments.

The Confederation had failed to measure up to the needs of the new republic mainly because its Congress had tried to do everything.   The ministers plenipotentiary who had negotiated treaties with foreign nations, had had to confide momentous diplomatic secrets to an ill-regulated legislative body whose members could not be prevented from blabbing. The chiefs of the executive departments of war and finance had been subject to the whims and caprices of a Congress, the make-up of which had changed frequently. The makers of the Constitution, according to the resolution of Congress under which they had met, were so to revise the Articles of Confederation as to "render the Federal Constitution adequate to the exigencies of the government and the preservation of the Union."[1] They fulfilled that duty, in part at least, by entrusting to the President and the Senate the control of foreign relations and governmental appointments.

He shall have Power, by and with the Advice and Consent of the Senate, to make Treaties, provided two-thirds of the Senators present concur.

"However proper and safe," said Hamilton in the *Federalist*,[2] "it may be in governments where the executive magistrate is an hereditary monarch, to commit to him the entire power of making treaties, it would be utterly unsafe and improper to intrust that power to an elective magistrate of four years' duration. . . . The history of human conduct does not warrant that exalted opinion of human virtue which would make it wise in a nation to commit interests of so delicate and momentous a kind, as those which concern its intercourse with the rest of the world, to the sole disposal of a magistrate created and circumstanced as would be a President of the United States.

"To have entrusted the power of making treaties to the Senate alone, would have been to relinquish the benefits of the Constitutional agency of the President in the conduct of foreign negotiations. . . . Though it would be imprudent to confide in him solely so impor-

of the whole number of members had been required, it would, in many cases, from the non-attendance of a part, amount in practise to a necessity of unanimity."

The President and Senate have exclusive control of the making of all treaties except those involving the expenditure of money. The courts so decided in 1852, when the question was presented in the case of *Turner vs. The American Baptist Missionary Union.*[1]

〔 In 1838, a man named Turner took up under the land laws a quarter-section (160 acres) of certain lands at the Falls of the Grand River in Michigan, upon which the Baptist missionaries then had their station. In 1842, he obtained another title from a man who had purchased a part of the land from the State of Michigan which under the provisions of the act of admission to the Union, had claimed title to all vacant lands. The missionaries had supposed they had a good title to the property under a treaty made by the United States with the Indians in March, 1836, in which it had been stipulated that "The mission establishment upon the Grand River shall be appraised and the proper value paid to the proper Boards." This treaty had been amended in the Senate by a provision that the missionary society should have the proceeds of the sale of 160 acres of land upon which their buildings stood. Because the treaty called for a payment of money, Congress had enacted a statute to give effect to its provisions. When Mr. Turner asserted his right to these lands, the missionary society brought an action for their recovery, and Turner retaliated by asking for an injunction restraining the missionaries from prosecuting their case. The United States Circuit Court of Ohio, where this case was heard, therefore, had before it questions which

[1] 5 McLean's Rep., 344.

called for explanations of the nature and application of the treaty power.   The Court said:

A treaty, under the federal constitution, is declared to be the supreme law of the land.   This, unquestionably, applies to all treaties, where the treaty-making power, without the aid of Congress, can carry it into effect.   It is not, however, and cannot be the supreme law of the land, where the concurrence of Congress is necessary to give it effect. Until this is exercised, as where the appropriation of money is required, the treaty is not perfect.   It is not operative, in the sense of the Constitution, as money cannot be appropriated by the treaty-making power.   This results from the limitations of our government.   The action of no department of the government can be regarded as a law until it shall have all the sanctions required by the Constitution to make it such.   As well might it be contended that an ordinary act of Congress, without the signature of the President, was a law, as that a treaty which engages to pay a sum of money, is in itself a law.   And in such a case, the representatives of the people and the States exercise their own judgments in granting or withholding the money.   They act upon their own responsibility, and not upon the responsibility of the treaty-making power.   It cannot bind or control the legislative action in this respect, and every foreign government may be presumed to know, that so far as the treaty stipulates to pay money, the legislative sanction is required.

The treaty-making power is limited to contracts which this government may make with other nations. The President has no authority to lay down any new rule of diplomacy or proclaim a foreign policy unconnected with the making of treaties.   Nevertheless the President can serve notice on all the world that the United States will not allow other governments to meddle with the internal affairs of any American republic or establish new colonies in any part of this hemisphere. This is the substance of the "Monroe doctrine."

In 1815, after the battle of Waterloo, the Emperors of Austria and Russia and the King of Prussia formed the Holy Alliance which had for its object the preservation of the rights and interests of European dynasties. It was an alliance of kings against the spirit of republicanism. The United States paid no attention to this alliance until 1823, when the royal association undertook to help the King of Spain regain his American dependencies which had declared their independence. Richard Rush, our minister to England, at once gave notice that the United States would object to any meddling in the affairs of this hemisphere, and on December 2, 1823, President Monroe took up the question in a message to Congress, which has been called the Second Declaration of Independence. He said in part:

We owe it, therefore, to candor and to the amicable relations existing between the United States and those powers, to declare that we should consider any attempt on their part to extend their system to any portion of this hemisphere as dangerous to our peace and safety. With the existing colonies or dependencies of any European power, we have not interfered and shall not interfere. But with the governments who have declared their independence and maintained it, and whose independence we have, on great consideration and on just principles, acknowledged, we could not view any interposition for the purpose of oppressing them or controlling in any other manner their destiny, by any European power, in any other light than a manifestation of an unfriendly disposition toward the United States. . . . The American continents, by the free and independent condition which they have assumed and maintain, are henceforth not to be considered as subjects for future colonization by any European powers.

He shall nominate, and by and with the Advice and Consent of the Senate, shall appoint Ambassadors, . . . Judges of the supreme Court, and all other Officers of the United States, whose Appointments are not herein otherwise provided for. "To what purpose then require the co-operation of the Senate in the appointment of public officers?" asked Hamilton in *The Federalist.*[2] "I answer that the necessity of their concurrence would have a powerful, though, in general, a silent operation. It would be an excellent check upon a spirit of favoritism in the President, and would tend greatly to prevent the appointment of unfit characters from state prejudice, from family connection, from personal attachment, or from a view to popularity. In addition to this, it would be an efficacious source of stability in the administration."

Who are "officers of the United States?" "An office," said Justice Miller of the Supreme Court in the case of *U. S. vs. Hartwell,*[3] "is a public station, or employment, conferred by the appointment of government. The term embraces the ideas of tenure, duration, emolument, duties. Unless a person in the service of the government . . . holds his place by virtue of an appointment by the President, or of one of the courts of justice, or heads of department, he is not . . . an officer of the United States."

The Supreme Court declared that the power to appoint officers includes, by necessary implication of law, the power to remove. This looks like amending

[1] Moore's *American Diplomacy,* p. 148.   [2] No. 75.
[3] 6 Wallace's Rep., 385, 393.

the supreme law of the land by judicial decision instead of by the method prescribed in the Constitution.

In the case of *Ex Parte Hennen*,[1] decided in 1839, it was brought to the attention of the Supreme Court that a Federal district judge in Louisiana had removed the clerk of his court without assigning any cause except that he wished to give the place to a friend. The clerk, thus removed, asked the judges of the Circuit Court to continue him in office upon the ground that he had been legally appointed to the clerkship and, not having resigned, was still legally clerk of the court. The circuit judges, not being able to agree upon the question thus presented, certified the case to the Supreme Court, which handed down a decision written by Justice Thompson, upholding the removal for the following reasons:

All offices, the tenure of which is not fixed by the Constitution or limited by law, must be held either during good behavior, or (which is the same thing in contemplation of law) during the life of the incumbent; or must be held at the will and discretion of some department of the government, and subject to removal at pleasure.

It cannot, for a moment, be admitted, that it was the intention of the Constitution, that those offices which are denominated inferior offices should be held during life. And if removable at pleasure, by whom is such removal to be made? In the absence of all constitutional provision, or statutory regulation, it would seem to be a sound and necessary rule to consider the power of removal as incident to the power of appointment.

Art. II., Sec. 2 (continued). The President shall have Power to fill up all Vacancies that may happen

[1] 13 Peters' Rep., 230.

during the Recess of the Senate, by granting Commissions which shall expire at the End of their next Session.

In the case of *In re Farrow*,[1] the United States Circuit Court had to pass upon the validity of a recess appointment to a vacancy which had occurred during a session of the Senate. The term of Henry P. Farrow, United States District Attorney for Georgia, had expired on April 19, 1880, and he had been reappointed by one of the justices to serve until an appointment should be made by the President. In May, 1880, while the Senate was still in session, the President had nominated John S. Bigby for the office, but the nomination had not been confirmed when the upper House had adjourned during the following month. Thereupon the President gave Bigby a recess appointment and issued his commission. Farrow refused to surrender the office on the ground that Bigby had been appointed to a vacancy which had happened during a session of the Senate, and not "during the recess of the Senate." Justice Woods decided the controversy mainly upon the authority of numerous opinions which had been rendered by attorney-generals of the United States, saying in part:

The first opinion given upon this point is that of Mr. William Wirt, attorney general under President Monroe, . . . in which he argues for the construction claimed in support of the President's action in this case. He says "in reason, it seems to me perfectly immaterial when the vacancy first arose, for, whether it arose during the session of the Senate or during their recess, it equally requires to be filled. The Constitution does not look to the moment of the origin of the vacancy, but to the state of things at the point of time at which the President is called on to act. Is

[1] 13 Federal Rep., 112.

the Senate in session? Then he must make a nomination
to that body. Is it in recess? Then the President must
fill the vacancy by a temporary commission. This seems
to me the only construction of the Constitution which is
compatible with its spirit, reason, and purpose, while at the
same time it offers no violence to its language, and these are,
I think, the governing points to which all sound construction
looks." . . . The only authority relied on to support the
other view is the case decided by the late Judge Cadwallader,
the learned and able United States District Judge for the
Eastern District of Pennsylvania. It is no disparagement
to Judge Cadwallader to say that his opinion, unsupported
by any other, ought not to be held to outweigh the authority
of the great number which are cited in support of the opposite view, and of the practise of the executive department
for nearly sixty years, the acquiescence of the Senate therein,
and the recognition of the power claimed by both houses of
Congress. I therefore shall hold that the President had
constitutional power to make the appointment of Bigby,
nothwithstanding the fact that the vacancy filled by his
appointment first happened when the Senate was in session.

**Art. II., Sect. 3. He [The President] shall from time
to time give to the Congress Information of the State
of the Union, and recommend to their Consideration
such Measures as he shall judge necessary and expedient; he may, on extraordinary Occasions, convene both
Houses, or either of them, and, in Case of Disagree-
ment between them, with Respect to the Time of Adjournment, he may adjourn them to such Time as he
shall think proper; he shall receive Ambassadors and
other public ministers; . . . and shall Commission
all the Officers of the United States.**

These are instructions which the People of the
United States have given to their chief executive officer.

The President, because he has these orders, has some control over the legislative body, although he has no direct legislative power. Being so instructed, he extends to the diplomatic representatives of other nations the formal recognition without which they could not act; yet the power of the Senate to a controlling voice in all negotiations with diplomatists is not modified or changed. It is the President's duty to enforce obedience to the laws of the nation by executing the mandates and orders of the courts; but this duty does not add to, or take away from, his power as supreme commander of the army and navy. The war powers of the Congress are not modified in any particular by the President's obligation to keep the peace.

He shall from time to time give to the Congress Information of the State of the Union, and recommend to their Consideration such Measures as he shall judge necessary and expedient. Our earlier Presidents thought they had performed their whole duty when they had told the Senators and Representatives what they ought to know about the state of the nation and what they ought to do about it. That rule no longer governs. The President now can speak his mind, if he chooses, in one of the 40,000-word addresses to the world which President Roosevelt used to send to the Congress to be read by relays of clerks to rows of empty benches at the joint session, and afterward read religiously by the bulk of the people in their homes. He can, like President Wilson, read in person short, pithy, eloquent addresses, worthy of ranking as classics. President Washington and the elder Adams, who were naturally stately and ceremonious, made set speeches, perhaps because they liked to deliver the President's message to Congress in the manner of an English King's speech from the throne.

Jefferson, who "wrote like an angel," but could not make a speech to save his life, set the fashion of written messages which prevailed until President Wilson revived the older custom.

He may, on extraordinary Occasions, convene both Houses, or either of them. The President quite frequently has called both Houses of Congress to meet in extra session; but, "the principal exercise of this power has been in proclamations in which the President has called the Senate together, at the close of a session of Congress, for the purpose of considering appointments to offices and sometimes treaties."[1]

And shall Commission all the Officers of the United States. It is the duty of the President to deliver their commissions to all properly appointed officers of the United States. For example, the Supreme Court ruled in the case of *Marbury vs. Madison*[2] that an appointment made by President John Adams during the last hours of his administration, was valid and binding because the commission to the appointee had been signed and sealed, though not delivered. Chief Justice Marshall stated in his opinion in that case that an officer so appointed had a legal right to his position for the term fixed by the act of Congress creating it, that the President was in duty bound to issue a commission to all persons who had been appointed to an office created by an act of Congress, and that if the President had refused to perform his duty in such a case, the Supreme Court had a constitutional right to direct him to do so. Chief Justice Marshall said:

By the Constitution of the United States, the President is vested with certain important political powers, in the

---

[1] Miller, *On the Constitution*, p. 170.   [2] 1 Cranch's Rep., 137.

exercise of which he is to use his own discretion, and is accountable only to his country in his political character, and to his own conscience.　To aid him in the performance of these duties, he is authorized to appoint certain officers, who act by his authority and in conformity with his orders. In such cases their acts are his acts; and whatever opinion may be entertained of the manner in which executive discretion may be used, still there exists, and can exist, no power to control that discretion.　Their subjects are political.　They respect the nation, not individual rights, and being intrusted to the executive, the decision of the executive is conclusive.　The application of this remark will be perceived by adverting to the act of Congress for establishing the department of foreign affairs.　This officer, as his duties were prescribed by that act, is to conform precisely to the will of the President.　He is the mere organ by whom that will is communicated.　The acts of such an officer, as an officer, can never be examinable by the courts.

But when the legislative proceeds to impose on that officer other duties, when he is directed peremptorily to perform certain acts; when the rights of individuals are dependent on the performance of those acts; he is so far the officer of the law; is amenable to the laws for his conduct; and cannot at his discretion sport away the vested rights of others. . . .

This, then, is a plain case for a mandamus [court order], either to deliver the commission, or a copy of it from the record; and it only remains to be inquired, Whether it can issue from that Court. . . .

The Constitution vests the whole judicial power of the United States in one Supreme Court, and in such inferior courts as Congress shall, from time to time, ordain and establish.　This power is expressly extended to all cases arising under the laws of the United States; and, consequently, in some form, may be exercised over the present case, because the right claimed is given by a law of the United States.

Art. II., Sec. 3. (Part of.)   He shall take Care that the Laws be faithfully executed.

The command to "take care that the laws be faithfully executed," being fully interpreted, signifies that
the laws are to be carried into execution "as they are
expounded and adjudged" by the judiciary.   This point
was made by Chief Justice Taney in his opinion in the
case of *Ex Parte Merryman*,[1] which grew out of the first
incidents of the Civil War.

The President executes the Constitution, laws, and
treaties of the United States in his own way until the
courts decide upon the meaning and application of the
written law of the United States.   For example, until
the *Chinese Exclusion Case*[2] was decided in 1888, the
President through his officers obeyed the instructions of
Congress concerning restricting the admission of Chinese laborers.   The Supreme Court in passing upon this
case, which is more correctly called *Chae Chan Ping vs.
United States*, explained the policy of the United States
on the whole subject of immigration.   Chae Chan Ping,
a Chinese subject who had resided in San Francisco
since 1875, went back to China on a visit in 1887, having
first obtained a certificate or license issued under the
Chinese Exclusion Act of 1882, entitling him to re-
admission to the United States.   On September 7, 1888,
he left Hong Kong on his return voyage, arriving at
San Francisco on October 8, 1888.   On October 1, 1888,
Congress had passed an act supplementary to the Exclusion Act of 1882, declaring null and void all certificates authorizing re-admission which had been issued
to Chinese laborers who had left the United States and
had not returned prior to the passage of the act.   The

[1] Taney's Decisions, 246.   [2] 130 U. S. Rep., 581.

lector of Customs of San Francisco, therefore refused to ... Chae Chan Ping's certificate and ordered him to ... deported to China. The Chinaman then brought an action in the United States Circuit Court of California, in which he claimed that he had been unlawfully excluded from the United States. This case was taken to the Supreme Court which decided that he had no ... right ... admitted to the United States. Justice Field, himself a Californian, delivered the opinion of the court in words which showed plainly that while he believed in the policy of excluding Chinese laborers, he thought Congress had not been quite fair in the way it had dealt with them. He said:

> ... discovery of gold in California in 1848 ... allowed by a large immigration ... citizens from all parts of the world, attracted not only to the mines, but ... to ... labor. The news of their ... discoveries ... laborers came from ... great numbers ...

not suffice for our laborers and artisans. The competition between them and our people was for this reason altogether in their favor, and the consequent irritation, proportionately deep and bitter, was followed, in many cases, by open conflicts to the great disturbance of the public peace. . . .

So urgent and constant were the prayers for relief against existing and anticipated evils, both from the public authorities of the Pacific Coast and from private individuals that Congress was impelled to act on the subject. Many persons, however, both in and out of Congress, were of opinion that so long as the treaty [with China, negotiated by Anson Burlingame in 1868] remained unmodified, legislation restricting immigration would be a breach of faith with China. A statute was accordingly passed appropriating money to send commissioners to China to act with our minister there in negotiating and concluding by treaty a settlement of such matters of interest between the two governments as might be confided to them. . . . Such commissioners were appointed, and as the result of their negotiations the supplementary treaty of November 17, 1880, was concluded and ratified in May of the following year. . . . It declares in its first article that "Whenever, in the opinion of the Government of the United States, the coming of Chinese laborers to the United States or their residence therein, affects or threatens to affect the interests of that country, or to endanger the good order of the said country or of any locality within the territory thereof, the Government of China agrees that the Government of the United States may regulate, limit, or suspend such coming or residence, but may not absolutely prohibit it. The limitation or suspension shall be reasonable and shall apply only to Chinese who may go to the United States as laborers, other classes not being included in the limitations. Legislation taken in regard to Chinese laborers will be of such a character only as is necessary to enforce the regulation, limitation, or suspension of immigration, and immigrants shall not be subject to personal maltreatment or abuse."

tion of express stipulations of the treaty of 1868 and of the supplemental treaty of 1880, but it is not on that account invalid or to be restricted in its enforcement. The treaties were of no greater legal obligation than the act of Congress. By the Constitution, laws made in pursuance thereof and treaties made under the authority of the United States are both declared to be the supreme law of the land, and no paramount authority is given to one over the other. A treaty . . . is in its nature a compact between nations and is often merely promissory in its character, requiring legislation to carry its provisions into effect. Such legislation will be open to future repeal or amendment. If a treaty operates by its own force, and relates to a subject within the power of Congress, it can be deemed in that particular only the equivalent of a legislative act, to be repealed or modified at the pleasure of Congress. In either case the last expression of the sovereign will must control. . . .

That the government of the United States, through the action of its legislative department, can exclude aliens from its territory is a proposition which we do not think open to controversy. Jurisdiction over its own territory to that extent is an incident of every independent nation. It is a part of its independence. If it could not exclude aliens, it would be to that extent subject to the control of another power. . . .

The power of exclusion of foreigners being an incident of sovereignty belonging to the government of the United States, as a part of those sovereign powers delegated by the Constitution, the right to its exercise at any time when, in the judgment of the government, the interests of the country require it, cannot be granted away or restrained on behalf of any one. The powers of government are delegated in trust to the United States, and are incapable of transfer to any other parties. They cannot be abandoned or surrendered. Nor can their exercise be hampered, when needed for the public good, by any considerations of private interest. The exercise of these public trusts is not the sub-

enter into contract. Whatever license the immigrant may have obtained, previous to the moment of his departure, to return to the United States at his pleasure, and subject to the will of the government, is revocable at its pleasure. Whether a ruler or a government of its previous laws or a government the nation whose subjects are affected thereby ought to have qualified its inhibitions and made it applicable only to persons departing from the country, are not questions which concern us. If there be any just complaint of the enforcement it must be made to the political department which alone is competent to act in the case.

. . . .

. . . . the German Empire . . . . United States . . . surrender the German . . . . committing forgery in a grand . . . . and escaped to the United States . . . arrested in Chicago on complaint of the . . . and brought before a commissioner of . . . .

the United States Court, who ordered that he be held for extradition. The rogue then petitioned the United States Court for an order directing his release upon the ground that the German Empire could not properly demand his surrender to Prussia for trial, because the treaty of 1852 between the United States and Prussia had been terminated by the establishment in 1871 of the German Empire. Therefore he claimed that there was no treaty under which he could be surrendered. Chief Justice Fuller, who gave the decision of the court, said:

The application of the foreign government was made through the proper diplomatic representative of the German Empire, . . . and the complaint before the commissioner was made by the proper consular authority representing the German Empire. . . . We concur in the view that the question whether power remains in a foreign State to carry out its treaty obligations is in its nature political and not judicial, and that the courts ought not to interfere with the conclusions of the political department in that regard. . . . Extradition may be sufficiently defined to be the surrender by one nation to another of an individual accused or convicted of an offence outside of its own territory, and within the territorial jurisdiction of the other, which, being competent to try and to punish him, demands his surrender. . . . If it be assumed . . . that the commissioner, on hearing, deemed the evidence sufficient to sustain the charges, and certified his findings and the testimony to the Secretary of State, and a warrant for the surrender of Terlinden on the proper requisition was duly issued, it cannot be successfully contended that the courts could properly intervene on the ground that the treaty under which both governments had proceeded, had terminated by reason of the adoption of the constitution of the German Empire, notwithstanding the judgment of both governments to the contrary. The decisions of the Executive Department in

Art. II., Sec. 4. The President, Vice President, and all civil Officers of the United States, shall be removed from Office on Impeachment for, and Conviction of, Treason, Bribery, or other high Crimes and Misdemeanors.

In the decision of the case of *Langford vs. The United States*,[1] the Supreme Court pointed out this difference between ours and other forms of government: that the officers of the United States, however exalted, are themselves accountable for their misdeeds. They cannot shift the consequences upon their subordinates. Langford, as assignee of the American Board of Commissioners for Foreign Missions, had brought action against the United States in the Court of Claims upon his complaint that certain Indian agents had taken forcible possession of buildings which the Board had erected and owned. The claim of the United States was that upon the old English common law principle that the king can do no wrong, the government, "in taking and using the property of an individual against his consent, cannot be guilty of . . . a wrongful act for which it is answerable to a court." Justice Miller ruled to the contrary, saying:

It is not easy to see how the first proposition [that the King can do no wrong] can have any place in our system of government. We have no king to whom it can be applied. The President, in the exercise of the executive functions, bears a nearer resemblance to the limited monarch of the English government than any other branch of our government, and is the only *individual* to whom it could possibly have any relation. It cannot be applied to him, because the Constitution admits that he may do wrong, and has provided, by the proceeding of impeachment, for his trial for wrong-doing, and his removal from office if found guilty. None of the eminent counsel who defended President John-

[1] 101 U. S. Rep., 341.

son on his impeachment trial asserted that by law he was incapable of doing wrong, or that, if done, it could not, as in the case of the King, be imputed to him, but must be laid to the charge of the ministers who advised him. It is to be observed that the English maxim does not declare that the government, or those who administer it, can do no wrong; for it is a part of the principle itself that wrong may be done by the governing power, for which the ministry, for the time being, is held responsible; and the ministers personally, like our President, may be impeached; or if the wrong amounts to a crime, they may be indicted and tried at law for the offense. We do not understand that either in reference to the government of the United States, or of the several States, or of any of their officers, the English maxim has an existence in this country.

PART VII

Judicial Government in the United States

CHAPTER XX

Art. III., Sec. 1. The judicial Power of the United States shall be vested in one supreme Court, and in such inferior Courts as the Congress may from time to time ordain and establish. The Judges, both of the supreme and inferior Courts, shall hold their Offices during good Behaviour, and shall, at stated Times, receive for their Services, a Compensation, which shall not be diminished during their Continuance in Office.

In April, 1851, Justice Nelson of the Supreme Court gave a definition of the words "judicial power" in the course of a special charge to a grand jury,[1] in which he said:

The judicial power mentioned in the Constitution and vested in the courts, means the power conferred upon courts ordained and established by and under the Constitution, in the strict and appropriate sense of that term —courts that compose one of the three great departments of the government prescribed by the fundamental law the same as the other two, the legislative and the executive.

The judicial Power . . . shall be vested in one supreme Court. "In modern times, and under our form of government," said Judge McCabe in *White County Commissioners vs. Givin,*[2] "the judicial power is exer-

[1] Blatchford's Rep., 635, 643.　　　[2] 136 Indiana Rep., 562.

349

cised by means of courts. A court is an instrumentality of government. It is a creation of the law, and in some respects it is an imaginary thing, that exists only in legal contemplation, very similar to a corporation. A time when, a place where, and the persons by whom judicial functions are to be exercised, are essential to complete the idea of a court. It is in its organized aspect, with all these constituent elements of time, place, and officers, that it completes the idea of a court in the general legal acceptance of the term."

A "supreme court" contains another idea. "The word 'supreme' means highest in the sense of final or last resort," said Judge Dent of the Supreme Court of West Virginia in the case of *Koonce vs. Doolittle.*[1] "Here all litigation must end, and when this court has once finally determined a question it has no power to reopen it." The supreme courts of States are courts of last resort in all matters reserved to the States; the Supreme Court of the United States is the final authority in all federal matters.

The judicial power of the United States is something which must be reckoned with, because the courts of the United States can and will summon all the civil officers and the whole military power of the People of the United States for the enforcement of their orders and mandates. For example, within twenty years after the Constitution had been adopted, Pennsylvania was taught in a very masterly way that the whole power of the richest and perhaps most powerful State in the Union would have to yield before the simple command of the Supreme Court of the United States.

This lesson was given by a decree in the case of *United States vs. Peters,*[2] in which United States District

---

[1] 48 West Va. Rep., 592.   [2] 3 Dallas' Rep., 135.

Judge Peters of Philadelphia was directed to enforce a judgment of his court, which the State legislature had ordered the governor of Pennsylvania to resist by military force if necessary. This conflict of authority between a great State of the United States and the Supreme Court of the United States had grown out of an incident of the War for Independence. In 1776, Gideon Olmsted, a Connecticut ship captain on a trading voyage in the West Indies, was captured by the British and put on board a sloop of war bound for New York with supplies for Sir William Howe's army. Captain Olmsted and three other prisoners below the decks melted their pewter spoons and dishes into a substitute for bullets, broke open the hatches, overpowered the captain and crew of the sloop, and drove them below the decks, where they had to stay because Olmsted had got possession of a swivel gun and trained it on the hatchway. The British officer and his men, however, did not give up the struggle. On the contrary, hoping to make the vessel unmanageable, they cut a hole in the stern and wedged the rudder. After two days of hunger and thirst, however, they surrendered. The new commander then sailed for Egg Harbor on the New Jersey coast. Almost in sight of land, he was overhauled by two armed vessels—the *Convention*, owned by the State of Pennsylvania, and the *Le Gerard*, a privateer. The captains of the vessels were sure that Olmsted's story of having captured this ship of war with only three men was a pretense. They insisted that the British captain, perceiving that his ship was sure to be captured, had fixed up a scheme with Olmsted to let him appear to be the captor, and later divide up the proceeds of the prize sale.

The case was heard in the Philadelphia Admiralty

Court which decided that the sloop and its cargo should be sold, and that Olmsted should have one fourth of the proceeds of the sale, the balance to be divided between the State of Pennsylvania and the owners of the *Le Gerard*. Olmsted, who was not the man to submit to injustice, promptly appealed to a committee of the Continental Congress which, at that time, constituted the "United States Court of Commissioners of Appeals in Admiralty Cases." In September, 1778, the Commissioners of Appeals reversed the decision of the Philadelphia Admiralty Court and directed that the captured vessel and cargo should be sold and the proceeds paid over to Olmsted. The marshal of the Philadelphia court, after selling the property for £47,981. 2s. 5d. proclamation money, which later became of some value, paid over that sum, not to Olmsted but to Judge Ross of Philadelphia, who in turn handed it over to David Rittenhouse, treasurer of Pennsylvania.

In 1790, Judge Ross died. Olmsted then brought an action against his executors to recover the proceeds of the sale, and they in turn sued State Treasurer Rittenhouse and obtained a judgment, which he did not see fit to pay.

In 1795, the Supreme Court decided, in the great case of *Penhallow vs. Doane*,[1] that it had power to carry out and enforce decisions of the old Court of Commissioners of Appeals. This gave Olmsted another chance. He sued Mrs. Sergeant and Mrs. Waters, the daughters and heirs of Rittenhouse who had died, and obtained a judgment against them in the United States District Court at Philadelphia. This judgment contained an order by which the two ladies were commanded to deliver to the United States Marshal the certificates of

[1] 3 Dallas' Rep., 54.

public debt in which their father had invested the money paid over to him by Judge Ross. Then the Pennsylvania legislature enacted a law ordering the certificates to be turned over to the State treasury, and directing the governor to defend the Rittenhouse heirs against the execution of any process issued out of the national courts. Again the parties stood still and looked at each other, because Judge Peters quite reasonably did not wish to defy the State of Pennsylvania.

In 1808, however, more than thirty years after the trouble began, Olmsted applied again to the Supreme Court and this time the court issued an order commanding Judge Peters to enforce the judgment against the Rittenhouse heirs. He obeyed, but when the United States Marshal went to the house where Mrs. Sergeant and Mrs. Waters lived, he found himself barred out by the State militia acting under the orders of the governor. As nothing could be done at the moment, the marshal read his warrant, made a speech, and went back to report to the court. He then named a day four weeks ahead on which he said he would serve the warrant, and issued summonses to 2,000 citizens to aid him as a *posse comitatus* (a company of persons called upon to aid a public officer).

The marshal's act brought the matter to a point where the State of Pennsylvania had to settle the case or undertake a fight against the whole United States. The State legislature appropriated a sum of money, which the governor paid. Then the whole matter was dropped. This sounds like a very tame ending, but it did not seem so at the time. It was an exhibition of the judicial power of the United States in its most convincing form. No second example has had to be made in order to satisfy every one that a mandate of the Su-

... held his office during with ... in drawing a salary while receiving ... ought to be paid a uniform ... of the United States went ... was not always a ... Signer of the Declaration ... a member of the Colonial ... served on the old Court of Appeals ... President Washington to a seat ... Supreme Court in 1796. He was ... American ... on the bench, and, that ... position would not rise he was in ... for this apparently beyond the ... neither prevarication nor ... partisanship could be considered high crimes ... for which civil officers might be ... impeachment; nevertheless, when the ... Court had handed down its famous decision ... Hylton v. Hylton, in which the executive depart... ... and ... jointly that it had wrongfully held ... commission of a duly appointed government ... the ... and especially Justice Chase had ... if they had been more prudent.

... impeachment for misconduct in office were ... against Justice Chase, perhaps because it was sup... ... the feeble unpopular, could be removed with... ... much public disapproval. Also, it was openly said that other judges were to be dealt with summarily until the make-up of the Court should be wholly changed. The Jeffersonians could have carried the program through if they had chosen, because they had majorities in both Houses of Congress. Judge Chase, however, escaped removal from office, though the vote against him in the Senate was unpleasantly near the number required by law.

In 1808, John Pickering, a District Court Judge in New Hampshire, was removed for wrongful rulings and intoxication while on duty; but there was evidence that he was insane at the time. In 1862, Judge Humphreys of the District Court of Tennessee was impeached for assisting the cause of the South in the Civil War by refusing to perform his duties as an officer of the United States. In 1912, Robert W. Archbald, a Circuit Judge, who had been designated a member of the Commerce Court (now abolished), was turned out of office for having made improper use of his official credit and accepting money favors which might have influenced his conduct as a judge.

CHAPTER XXI

JURISDICTION OF COURTS OF THE UNITED STATES

Art. III., Sec. 2. The judicial Power shall extend to all Cases, in Law and Equity, arising under this Constitution, the Laws of the United States, and Treaties made, or which shall be made, under their Authority; — to all cases affecting Ambassadors, other public Ministers and Consuls; — to all Cases of admiralty and maritime Jurisdiction; — to Controversies to which the United States shall be a Party; — to Controversies between two or more States; — between a State and Citizens of another State; — between Citizens of different States; — between Citizens of the same State claiming Lands under Grants of different States, and between a State, or the Citizens thereof, and foreign States, Citizens or Subjects.

Americans are justly proud of the great system of jurisprudence which five generations of justices of the Supreme Court have built up under the authority of this clause of the Constitution. They realize that the world has been made richer by a distinct addition to a science which is most necessary for the preservation of society.

"This 'jurisprudence' or common law, in some nations," said Judge Porter of Louisiana in the decision of *Saul vs. His Creditors*,[1] "is found in the decrees of their courts; in others, it is furnished by private individuals, eminent in their learning and integrity, whose superior wisdom has enabled them to gain the proud distinction of legislating, as it were, for their country, and enforcing their legislation by the most noble of all means;—that of reason alone. After a long series of years, it is sometimes difficult to say, whether these opinions and judgments were originally the effect of principles previously existing in society, or whether they were the cause of the doctrines, which all men at last recognize. But whether the one or the other, when acquiesced in for ages, their force and effect cannot be distinguished from statutory law. No civilized nation has been without such a system. None, it is believed, can do without it; and every attempt to expel it, only causes it to return with increased strength on those, who are so sanguine as to think it may be dispensed with."

The judicial Power shall extend. These words declare that the courts of the United States shall have a "jurisdiction" or right to judge. "Jurisdiction," said Chief Justice Beasley of New Jersey in the decision of *Munday vs. Vail*,[2] "may be defined to be the right to adjudicate, to judge concerning the subject matter in the given case. To constitute this, there are three essentials: First. The court must have cognizance of the class of cases to which the one to be judged belongs. Second. The proper parties must be present. And, Third. The point to be decided must be, in substance and effect, within the issue. That a court cannot go out of its appointed sphere, and that its

[1] 5 Martin's (La) N. S., 569, 582.
[2] 34 New Jersey Law Rep., 418.

action is void with respect to persons who are strangers to its proceedings, are propositions established by multitudes of authorities."

The judicial Power shall extend to all Cases . . . [and] Controversies. The word "cases" in this clause of the Constitution refers to the nature or subject matter of litigation which may be adjudicated in the Federal courts; and the word "controversies" is used when persons or parties are spoken of as the persons or parties arrayed against each other. In his opinion in the case of *King vs. McLean Asylum,* Circuit Judge Putnam said:

The appellees rely on a supposed distinction between the use of the word "cases" and the word "controversies" in the section of the Constitution defining the federal judicial power. That section used the word "cases" in the first three clauses, namely, "cases in law and equity," arising under the Constitution and the laws and treaties of the United States, "cases affecting ambassadors, other public ministers and consuls," and "cases of admiralty and maritime jurisdiction" . . . for it has relation mainly, although not entirely, to the subject matter of the litigation, and not to the parties involved . . . then changes to the word "controversies," and uses this with reference to "controversies to which the United States shall be a party," "controversies between two or more States, and then, without repeating the word, continues "between a State and citizens of another State, between citizens of different States, . . . citizens of the same State claiming lands under grants of different States, and between a State, and . . . other States, citizens or subjects."

. . . change under consideration from the word "cases" . . . to "controversies" will be found to have . . . matter of style, and to have no relation to any . . . of the class of questions to be ad-

. . . 33', 335.

judicated. As we have already said, so long as this section
of the Constitution speaks specially with reference to the
nature of the questions involved, it uses the word "cases,"
but, when it considers more particularly proceedings having
relation to the existence of parties, it uses the word "controversies," probably because, when parties are spoken of
as arrayed against each other, literary style suggested the
change."

*The judicial Power shall extend to all Cases, in Law and
Equity.* When the Constitution was made, "law"
was one thing and "equity" was something very
different. In very old times the word "law" had meant
what we mean by the word "right." A man's "law"
was a part of his property. It was an imaginary thing
which he owned and possessed against all the world.
Whatever land he occupied was his by his "law" or
property right. He possessed a "law" or right to
defend himself and his family against the violence of
others. Lawsuits had to be decided when one man's
"law" or right conflicted with some other man's real
or supposed "law" or right. For example, if one man
thought it was his "law" or right to occupy a farm
which another man held and occupied, he would go
upon the land and pick up a twig or some other trifle
as a way of claiming that it was his "law" to have the
land. The other man, by interfering, would assert a
conflicting "law" or right.

In old times, disputes of this sort were settled by all
the people in their tribal assemblies. Each party to
the lawsuit brought witnesses to swear that it was his
"law" or right to possess the land. These witnesses
were sworn and thus were called "jurors" from the
Latin word *jurare*, which means "to swear." Apparently the land went to the one who presented the larger

~~number of jurors. Later on, the jurors became judges of all the circumstances which ought rightly to be considered in deciding lawsuits. Thus it came about that~~ a lawsuit or a "case in law," as this clause puts it, meant a case which had to be tried by a jury.

A "case in equity," on the other hand, means a case which is decided by a judge alone. The technicalities and formalities, which had been invented to protect the weak or ignorant from the strong and clever, often had made the process of justice a cruel practical joke. Those who had the right in a controversy often had been denied justice. English kings had tried to remedy this evil by holding what were called "equity" courts, in which the rules of law were suspended and the decisions were dictated by the royal conscience. New rules and many of them were soon adopted; and, in the end, it was doubtful whether the suitor in equity was not more unfortunate than the suitor at law.

Each of these ways of administering justice was in force throughout the United States when the Constitution was framed. The Americans of that day were accustomed to courts in which cases in law and cases in equity were heard and decided. Hence, because it was the natural thing to do, they gave the courts of the new constitutional government power to judge cases of both kinds. Although abolished in nearly all the States, the distinction between law and equity has been retained in the Federal courts.

The difference between a case in law and a case in equity was explained by the Supreme Court of Wisconsin in the case of *Callanan vs. Judd*,[1] decided in 1868, an action to foreclose a mortgage. Judd had given a mortgage upon his property at Fox Lake, Wisconsin, to the

[1] 13 Wisconsin Rep., 343, 349.

La Crosse and Milwaukee Railroad Company in return for a promise that the railroad would be built through the village and the station so located as to increase the value of the rest of his property. As often happened in those boom times, the railroad went somewhere else, but Mr. Judd had been called upon to pay the mortgage or lose his property. The legislature of Wisconsin had enacted a law requiring the trial by a jury of all actions to foreclose mortgages in which the defense was that the mortgage had been paid or that no consideration in money had been given to the maker. The law was intended to cover cases in which the mortgagees had been swindled. The jury had decided this case in favor of the defendant, and an appeal had been taken which presented this question: Can an action to foreclose a mortgage, which is an action in equity, be tried by a jury under a statute which so provides? The decision of the Supreme Court of Wisconsin in this case had hinged upon the meaning of the clause in the State constitution, which provided that "the judicial power of this State, both as to matters of law and equity, shall be vested in a supreme court, circuit courts, courts of probate and justices of the peace." Judge Paine said:

In order to determine the meaning of the phrase "judicial power as to matters of law and equity," it is only necessary to recur to the system of jurisprudence established in this country and derived from England, in which the courts had certain well-defined powers in those two classes of actions. In actions at law they had the power of determining questions of law, and were required to submit questions of fact to a jury. When the constitution, therefore, vests in certain courts judicial power in matters at law, this would be construed as vesting such power as the courts, under the English and American systems of jurisprudence, had always exercised in that class of actions. It would not import that they were to decide questions of fact, because such was not the judicial power in such actions. . . .

Under the old equity system, the chancellor might at any time refer questions of fact to a jury, but it was merely to inform his conscience. He might, if he saw fit, disregard their verdict, and take it upon himself to dispose of the questions of fact absolutely, as he could have done in the first instance.

The judicial Power shall extend to all Cases . . . arising under this Constitution, [and] the Laws of the United States. A case under the Constitution of the United States arises when a State makes a law which the Constitution forbids. In the case of *Dartmouth College vs. Woodward,* the story of which already has been told, one question before the Supreme Court was whether a case under the Constitution of the United States arose when the State of New Hampshire passed a law which impaired the obligation of a contract contained in the charter granted by King George the Third to Dartmouth College. Chief Justice Marshall said:

The only question now to be considered is, do the acts to which the verdict refers violate the Constitution of the United States? . . . On more than one occasion, this Court . . . has declared that, in no doubtful case, would it pronounce a legislative act to be contrary to the Constitution. But the American people have said, in the Constitution of the United States, that "no State shall pass any bill of attainder, *ex post facto* law, or law impairing the obligation of contracts." In the same instrument they have also said "that the judicial power shall extend to all cases in law and equity arising under the Constitution." On the judges of this Court, then, is imposed the high and solemn duty of protecting, even from legislative violation, those contracts which the Constitution of our country has placed beyond legislative control; and, however irksome the task may be, this is a duty from which we dare not shrink.

A case under the Constitution and laws of the United States arises when a State makes a law which is inconsistent with and repugnant to a valid law of the United States. Justice Paterson of the Supreme Court, who as a member of the Constitutional Convention had been one of the most ardent supporters of the rights of the smaller States, presided as circuit judge at the trial, in 1795, of the great case of *Van Horne vs. Dorrance*,[1] the report of which begins with these quaint words: "This was a cause of great expectation involving several important questions of constitutional law." One of the questions in that case was whether the words which extend the judicial power to "a case arising under the Constitution and laws of the United States" mean that the Supreme Court can set aside a State law which is inconsistent with a national law. Justice Paterson said in his charge to the jury:

I take it to be a clear position; that if a legislative act oppugns a constitutional principle, the former must give way, and be rejected on the score of repugnance. I hold it to be a position equally clear and sound, that, in such case, it will be the duty of the court to adhere to the Constitution and to declare the act null and void. The Constitution is the basis of legislative authority; it lies at the foundation of all law, and is a rule and commission by which both legislators and judges are to proceed.

In the case of *McCulloch vs. Maryland*,[2] the following facts appeared. In April, 1816, Congress had incor-

[1] 2 Dallas' Rep., 304.   [2] 4 Wheaton's Rep., 316, 425, 426.

toms laws, a State law imposing a tax upon importers.

The Supreme Court decided in *Dobbins vs. Erie County*,[1] that a State could not compel an official of the United States to pay a tax upon his salary, because the local taxing law conflicted with the national statute which entitled him to receive for his services a specified compensation.

In the *Passenger Cases*,[2] the Supreme Court set aside, because of inconsistency with the laws of the nation, for the regulation of commerce, a State law which compelled captains of vessels to pay a head-money tax on the immigrants they brought to this country.

In the case of *Barron vs. Burnside*,[3] the Supreme Court declared unconstitutional and void an Iowa law which required all foreign corporations, before doing business in that State, to stipulate not to remove to the Federal courts certain kinds of actions to which they might be made parties. The justices said this statute was inconsistent with the laws of the United States giving to the national courts jurisdiction in those actions.

A case under the Constitution also arises whenever Congress makes a law which it has no constitutional power to enact.

John Marshall, Chief Justice of the United States from 1801 to 1835, explained in his opinion in the case of *Marbury vs. Madison*,[4] just how the courts of the United States must deal with an unconstitutional national law. He said:

If an act of the legislature [Congress] repugnant to the Constitution, is void, does it, notwithstanding its invalidity

---

[1] 16 Peters' Rep., 435.
[2] 121 U. S. Rep., 186.
[3] 7 Howard's Rep., 283.
[4] 1 Cranch's Rep., 137.

bind the courts, and oblige them to give it effect? Or, in other words, though it be not law, does it constitute a rule as operative as if it was a law? This would be to overthrow in fact what was established in theory; and it would seem, at first view, an absurdity too gross to be insisted on. It shall, however, receive a more attentive consideration. It is emphatically the province and duty of the judicial department to say what the law is. Those who apply the rule to particular cases, must of necessity expound and interpret that rule. If two laws conflict with each other, the courts must decide on the operation of each. So if a law be in opposition to the Constitution; if both the law and the Constitution apply to a particular case, so that the Court must either decide that case conformably to the law, disregarding the Constitution, or conformably to the Constitution, disregarding the law, the Court must decide which of these conflicting rules governs the case. This is of the very essence of judicial duty.

. . . . curse . . . . McCulloch v. Maryland . . . .

. . . .

. . . . . . in the case of Dred Scott v. Sanford. The . . . . in passing the Missouri . . . . Act of 1820, which had limited the spread

. . . .

of slavery, Congress had, "under pretext of executing its powers," passed a law "for the accomplishment of objects not entrusted to the government." Chief Justice Taney, speaking for himself and five others of the nine justices, decided that the Missouri Compromise Act was unconstitutional because Congress had had no power to enact a law which took away the master's right of property in a slave, that had been taken into free territory. He said:

The powers of the government [of the United States], and the rights of the citizen under it, are positive and practical regulations plainly written down. The people of the United States have delegated to it certain enumerated powers, and forbidden it to exercise others. It has no power over the person or property of a citizen but what the citizens of the United States have granted. And no laws or usages of other nations, or reasoning of statesmen or jurists upon the relations of master and slave, can enlarge the powers of the government, or take from the citizens the rights they have reserved. And if the Constitution recognizes the right of property of the master in a slave and makes no distinction between that description of property and other property owned by a citizen, no tribunal, acting under the authority of the United States, whether it be legislative, executive, or judicial, has a right to draw such a distinction, or deny to it the benefit of the provisions and guarantees which have been provided for the protection of private property against the encroachments of the government. . . . Upon these considerations, it is the opinion of the Court that the act of Congress [Missouri Compromise], which prohibited a citizen from owning and holding property of this kind in the territory of the United States north of the line therein mentioned, is not warranted by the Constitution, and is therefore void; and that neither Dred Scott himself, nor any of his family were

made free by being carried into this territory; even if they
had been carried there by the owner, with the intention of
becoming a permanent resident.

From the beginning until the end of the Civil War,
the People of the United States dealt with governmental
problems as well as they could, but without much
regard to constitutional limitations. Their chief task
then was to keep the Union intact in one way or another
and settle questions of regularity afterward. The press-
ing problem was to equip, feed, and pay the Union
army. In 1863, when hard money was not to be had,
Congress solved this problem by making a law under
which paper dollars were printed, issued by the million,
and made a legal tender for the payment of debts.
The Constitution nowhere says that Congress may make
laws for the issuance of paper money, and many members of the Constitutional Convention had said that the
Constitution did not confer any such power. Nevertheless, our people accepted the Civil War "shin-
plaster" currency and were glad to get it, because paper
money was better than none. In December, 1869,
however, the power of Congress to pass the paper-
money law was challenged in the case of *Hepburn vs.
Griswold*,[1] and the justices of the Supreme Court declared the act unconstitutional. The Supreme Court
had not then fully recovered the popularity it had lost
by its decision in the Dred Scott case. Its power to
annul and set aside a law of Congress for unconstitutionality, which had been exercised only in the case of
Marbury vs. Madison,[2] in which the decision had not
been enforced, and in the *Dred Scott* case,[3] in which the

---

[1] 8 Wallace's Rep., 603.   [2] *Vide supra.*
[3] *Vide supra.*

decision was regarded as indefensibly wrong, was not generally conceded. But Chief Justice Taney was dead, and his successor, Salmon P. Chase of Ohio, was a tried and trusted supporter of the Union. Hence, this decision, setting aside another national law, was received respectfully. Chief Justice Chase said:

It is not necessary . . . in order to prove the existence of a particular authority to show a particular and express grant. The design of the Constitution was to establish a government competent to the direction and administration of the affairs of a great nation. To this end it was needful only to make express grants of general powers, coupled with a further grant of such incidental and auxiliary powers as might be required for the exercise of the powers expressly granted. These powers are necessarily extensive. It has been found, indeed, in the practical administration of the government, that a very large part, if not the largest part, of its functions have been performed in the exercise of powers thus implied. . . . All powers of this nature are included under the description of "power to make all laws necessary and proper for carrying into execution the powers expressly granted to Congress or vested by the Constitution in the government or in any of its departments or officers."

It must be taken . . . as finally settled, so far as judicial decisions can settle anything, that the words "all laws necessary and proper for carrying into execution" powers expressly granted or vested, have, in the Constitution, a sense equivalent to that of the words, laws, not absolutely necessary indeed, but appropriate, plainly adapted to constitutional and legitimate ends; laws not prohibited, but consistent with the letter and spirit of the Constitution; laws really calculated to effect objects intrusted to the government.

We are obliged to conclude that an act making mere promises to pay dollars a legal tender in payment of debts

... a year later, the Supreme ... bench, changed ... and decided that ... constitutional. The ... which ... was void were now ...

... to the government ... utterly every ... and for the ... such a right, we hold ... eighth section of the ... immunities referred to it ... enumerated, or defined ... and specification were ... discretion of Congress ... they be not prohibited. ... carrying into execution the ... and all other powers ... States, or in any ...

... which has been ad- ... the legal tender ... the spirit of the ... were what we have ... appropriate means for legitimate ends. ... the authority vested in

In 1894, the Supreme Court again set aside a national law. Congress had enacted a law imposing taxes upon incomes. It was then generally supposed that such taxes were included among the "excises," authorized by the Art. I., Sec. 8., of the Constitution. Indeed, the Supreme Court had so ruled in the case of *Springer vs. United States.*[1] The constitutionality of income taxation, however, was challenged in the case of *Pollock vs. Farmers Loan and Trust Co.*,[2] upon the ground that a tax upon incomes derived in part from rents of real estate, not apportioned to the States according to population, was such a direct tax, as, under the provisions of the ninth section of the first article of the Constitution, Congress was forbidden to enact. Chief Justice Fuller, after reviewing the history of the clause forbidding direct taxes not apportioned to the States in proportion to population, said:

Thus was accomplished one of the great compromises of the Constitution, resting on the doctrine that the right of representation ought to be conceded to every community on which a tax is to be imposed, but crystallizing it in such form as to allay jealousies in respect of the future balance of power; to reconcile conflicting views in respect of the enumeration of slaves; and to remove the objection that, in adjusting a system of representation between the States, regard should be had to their relative wealth, since those who were to be most heavily taxed ought to have a proportionate influence in the government. The compromise, in embracing the power of direct taxation, consisted not simply in including part of the slaves in the enumeration of population, but in providing that as between State and State, such taxation should be proportioned to representation. . . .

[1] 102 U. S. Rep., 396.   [2] 157 U. S. Rep., 429.

is apparent: 1. That the distinction between direct and indirect taxation was well understood by the framers of the Constitution and those who adopted it. 2. That under the State systems of taxation all taxes on real estate or personal property or the rents or income thereof were regarded as direct taxes. 3. That the rules of apportionment and of uniformity were adopted in view of that distinction and those systems. . . . 5. That the original expectation was that the power of direct taxation would be exercised only in extraordinary exigencies, and . . . down to August 15, 1894 (the date of the income tax law under consideration), this expectation has been realized. The act of that date was passed in a time of profound peace, and if we assume that no special exigency called for unusual legislation, and that resort to this mode of taxation is to become an ordinary and usual means of supply, that fact furnishes an additional reason for circumspection and care in disposing of the case.

The requirement of the Constitution is that no direct tax shall be laid otherwise than by apportionment—the prohibition is not against direct taxes . . .

. . . Supreme Court, in order to . . . more or less . . . regulations when it sets aside a national . . . inconsistency with the Constitution. In the . . . of a majority of the justices in the *Employers'*

Liability Case,[1] handed down in 1907, for example, Chief Justice White said that the court was in duty bound to annul the Employers' Liability Act of 1906, because *it regulated the persons who engage in interstate commerce*, and did not regulate the business of interstate commerce.   He said:

The act . . . being addressed to all common carriers engaged in interstate commerce, and imposing a liability upon them in favor of any of their employes, without qualification or restriction as to the business in which the carriers or their employes may be engaged at the time of the injury, of necessity includes subjects wholly outside of the power of Congress to regulate commerce. . . .

Concluding, as we do, that the statute, whilst it embraces subjects within the authority of Congress to regulate commerce, also includes subjects not within its constitutional power, and that the two are so interblended in the statute that they are incapable of separation, we are of opinion that the courts below rightly held the statute to be repugnant to the Constitution.

Our courts construe and interpret the laws whenever there is any doubt about either meaning or application. Therefore it is needful to know exactly what is meant by construction and interpretation of law; also by what right the justices of the Supreme Court construe and interpret the laws.

These points were discussed by Chief Justice Jones of the Supreme Court of Washington Territory in the case of *Bloomer vs. Todd*,[2] in which the question was whether a law of the legislature of Washington Territory, enacted in 1888, giving women the right to vote,

was consistent with the act of Congress by which the
Territory had been established. Section 1859 of the
Revised Statutes of the United States concerning
the government of Territories gave the suffrage at the
first territorial election to "male citizens," and section
1860 gave the legislature power to regulate future elections at its pleasure, subject only to the limitation that
the suffrage must be confined to "citizens," omitting
the word "male." It was argued that this omission
gave the territorial legislature power to confer the
suffrage upon women. The Territorial Supreme Court
ruled against woman suffrage on the ground that this
omission did not signify anything of the kind, and,
further, that in the original act establishing the Territory, the word "citizen" in the proviso stands opposed
to the words "white male inhabitants" in the enacting
clause. That is to say the court took it upon itself to
decide what the laws of the nation for the establishment
and government of the Territory *meant.* Chief Justice
Jones said:

Interpretation differs from construction in this: that it is
used for the purpose of ascertaining the true sense of any
form of words; while construction involves the drawing of
conclusions regarding subjects that are not always included
in the direct expression. In all constitutional governments
the powers of government are divided or allotted to different
officers or departments, and each of these has by constitutional limitation certain powers, generally independent of
each other, and usually involving the duty of interpretation,
and often of construction, upon each of the several departments or officers who have the administration of the
government in charge. Constitutions have not as a rule
provided for a tribunal whose specific duty is that of solving
difficult questions which may arise under it prior to the

necessary solution resulting from litigation. . . . As a rule the construction and interpretation of the laws arise after enactment. To illustrate further, the administration of public justice, in this territory, is conferred upon the courts, and the courts perform that duty by first ascertaining the facts in any case, and giving effect to their conclusion of fact by applying the laws to the facts ascertained. In doing so, a construction or interpretation of law is necessary. The right and power of the courts to do this is so universal that their conduct in that regard is unquestioned.

The judicial Power shall extend to all Cases . . . arising under . . . Treaties made . . . under their [United States] Authority. A case under a treaty, sifted down, is a case under a contract made by one nation, acting for its citizens, with one or more other nations, acting for their citizens. Those citizens may have rights like rights under a contract which may be referred to the courts. Under this provision of the Constitution, such disputes may be referred to the courts of the United States whenever they arise in the United States under any treaty giving rights to persons, apart from the rights reserved to the nations which make it.

There is a broad distinction between a political case arising under a treaty, with which the Federal courts cannot deal, and a judicial case arising under a treaty, to which the judicial power of the United States extends. For example, in 1829, the Supreme Court refused to decide the case of *Foster vs. Neilson*,[1] in which the petitioners asked for a judicial decree to confirm them in the possession, under an old Spanish land grant, of certain lands in West Florida, now Louisiana. An article in the treaty of 1819 with Spain, ceding East and West Florida to the United States, had stipulated

[1] 2 Peters' Rep., 253, 314.

that all grants of land made by the King of Spain before January 24, 1818, should be ratified and confirmed to the persons in possession. Chief Justice Marshall, referring to the provisions of the treaty of 1803, by which France had ceded Louisiana to the United States, explained that the confirming of such a land grant under the provisions of a treaty was an act which only the legislature could perform. He said:

Our Constitution declares a treaty to be the law of the land. It is, consequently, to be regarded in courts of justice as equivalent to an act of the legislature, whenever it operates of itself without the aid of any legislative provision. But when the terms of the stipulation import a contract, when either of the parties engages to perform a particular act, the treaty addresses itself to the political, not the judicial department; and the legislature must execute the contract before it can become a rule for the court.

In the *Head Money Cases*,[1] the Supreme Court passed upon questions in which the Cunard Line and a firm of steamship agents doing business in New York City were interested. The claim set up was that the national law imposing a tax upon immigrants of fifty cents a head, to be paid by the company which brought them, was inconsistent with the provisions of our treaties with the nations from which the immigrants came. Justice Miller said:

A treaty is primarily a compact between independent nations. It depends for the enforcement of its provisions on the interest and the honor of the governments which are parties to it. If these fail, its infraction becomes the subject of international negotiations and reclamations, so far as the injured party chooses to seek redress, which may in

[1] 112 U. S. Rep., 580.

the end be enforced by actual war. It is obvious that with all this the judicial courts have nothing to do and can give no redress. But a treaty may also contain provisions which confer certain rights upon the citizens or subjects of one of the nations residing in the territorial limits of the other, which partake of the nature of municipal law, and which are capable of enforcement as between private parties in the courts of the country. An illustration of this character is found in treaties, which regulate the mutual rights of citizens and subjects of the contracting nations in regard to rights of property by descent or inheritance, when the individuals concerned are aliens. The Constitution of the United States places such provisions as these in the same category as other laws of Congress by its declaration that "this Constitution and the laws made in pursuance thereof, and all treaties made or which shall be made under authority of the United States, shall be the supreme law of the land." A treaty then, is the law of the land as an act of Congress is, whenever its provisions prescribe a rule by which the rights of the private citizen or subject may be determined. And when such rights are of a nature to be enforced in a court of justice, that court resorts to the treaty for a rule of decision for the case before it as it would to a statute.

The judicial Power shall extend to all Cases . . . affecting Ambassadors, other public Ministers and Consuls. Chief Justice Marshall defined a case "affecting ambassadors, other public ministers, and consuls" in his opinion in the case of *Osborn vs. Bank of United States.*[1] He said:

If a suit be brought against a foreign minister, the Supreme Court alone has original jurisdiction, and this is shown on the record. But suppose a suit to be brought which affects the interest of a foreign minister, or by which

[1] 9 Wheaton's Rep., 251.

country or government which the consul represents. This is the light in which foreign ministers are considered by the law of nations, and our Constitution and law seem to put consuls on the same footing in this respect. If the privilege or exemption was merely personal, it can hardly be supposed that it would have been thought a matter sufficiently important to require a special provision in the Constitution and laws of the United States. Higher considerations of public policy doubtless led to the provision. It was deemed fit and proper that the courts of the government, with which rested the regulation of all foreign intercourse, should have cognizance of suits against the representatives of such foreign governments.

The judicial Power shall extend . . . to all Cases of admiralty and maritime Jurisdiction. The law of the seas is called admiralty law because at one time all English marine cases were tried in the Lord High Admiral's Court. The law, however, dates back to those early times when men first felt the need of tribunals to settle disputes over commercial transactions. The courts which decided cases arising on land had no power over cases arising on the high seas. The process of the land court which seized the property or body of a debtor to compel him to satisfy a judgment, was ineffective against strangers who came across the seas to barter their wares for local products. Therefore, under the law of the seas, the ships themselves were made responsible for the debts of those who owned or sailed them. Such was the origin of those actions *in rem* (against a thing) which are puzzling to those not familiar with maritime law.

Justice Bradley, in the decision of the case of *New England Insurance Co. vs. Dunham,*[1] explained the

[1] 11 Wallace's Rep., 1, 23.

... generally entrusted to the ... monarchs of Europe for the ... administration of ... courts in matters touching ... law itself ... a level ... any particular country, but ... In all countries bordering on the Atlantic the marine courts, ... admiralty courts or otherwise, ... jurisdiction of all matters arising ... as other marine matters of ... committed on the sea, ... But in England, ... succeeded in establishing this ... jurisdiction of the admiralty was ... entirely excluded from transactions within the body of a country, such as ... of the sea, as far out as the naked ... from shore to shore, as well as ... on the land, though relating to ... But this narrow view has not ... it would be contrary to the first ... men was formed to confine them ... bordering on the Atlantic, and to the ... with it, and to deny them to the ... of the river, and the great navigable ... flowing through the western States.

... to all cases ... in Controversies ... the United States shall be a Party. In ... United States v. Texas, the Attorney ... of the United States had raised the

Supreme Court to fix the northern boundary line of the State of Texas. One defense presented by that State was that the United States had no power under the Constitution to sue a State. Justice Harlan, in the course of his opinion overruling this defense and sustaining the right of the United States to sue a State, said:

We cannot assume that the framers of the Constitution, while extending the judicial power of the United States to controversies between two or more States of the Union, and between a State of the Union and foreign States, intended to exempt a State altogether from suit by the General Government. They could not have overlooked the possibility that controversies, capable of judicial solution, might arise between the United States and some of the States, and that the permanence of the Union might be endangered if to some tribunal was not entrusted the power to determine them according to the recognized principles of law. . . . It would be difficult to suggest any reason why this court should have jurisdiction to determine questions of boundary between two or more States, but not jurisdiction of controversies of like character between the United States and a State.

The judicial Power shall extend . . . to Controversies between two or more States. In the case of *Rhode Island vs. Massachusetts,*[1] in which an old boundary line quarrel had been referred to the Supreme Court, the first question was whether an action by one State against another could be decided by the Supreme Court of the United States. Justice Baldwin said:

Those States, in their highest sovereign capacity, in the convention of the people thereof; on whom, by the Revolu-

[1] 12 Peters' Rep., 657, 720.

issuance of a judgment because he thought Congress had not passed any act which authorized the Supreme Court to proceed with such an action. Justice Wilson said that the Constitution had expressly authorized the Court to give Chisholm the remedy he sought. Justice Cushing's opinion was that the Constitution had given the Supreme Court jurisdiction under this clause because, if not submitted to a disinterested tribunal, controversies between a State and citizens of another State might cause bloodshed. Chief Justice Jay insisted that the judicial power had been extended to suits by a citizen of a State against another State in order to "establish justice," one of the chief objects stated in the Preamble to the Constitution. Justice Blair, an eminent Virginian jurist, urged that the Supreme Court had jurisdiction, saying:

It seems to me that if this Court should refuse to hold jurisdiction of a case where a State is defendant, it would renounce part of the authority conferred, and consequently part of the duty imposed on it by the Constitution; because it would be a refusal to take cognizance of a case where a State is a party.

This decision was good law because the justices had said so, but it lasted only until the advocates of State sovereignty could lay hands on it. In 1798, the States adopted the Eleventh Amendment, which effectually deprived the Federal Courts of jurisdiction in any case brought by a private citizen against a State.

Eleventh Amendment. The Judicial power of the United States shall not be construed to extend to any suit in law or equity, commenced or prosecuted against one of the United States by Citizens of another State, or by Citizens or Subjects of any Foreign State.

In the case of *Hollingsworth vs. Virginia*,[1] decided in 1798, the Supreme Court was asked by the Attorney General of the United States to decide whether the Eleventh Amendment applied to lawsuits which had already been brought. The Court delivered its unanimous opinion "that the amendment being constitutionally adopted, there could not be exercised any jurisdiction, in any case, past or future, in which a State was sued by citizens of another State, or by citizens or subjects of any foreign State."

In 1821, the Supreme Court was called upon to decide whether it had power to revise judgments of State courts in cases in which a State was a party. The question in the case of *Cohens vs. Virginia*[2] was upon the constitutionality of a Virginia law forbidding the sale of lottery tickets. Two men named Cohen had been convicted at Norfolk, Va., of selling tickets in a lottery which had been authorized by an act of Congress. They took the case to the Supreme Court on the claim that they had been convicted under a State law, which was void because inconsistent with a law of the United States. The Supreme Court decided that the Constitution as amended did not prevent the courts of the United States from passing upon the constitutionality of a State law which had been challenged on the ground of repugnancy to a national law. Chief Justice Marshall said:

It is a part of our history, that, at the adoption of the Constitution, all the States were greatly indebted; and the apprehension that these debts might be prosecuted in the federal courts, formed a very serious objection to that instrument. Suits were instituted; and the court main-

---

tained its jurisdiction. The alarm was general; and to quiet the apprehensions that were so extensively entertained this [Eleventh] amendment was proposed in Congress and adopted by the State legislatures. That its motive was not to maintain the sovereignty of a State from the degradation supposed to attend a compulsory appearance before the tribunal of the nation, may be inferred from the terms of the amendment. It does not comprehend controversies between two or more States, or between a State and a foreign State. The jurisdiction of the Court still extends to these cases; and in these a State may still be sued. We must ascribe the amendment, then, to some other cause than the dignity of a State. There is no difficulty in finding this cause. Those who were inhibited from commencing a suit against a State, or from prosecuting one which might be commenced before the adoption of the amendment, were persons who might probably be its creditors. . . . The amendment therefore extended to suits commenced or prosecuted by individuals, but not to those brought by States.

The judicial Power shall extend to . . . Controversies . . . between Citizens of different States. During the whole of the colonial period, the provinces had done little trading with each other, partly because English law fostered a British monopoly of trade with the colonies, but mostly because the merchants of one colony could not safely extend credits to persons who lived in other colonies. By extending the judicial power to controversies between citizens of different States, the Constitution makers gave the People of the United States a chance to do business with each other on a sound basis. That basis was that, if a citizen of one State should be cheated by a citizen of another State, the aggrieved party could apply to the courts of the United States for relief.

a right under the law of the United States; and, on the facts in the case, the judge had no discretion to withhold that right.

The judicial Power shall extend . . . . to Controversies . . . between Citizens of the same State claiming Lands under Grants of different States. Before the Revolution, much territory in what is now Vermont and in the Mississippi Valley had been claimed by more than one colony. The States that succeeded these colonies had made many land grants to settlers, some of which overlapped. Many of the resulting disputes were unsettled at the time of the adoption of the Constitution. The members of the Federal Convention deemed it wise to give the Federal courts power to judge such disputes because the rights of different States were involved. For example, in the case of *Town of Pawlet vs. Clark*,[1] decided in 1815, it was shown that lands in the town of Pawlet in the western part of New Hampshire, which afterward became the State of Vermont, had been set apart by a New Hampshire grant for the support of a minister of the Church of England. The land had been held by Mr. Clark under a lease which provided for payment of the rents and profits to the Episcopal minister who preached in the local church. In 1805, however, the Vermont legislature had made a law by which it was declared that the title to all glebe lands in that State had, by the Revolution, become vested in the sovereignty of the State of Vermont, and had directed the selectmen of the different towns to bring actions to obtain possession of such lands. The case was taken to the national Supreme Court upon the question whether a grant made by the State of New Hampshire when it owned all of Vermont and a later grant of the same land by Vermont, were grants made by different States. Justice Story, in the course of this decision, said:

The Constitution intended to secure an impartial tribunal for the decision of causes arising from the grants of different States; and it was supposed that a State tribunal might not stand indifferent in a controversy, where the claims of its own sovereign were in conflict with those of another sovereign. It had no reference whatever to the antecedent situation of the territory, whether included in one sovereignty or another. It simply regarded the fact, whether grants arose under the same or under different States. Now it is very clear that, although the territory of Vermont was once a part of New Hampshire, yet the State of Vermont, in its sovereign capacity, is not, and never was the same as the State of New Hampshire. The grant of the plaintiffs emanated purely and exclusively from the sovereignty of Vermont; that of the defendants purely and exclusively from the sovereignty of New Hampshire. . . . The case is, therefore, equally within the letter and the spirit of the clause of the Constitution.

The judicial Power shall extend to . . . Controversies . . . between a State, or the Citizens thereof, and foreign States, Citizens or Subjects. In 1829, one John Twenty-man brought an action in the United States Court at New York against Daniel and Joseph Jackson in which, as a basis for obtaining relief in a Federal tribunal, he set forth the fact that he was a British subject. Unluckily he failed to claim that the Jacksons were citizens of the United States. The Circuit Court sustained the appeal of the defendants on the ground that Twenty-man had not shown, as required by the Constitution and by the Judiciary Act, which carries the judicial power into effect, that this was a controversy between a citizen of a State and a subject of a foreign state. The decision[1] says:

The court were of opinion that the 11th section of the Judiciary Act must be construed in connection with and in conformity to the Constitution of the United States. That, by the latter, the judicial power was not extended to private suits, in which an alien is a party, unless a citizen be an adverse party. It was indispensable, therefore, to aver the citizenship of the defendants, in order to show on the record the jurisdiction of the court. The omission to do so was fatal.

Art. III., Sec. 2 (continued). In all Cases affecting Ambassadors, other public Ministers and Consuls, and those in which a State shall be a Party, the supreme Court shall have original Jurisdiction. In all the other Cases before mentioned, the supreme Court shall have appellate Jurisdiction, both as to Law and Fact, with such Exceptions, and under such Regulations as the Congress shall make.

Certain persons and parties can, if they choose, bring lawsuits in the Supreme Court without first being heard in an inferior court. All other cases must be heard in some other court before being considered by the Supreme Court of the United States. This is the difference between "original jurisdiction" and "appellate jurisdiction" in the Federal courts.

"Original jurisdiction" does not mean "exclusive" jurisdiction. Congress though it cannot prevent suits

[1] *Jackson vs. Twentyman*, 2 Peters' Rep., 136.

affecting ambassadors, other public ministers, and consuls from being brought in the first instance in the Supreme Court, may authorize the hearing of such suits in the lower courts. The case of *Gittings vs. Crawford*, tried in the Federal Circuit Court at Baltimore, in 1838, was a suit against a British consul upon a promissory note. The action had been brought in the Federal District Court and the appeal to the Circuit Court taken by the British consul was based upon the contention that the Constitution did not give Congress power to authorize the trial in a Federal District Court of a case against a foreign consul. Chief Justice Taney, sitting as a circuit judge, explained what original jurisdiction is, saying:

> ...that the grant of original jurisdiction in ... the Supreme Court, means *exclusive* original ... and that it is not in the power of Congress to ... original jurisdiction, in the cases there mentioned, ... other court ... It would hardly have been ... tion of the statesmen who framed our Constitution. ... that one of our citizens who had a petty claim of ... five dollars against another citizen, who had ... some foreign government with the consular ... be compelled to go into the Supreme Court to ... summoned in order to enable him to recover it. ... no reason, either of policy or convenience, ... such a provision in the Constitution; and ... probability, impute such a design to ... men who, with so much wisdom and foresight ... the Constitution of the United States.

"Appellate jurisdiction" is exercised when the record of a decision of a lower court is reviewed in a higher tribunal. "It is the essential criterion of appellate jurisdiction," said Chief Justice Marshall in his opinion in the case of *Marbury vs. Madison*,[1] "that it revises and corrects the proceedings in a cause already instituted, and does not create that cause."

In *Cohens vs. Virginia*,[2] Chief Justice Marshall said:

The Constitution gives the Supreme Court original jurisdiction in certain enumerated cases, and gives it appellate jurisdiction in all others. Among those in which jurisdiction must be exercised in the appellate form, are cases arising under the Constitution and laws of the United States. . . . If a State be a party, the jurisdiction of this court is original; if a case arise under a constitution or a law, the jurisdiction is appellate. But a case to which a State is a party, may arise under the Constitution or a law of the United States. What rule is applicable to such a case? What, then, becomes the duty of the court? Certainly, we think, so to construe the Constitution as to give effect to both provisions, so far as it is possible to reconcile them, and not to permit their seeming repugnancy to destroy each other. . . . In one description of cases, the jurisdiction of the court is founded entirely on the character of the parties; and the nature of the controversy is not contemplated by the Constitution. The character of the parties is everything, the nature of the case nothing. In the other description of cases the jurisdiction is founded entirely on the character of the case, and the parties are not contemplated by the Constitution. In these the nature of the case is everything, the character of the parties nothing. When, then, the Constitution declares the jurisdiction, in cases where a State shall be a party, to be original, and in all cases arising under the Constitution or a law, to be appellate — the conclusion seems irresistible, that its framers de-

[1] 1 Cranch's Rep., 137.   [2] 6 Wheaton's Rep., 264, 392.

CHAPTER XXII

CRIMINAL PROCEDURE IN THE FEDERAL COURTS

Art. III., Sec. 2 (continued). **The Trial of all Crimes, except in Cases of Impeachment, shall be by Jury; and such Trial shall be held in the State where the said Crimes shall have been committed; but when not committed within any State, the Trial shall be at such Place or Places as the Congress may by Law have directed.**

Fifth Amendment (Part of). **No person shall be held to answer for a capital, or otherwise infamous crime, unless on a presentment or indictment of a Grand Jury, except in cases arising in the land or naval forces, or in the Militia, when in actual service in time of War or public danger;—**

Sixth Amendment (Part of). **In all criminal prosecutions, the accused shall enjoy the right to a speedy and public trial, by an impartial jury of the State and district wherein the crime shall have been committed, which district shall have been previously ascertained by law.**

The Trial of all Crimes, except in Cases of Impeachment, shall be by Jury. Justice Brewer, in the case of *Schick vs. The United States,*[1] which involved the constitutionality of laws regulating the sale of oleomargarine, defined the word "crimes" as follows:

[1] 195 U. S. Rep., 65, 68.

jurors, who have been specially assembled to decide what persons accused of crimes are to be tried by the courts. The grand jury holds the supreme, irresponsible power of the people for this purpose only. No person can be convicted legally in a court of the United States of a capital or otherwise infamous crime unless brought to trial upon such a presentment or indictment, even if he should plead guilty to a complaint in open court. In the case of *Ex Parte McClusky*,[1] the defendant had pleaded guilty in the Federal court of Arkansas to a complaint charging him with having stolen property worth more than twenty-five dollars, and was sent to the penitentiary. Then he was sorry he had confessed and asked the Federal Circuit Court for his release upon the ground that no indictment ever had been found against him. The court released him. Circuit Judge Parker said:

A party cannot waive a constitutional right when its effect is to give a court jurisdiction. . . . The fifth amendment to the Constitution, that no person shall be held to answer for a capital or otherwise infamous crime unless on a presentment or indictment of a grand jury, provides for a requisite to jurisdiction. . . . If the crime is of such a nature that an indictment to warrant a prosecution of the crime is required by the law, the court has no jurisdiction to try without such an indictment. Can a party consent to jurisdiction? Can he, by an agreement with the government, surrender his liberty for a stipulated time? Has any person the right to surrender his liberty in violation of a fundamental right, secured to him for the protection of the liberty of such person by the fifth amendment to the Constitution of the United States? No man and no power has a right to take away another person's

[1] 40 Federal Reporter, 71.

has had a reasonable time to prepare for the trial. Nor does a speedy trial mean a trial immediately upon the presentation of the indictment or the arrest upon it. It simply means that the trial shall take place as soon as possible after the indictment is found, without depriving the prosecution of a reasonable time for preparation.

A "public trial" is one at which all persons who have a proper interest in the matter at issue may be present. "By this is not meant," says Judge Cooley in his *Constitutional Limitations*,[1] "that every person who sees fit shall in all cases be permitted to attend criminal trials; because there are many cases where, from the character of·the charge and the nature of the evidence by which it is to be supported, the motives to attend the trial on the part of portions of the community would be of the worst character, and where a regard to public morals and public decency would require that at least the young be excluded from hearing and witnessing the evidences of human depravity which the trial must necessarily bring to light. The requirement of the public trial is for the benefit of the accused; that the public may see he is fairly dealt with and not unjustly

Our Constitution makes it impossible to drag persons accused of national crimes from one end of the country to the other for their trials.

In the case of *In re Rosdeitscher*,[1] the defendant had been arrested in Virginia upon a warrant which charged him with having passed a counterfeit twenty-dollar United States bank bill at Chester, Pennsylvania. The warrant of arrest had been issued by a commissioner of the United States Circuit Court of Virginia instead of by the United States court of Pennsylvania. Rosdeitscher had petitioned for release from arrest on the ground that an officer of the Federal court in Virginia had had no right to issue the warrant for his arrest for a crime

[1] 170 U. S. Rep., 343.   [2] 33 Federal Reporter, 657.

alleged to have been committed in Pennsylvania. District Judge Hughes ordered that he be discharged from custody for the following reasons:

My reasons for discharging the prisoner are founded on elementary principles. An indictment cannot be found in one State of this Union for an offense committed in another. This is forbidden by clause 3 of Section 2 of Article 3 of the national Constitution. . . . As there can be no original indictment for such a crime here, so there can be no original complaint against him here.

In the case of *Callan vs. Wilson*,[1] the question before the Court was whether the District of Columbia was a "State and district" which had been "ascertained by law" in accordance with the Sixth Amendment. A number of musicians who had been suspended from membership in Washington, D. C., Musical Assembly No. 4308, Knights of Labor, had continued to play at hotel dinners and public dances. The Knights of Labor had then boycotted the employers of the non-union musicians; and the boycotters had been prosecuted, found guilty, and fined in the United States court of the District of Columbia. They had appealed to the Supreme Court on the ground that the District of Columbia where they had been tried was not a "State and district" which had been "previously ascertained by law." Justice Harlan ruling upon this point said:

And as the guarantee of a trial by jury, . . . implied a trial in that mode and according to the settled rules of the common law, the enumeration, in the Sixth Amendment, of the rights of the accused in criminal prosecutions, is to be taken as a declaration of what those rules were, and is to be

[1] 127 U. S. Rep., 540.

referred to the anxiety of the people of the States to have in the supreme law of the land, and so far as the agencies of the General Government were concerned, a full and distinct recognition of those rules, as involving the fundamental rights of life, liberty, and property. This recognition was demanded and secured for the benefit of all the people of the United States, as well those permanently or temporarily residing in the District of Columbia, as those residing or being in the several States. There is nothing in the history of the Constitution or of the original amendments to justify the assertion that the people of this District may be lawfully deprived of the benefit of any of the constitutional guarantees of life, liberty, and property—especially of the privilege of trial by jury in criminal cases.

Persons who commit crimes against the laws of the United States cannot escape the consequences by running off to another State and district. The procedure in such cases is to obtain an indictment against the wrongdoer in the State and district in which the crime was committed. This indictment is sent to the State and district where the criminal has taken refuge, and the Federal Courts there order his arrest and removal to the place where the crime was committed. This puts the criminal in the custody of the Federal court which has power to punish him.

Art. III., Sec. 3. **Treason against the United States, shall consist only in levying War against them, or in adhering to their Enemies, giving them Aid and Comfort. No Person shall be convicted of Treason unless on the Testimony of two Witnesses to the same overt Act, or on Confession in open Court.**

Treason against the United States, the only crime defined in our Constitution, covers only the acts specified in this section. It does not include words spoken or plans made, which in other countries have been and are construed to be treasonable. Our people, even in the earliest colonizing era, never would have permitted judges to construe the acts or conduct of accused persons as being treason. An extreme case of such constructive treason, which happened in England in the reign of Edward the Fourth, was that of a gentleman, whose favorite deer had been killed by the king while hunting, and who thereupon had wished the buck, horns and all, in the king's belly; and he was executed for it.

Treason against the United States shall consist only in levying War against them. The Supreme Court explained the phrase "levying war against the United States" in the case of *Ex Parte Bollman; Ex Parte Swartwout.*[1] Dr. Bollman and Mr. Swartwout had been arrested under an order of the Federal court of the District of Columbia "to take their trial for treason against the United States by levying war against them." The prisoners had brought their case before the Supreme Court upon a petition for release upon the ground that no evidence of any treason had been presented to the court which had ordered their arrest. The evidence presented against them consisted of a deposition made by General Eaton about conversations with Colonel Burr concerning a number of projects the latter had in mind. There also was an affidavit of General Wilkinson containing the substance of a letter signed by Burr, relating to a military enterprise, which, if against Mexico, would have been a high misdemeanor; if against the United States and involving the employment of an assemblage of men, would have amounted to levying war against

[1] 4 Cranch's Rep., 75.

26

d States. The letter said: "Burr's plan of
tion is to move rapidly down from the Falls on
'5th of November with the first 500 or 1000 men in
boats now constructing for that purpose, to be at
Nez between the 5th and 15th of December, there
meet Wilkinson; then to determine whether it will
expedient, in the first instance, to seize on, or pass
Baton Rouge. The people of the country to which
we are going are prepared to receive us. Their agents,
now with Burr, say that if we will protect their religion,
and will not subject them to a foreign power, in three
weeks all will be settled." The words used by Swartwout were that "Colonel Burr was levying an armed
body of 7000 men." There was no evidence at all to
support a charge of treason against Bollman. It was
the unanimous opinion of the court that they could not
be tried in the District of Columbia because no crime
had been committed there. Chief Justice Marshall,
in his opinion in the decision that the prisoners should
be discharged from custody, gave the following definition of "treason by levying war":

"Treason against the United States, shall consist only in
levying war against them, or in adhering to their enemies,
giving them aid and comfort." To constitute that specific
crime for which the prisoners now before the court have been
committed, war must be actually levied against the United
States. However flagitious may be the crime of conspiring
to subvert by force the government of our country, such
conspiracy is not treason. To conspire to levy war, and
actually to levy war, are distinct offenses. The first must
be brought into open action by the assemblage of men for a
purpose treasonable in itself, or the fact of levying war cannot have been committed. . . . If war be actually
levied, that is, if a body of men be actually assembled for the

purpose of effecting by force a treasonable purpose, all those who perform any part, however minute, or however remote from the scene of action, and who are actually leagued in the general conspiracy, are to be considered as traitors. But there must be an actual assembling of men for the treasonable purpose, to constitute a levying of war.

Treason against the United States, shall consist . . . in adhering to their Enemies, giving them Aid and Comfort. Whoever tries to help the enemy, gives them aid and comfort. Justice Field said in the course of his charge to the jury in the case of *U.S. vs. Greathouse*[1]:

If, for example, a vessel fully equipped and armed in the service of the rebellion should fail in its attack upon one of our vessels and be itself captured, no assistance would in truth be rendered to the rebellion; but yet, in judgment of law, in legal intent, the aid and comfort would be given. So if a letter containing important intelligence for the insurgents be forwarded, the aid and comfort are given, though the letter be intercepted on its way. Thus Foster, in his treatise on *Crown Law* says: "And the bare sending of money or provisions, or sending intelligence to rebels or enemies, which in most cases is the most effectual aid that can be given them, will make a man a traitor, though the money or intelligence should happen to be intercepted; for the party in sending it did all he could; the treason was complete on his part, though it had not the effect he intended."

No Person shall be convicted of Treason unless on the Testimony of two Witnesses to the same overt Act, or on Confession in open Court. Chief Justice Marshall, in his charge to the jury at the trial of the case of *United States vs. Aaron Burr*,[2] commented as follows upon the requirement of two witnesses to the same overt act:

[1] 4 Sawyer's Rep., 457, 472. [2] 25 Federal Cases, 176.

of the men to the British. The jury rendered a verdict of not guilty, although Circuit Judge Duval ruled that what the Hodges had done was an overt act of treason. He said:

Hodges is accused of adhering to the enemy, and the overt act laid consists in the delivery of certain prisoners, and I am of opinion that the overt act laid in the indictment and proved by the witness is high treason against the United States. . . . When the act itself amounts to treason it involves the intention, and such was the character of this act.

The rule that no person shall be convicted of treason upon any confession not made in open court is founded upon common sense and common justice. The men of the constitutional era were familiar with English state trials in which many innocent men had been doomed to cruel and shameful death upon evidence of confessions which never had been made except in the imaginations of perjured witnesses. They did not intend to have our judicial annals disgraced by any scandals of that kind.

Art. III., Sect. 3 (continued). The Congress shall have Power to declare the Punishment of Treason, but no Attainder of Treason shall work Corruption of Blood, or Forfeiture except during the Life of the person Attainted.

Public opinion at the close of the Revolution was

which the condemned traitor was dragged to the gallows, hung up by the neck, and cut down while still alive, his entrails taken out and burned, his head cut off, and his body divided into four quarters; and by which the traitor's property of every kind was forfeited to the king, so that his innocent family suffered with him. Until 1862, the punishment of treason in this country had been death by hanging. Then, at President Lincoln's suggestion, the courts were authorized to impose either the death penalty or imprisonment at hard labor for not less than five years, a fine of not less than $10,000, and loss of capacity to hold any public office under the national government.

In the case of *Bigelow vs. Forrest*,[1] decided in 1869, the justices were asked to construe an act of Congress which authorized the seizure and confiscation of the property of those who had adhered to the Confederacy. Under this law, a tract of land in Virginia belonging to French Forrest, an officer in the Confederate navy, had been condemned and sold by order of court. Mr. Forrest died in 1866, and his son, Douglas Forrest, had brought this action to recover the land from the purchaser at the condemnation sale. The son's claim was that the forfeiture incurred by his father as a penalty for treason, did not extend beyond his lifetime, and that, upon his death, the property ought to have been passed over to his heirs. The courts of Virginia had held that the forfeiture incurred by French Forrest had ended with his life, and had given judgment in favor of the son. The persons in possession of the land had then appealed to the Supreme Court, and had again been defeated. Justice Strong, in his opinion in this case, said:

The fifth section of the Confiscation Act of July 17, 1862, enacted that it should be the duty of the President of the United States to cause the seizure of all the estate and property, moneys, stocks, credit, and effects of certain persons described in six classes, and to apply and use the same and the proceeds thereof for the support of the army. To one or more of these classes French Forrest belonged. That it was not intended that the mere act of seizure should vest the property seized in the United States is plain from the provisions of the seventh section, which enacted that to secure the condemnation and sale of any such property, after the same shall have been seized, proceedings *in rem* should be instituted in a district court, and that if it should be found to have belonged to a person engaged in rebellion, or who had given aid or comfort thereto, it should be condemned as enemy's property, and become the property of the United States, and that it might be disposed of as the court might decree. Concurrently with the passage of this act, Congress also adopted a joint resolution explanatory of it, whereby it was resolved that no punishment or proceedings under the act should be so construed as to work a forfeiture of the real estate of the offender beyond his natural life. It is a well known fact in our political history that this resolution was adopted in consequence of doubts which the President entertained respecting the power of Congress to prescribe a forfeiture of longer duration than the life of the offender. Be this as it may, the act and the resolution are to be construed together, and they admit of no doubt that all which could, under the law, become the property of the United States, or could be sold by virtue of a decree of condemnation and order of sale, was a right to the property seized, terminating with the life of the person for whose act it had been seized.

Fourteenth Amendment. Sec. 3. No person shall be a Senator or Representative in Congress, or elector of President and Vice President, or hold any office,

States of America. In 1868, an indictment for treason was filed against him in the United States Circuit Court of Virginia. The defense offered was that "prior to such insurrection or rebellion and in the year 1845, the said defendant was a member of the Congress of the United States, and as such member took an oath to support the Constitution of the United States in the usual manner and as required by law in such cases and the defendant alleges in bar of any proceedings upon said indictments or either of them, the penalties and disabilities denounced against and inflicted on him by the Third Section of the Fourteenth Article of the Constitution of the United States, forming an amendment to said Constitution." Mr. Davis' contention thus was that no penalty except disqualification for Federal office could be inflicted upon a Federal officeholder who afterward had committed acts of treason against the United States. After the case had been argued by counsel on both sides, Chief Justice Chase announced that the judges could not agree upon the question. A proclamation of general amnesty soon afterward, made any further prosecution of this case unnecessary; hence the point is still debatable. Chief Justice Chase, however, instructed the reporter of the case to record him as having been of the opinion "that the indictment should be quashed and all further proceedings barred by the effect of the Fourteenth Amendment of the Constitution of the United States."

PART VIII

The Federal Compact

CHAPTER XXIII

CONSIDERATIONS OF THE AGREEMENT OF UNION

"EVERY State constitution," said Chief Justice Jay in his opinion in *Chisholm vs. Georgia*,[1] "is a compact made by and between the citizens of a State to govern themselves in a certain manner; and the Constitution of the United States is likewise a compact, made by the people of the United States to govern themselves as to general objects in a certain manner."

The Constitution of the United States, at bottom, is a contract which the People of the United States have made with the States of the United States in order to obtain the advantages of a strong united government. By that Constitution, the People of the United States *constituted* a national Congress with power to make laws which are executed by a national President under the instructions of a national Supreme Court. By ratifying that Constitution, the States of the United States agreed that the powers of government which they had surrendered to the nation should be exercised by these three great departments of authority. The constitutional compact so made is valid and binding upon the contracting parties, the People of the United States and the States of the United States, because they have accepted the considerations or benefits which it provides.

[1] 2 Dallas' Rep., 419, 471.

payment in another State, to prove for a second time that the debtor owes the amount of the judgment. Upon proof in an action upon the judgment, that it has been legally obtained, the courts of the second State will, upon request, issue judgment upon the first judgment and award execution against the debtor, because each State is bound to give full faith and credit to the judicial proceedings of the other States. If the rule were otherwise, a debtor could, by moving across State lines whenever prosecuted, compel his creditor either to abandon the debt or carry, wherever the absconder might seek refuge, witnesses to the validity of the claim.

In the case of *Mills vs. Duryea*,[1] the question before the Supreme Court was whether the defendant in a suit brought in a Federal Court upon a judgment of a court of the State of New York had a right to a second trial upon questions which had been decided in the State court. In other words, the Supreme Court had to say whether the State court could decide finally upon all matters of fact which had been tried out before it. The Supreme Court ruled that the judgment of the State court was final, because otherwise the "full faith and credit" clause of the Constitution would not mean anything. Justice Story said:

By the act of 26th May, 1790, c. II., Congress provided for the mode of authenticating the records and judicial proceedings of the State courts, and further declared that: "the records and judicial proceedings, authenticated as aforesaid, shall have such faith and credit given to them in every court within the United States as they have by law and usage in the courts of the State from whence the said records are or shall be taken." It is argued that this act

[1] 7 Cranch's Rep., 481.

Jersey court had had no right to render this judgment. Thus the question which the United States Circuit Court had to decide first of all was whether it had power to inquire into the jurisdiction of the New Jersey court which had made the decree of condemnation. The decision was that the inquiry could be made; and the case then went on appeal to the Supreme Court, where Justice Bradley wrote the decision of the court on this point as follows:

It has been supposed that this act [prescribing the manner in which the public acts, records, and judicial proceedings of a State shall be proved and their effect], in connection with the constitutional provision which it was intended to carry out, had the effect of rendering the judgments of each State equivalent to domestic judgments in every other State, or at least of giving to them in every other State the same effect, in all respects, which they have in the State where they are rendered. . . . But where the jurisdiction of the court which rendered the judgment has been assailed, quite a different view has prevailed. Justice Story, . . . in his *Commentary on the Constitution* (Sec. 1313), . . . adds: "But this does not prevent an inquiry into the jurisdiction of the court in which the original judgment was given, to pronounce it; or the right of the State itself to exercise authority over the person or the subject matter. The Constitution did not mean to confer [upon the States] a new power or jurisdiction, but simply to regulate the effect of the acknowledged jurisdiction over the persons and things within their territory." . . . On the whole, we think it clear that the jurisdiction of the court by which a judgment is rendered in any State may be questioned in a collateral proceeding in another State, notwithstanding the provision of the fourth article of the Constitution and the law of 1790, and notwithstanding the averments contained in the record of the judgment itself.

foreign jurisdiction depended upon their conceptions of
duty and comity. Besides, it must be conceded that the
Constitution delegated no authority to the government of
the United States on the subject of marriage and divorce.
Yet, if the proposition be maintained, it would follow that
the destruction of the power of the States over the dissolution of marriage, as to their own citizens, would be brought
about by the operation of the full faith and credit clause
of the Constitution. That is to say, it would come to pass
that, although the Constitution of the United States does
not interfere with the authority of the States over marriage,
nevertheless the full faith and credit clause of that instrument destroyed the authority of the States over the marriage
relation. And as the Government of the United States has
no delegated authority on the subject, that Government
would be powerless to prevent the evil thus brought about
by the full faith and credit clause. Thus neither the States
nor the National Government would be able to exert that
authority over the marriage tie possessed by every other
civilised government. . . .

The denial of the power to enforce in another State a
decree of divorce rendered against a person who was
not subject to the jurisdiction of the State in which the
decree was rendered obviates all the contradictions and
inconveniences which are above indicated. It leaves un-
curtailed the legitimate power of all the States over a
subject peculiarly within their authority, and thus not only
enables them to maintain their public policy but also to
protect the individual rights of their citizens. . . . It
causes the full faith and credit clause of the Constitution to
operate upon decrees of divorce in the respective States
just as that clause operates upon other rights—that is, it
compels all the States to recognize and enforce a judgment
of divorce rendered in other States where both parties were
subject to the jurisdiction of the State in which the decree
was rendered, and it enables the States rendering such
decrees to take into view for the purpose of the exercise

of their authority the existence of a matrimonial domicil from which the presence of a party not physically present within the borders of a State may be constructively found to exist. . . .

Without questioning the power of the State of Connecticut to enforce within its own borders the decree of divorce which is here in issue, and without intimating a doubt as to the power of the State of New York to give to a decree of that character rendered in Connecticut, within the borders of the State of New York and as to its own citizens, such efficacy as it may be entitled to in view of the public policy of that State, we hold that the decree of the court of Connecticut rendered under the circumstances stated was not entitled to obligatory enforcement in the State of New York by virtue of the full faith and credit clause.

Art. IV., Sec. 2. The Citizens of each State shall be entitled to all Privileges and Immunities of Citizens in the several States.

"The great object to be attained [by the equal rights clause]," said Chief Justice Johns of Delaware in his opinion in the case of *Douglass vs. Stephens*, [1] "was to prevent a citizen of one State from being considered an alien in another State."

In the case of *Ward vs. Maryland*, [2] it was shown to the court that a statute of Maryland, enacted in 1870, had required all merchants residing in that State to take out trading licenses for which they had to pay from $12 up to $150 a year according to the value of their stock-in-trade. One section of this law declared that all non-residents who sold goods, wares, and merchandise in Maryland, should pay an annual license fee of three hundred dollars. A New Jersey man named

[1] 1 Del. Ch. Rep., 465. [2] 12 Wallace's Rep., 418.

Ward, who had sold harnesses by sample at Baltimore without having taken out a trading license, had been convicted and fined $200 in the State court. He had then taken the case to the Supreme Court, which decided that the Maryland law did not give to citizens of other States the same privileges in Maryland as it did to residents. Justice Clifford said:

Imposed as the exaction is upon persons not permanent residents in the State, it is not possible to deny that the tax is discriminating with any hope that the imposition could be sustained by the court. Comprehensive as the power of the States is to lay and collect taxes and excises, it is nevertheless clear, in the judgment of the court, that the power cannot be exercised to any extent in a manner forbidden by the Constitution; and inasmuch as the Constitution provides that the citizens of each State shall be entitled to all privileges and immunities of citizens in the several States, it follows that the defendant might lawfully sell or offer or expose for sale within the district described in the indictment any goods which the permanent residents of the State might sell or offer or expose for sale in that district, without being subjected to any higher tax or excise than that exacted of any of such permanent residents.

Ten years after, in 1871, the Supreme Court of Kentucky, in the case of Amy v. Smith, defined the word "citizen" as used in this section of the Constitution. A colored woman, a slave, who had lived in Pennsylvania, asserted that, as she had been a citizen of a free State, her privileges and immunities were violated by the Kentuckians who claimed her as a slave. This contention, brought before the court, raised the question, whether a slave woman, by residing in a free State, might become entitled to all the privileges and immunities of citizens of that State. The court decided that she was not a citizen of a State and therefore was not entitled to the benefits of the Constitution. The court said:

The term, citizen, is derived from the Latin word, *civis*, and in its primary sense signifies one who is vested with the freedom and privileges of a city. At an early period after the subversion of the Roman Empire, when civilization had again begun to progress, the cities in every part of Europe, either by usurpation or concession from their sovereigns, obtained extraordinary privileges, in addition to those which were common to the other subjects of their respective countries; and one who was invested with those extraordinary privileges, whether he was an inhabitant of the city or not, or whether he was born in it or not, was deemed a citizen. . . . In England, a citizen is not only entitled to all the local privileges of the city to which he belongs, but he has also the right of electing and being elected to parliament, which is itself rather an extraordinary privilege since it does not belong to every class of subjects. . . . If we go back to Rome, whence the term, citizen, has its origin, we shall find, in the illustrious period of her republic, that citizens were the highest class of subjects to whom the *jus civitatis* (right of the city) belonged, and that *jus civitatis* conferred upon those who were in possession of it, all rights and privileges, civil, political, and religious. . . . When the term came to be applied to the inhabitants of a state, it necessarily carried with it the same signification, with reference to the privileges of the state, which had been implied by it with reference to the privileges of a city, when it was applied to the inhabitants of the city; and it is in this sense, that the term, citizen, is believed to be generally, if not universally, understood in the United States. . . . No one can, . . . in the correct sense of the term, be a citizen of a state, who is not entitled, upon

munities which are, in their nature, fundamental; which belong, of right, to the citizens of all free governments; and which have, at all times, been enjoyed by the citizens of the several states which compose this Union, from the time of their becoming free, independent, and sovereign. What these fundamental principles are, it would perhaps be more tedious than difficult to enumerate. They may, however, be all comprehended under the following general heads: protection by the government; the enjoyment of life and liberty, with the right to acquire and possess property of every kind, and to pursue and obtain happiness and safety; subject nevertheless to such restraints as the government may justly prescribe for the general good of the whole. The right of a citizen of one state to pass through, or to reside

4 Washington C. C. Rep., 380.

in, any other State, for purposes of trade, agriculture, professional pursuits, or otherwise; to claim the benefit of the writ of habeas corpus; to institute and maintain actions of any kind in the courts of the State; to take, hold, and dispose of property, either real or personal; and an exemption from higher taxes or impositions than are paid by the other citizens of the State; may be mentioned as some of the particular privileges and immunities of citizens, which are clearly embraced by the general description of privileges deemed to be fundamental: to which may be added, the elective franchise, as regulated and established by the laws or constitution of the State in which it is to be exercised. These, and many others which might be mentioned, are, strictly speaking, *privileges* and *immunities*, and the enjoyment of them by the citizens of each State, in every other State, was manifestly calculated (to use the expressions of the preamble of the corresponding provision in the old articles of confederation), "the better to secure and perpetuate mutual friendship and intercourse among the people of the different States of the Union."

Art. IV., Sec. 2 (continued). A person charged in any State with Treason, Felony, or other Crime, who shall flee from Justice, and be found in another State, shall on Demand of the executive Authority of the State from which he fled, be delivered up, to be removed to the State having Jurisdiction of the Crime.

Extradition, nowadays provided for in all treaties between civilized nations, is almost an American invention. In old times, nations which happened to be on unusually friendly terms or wished to be obliging, had at intervals surrendered to one another fugitive offenders. But there had been no regular practise on the subject. Chief Justice Taney, in the case of *Ken-*

tucky vs. Dennison,[1] traced the history of extradition, saying:

It is manifest that the statesmen who framed the Constitution were fully sensible that, from the complex character of the government, it must fail unless the States mutually supported each other and the general government; and that nothing would be more likely to disturb its peace, and end in discord, than permitting an offender against the laws of a State, by passing over a mathematical line which divides it from another, to defy its process, and stand ready, under the protection of the State, to repeat the offense as soon as another opportunity offered.

Indeed, the necessity of this policy of mutual support, in bringing offenders to justice, without any exception as to the character and nature of the crime, seems to have been first recognized and acted upon by the American colonies; for we find by Winthrop's *History of Massachusetts*, vol. 2, pages 121 and 126, that as early as 1643, by "Articles of Confederation between the plantation under the government of Massachusetts, the plantation under the government of New Plymouth, the plantation under the government of Connecticut and the government of New Haven, with the plantations in common therewith," these plantations pledged themselves to each other that, "upon the escape of any prisoner or fugitive for any criminal cause, whether by breaking prison, or getting from the officer, or otherwise escaping, upon the certificate of two magistrates of the jurisdiction out of which the escape was made that he was a prisoner or such an offender at the time of the escape, the magistrate, or some of them, of the jurisdiction where, for the present, the said prisoner or fugitive abideth, shall forthwith grant such a warrant as the case will bear, for the apprehending of any such person, and the delivery of him into the hands of the officer or other person who pursueth him; and if there be help required for the safe returning

[1] 24 Howard's Rep., 66.

of any such offender, then it shall be granted unto him that craves the same, he paying the charges thereof." It will be seen that this agreement gave no discretion to the magistrate of the government where the offender was found; but he was bound to arrest and deliver, upon the production of the certificate under which he was demanded.

When the thirteen colonies formed a confederation for mutual support, a similar provision was introduced, most probably suggested by the advantages which the plantations had derived from their compact with one another. But, as the colonies had then, by the declaration of independence, become separate and independent sovereignties, against which treason might be committed, their compact is carefully worded, so as to include treason and felony —that is, political offenses—as well as crimes of an inferior grade. It is in the following words:

"If any person, guilty of or charged with treason, felony, or other high misdemeanor, in any State, shall flee from justice, and be found in any other of the United States, he shall, upon demand of the governor or executive power of the State from which he fled, be delivered up and removed to the State having jurisdiction of his offense."

And when these colonies were about to form a still closer union by the present Constitution, but yet preserving their sovereignty, they had learned from experience the necessity of this provision for the internal safety of each of them, and to promote concord and harmony among their members; and it is introduced in the Constitution substantially in the same words, but substituting the word "crime" for the words "high misdemeanor," and thereby showing the deliberate purpose to include every offense known to the law of the State from which the party charged had fled.

The treasons, felonies, or other crimes, for which a fugitive from justice may be removed from one State to another, according to *Watson on the Constitution*,[1]

[1] ii, 1234.

other New York gentlemen were called upon to defend
themselves in the Court of General Sessions of the
Peace upon a charge of treason against the State of
New York, committed by furnishing provisions to the
British ship of war *Bulwark*. The court ruled that this
was treason against the United States and not against
the State of New York, but indicated in the course
of the opinion that there was such a crime as treason
against a State. The court said:

For there can be no doubt but such a state of things
might exist, as that treason against the people of this
State might be committed. This might be, by an open and

' 115 North Carolina Rep., 811.
' 11 Johnson's N. Y. Rep., 549.

armed opposition to the laws of the State, or a combination and forcible attempt to overturn and usurp the government.

A fugitive from justice, according to the opinion of Justice Harlan in the case of *Appleyard vs. Massachusetts*,[1] is a person who commits a crime in one State and then goes to another State. In this case, a man who had been indicted on a charge of crime in Buffalo, New York, insisted that he ought not to be extradited from Massachusetts because he had left Buffalo of his own accord and without any idea that he was running away from a charge of crime. Justice Harlan said:

A person charged by indictment or by affidavit before a magistrate with the commission within a State of a crime covered by its laws, and who, after the date of the commission of such crime, leaves the State—no matter for what purpose or with what motive, nor under what belief—becomes from the time of such leaving and within the meaning of the Constitution and the laws of the United States, a fugitive from justice, and if found in another State must be delivered up by the Governor of such State to the State whose laws are alleged to have been violated, on the production of such indictment or affidavit, certified as authentic by the Governor of the State from which the accused departed.

The Supreme Court has often been appealed to in cases in which, for one reason or another, a State governor has refused to order the extradition to another State of a person charged with crime. The court always has declined to interfere. For instance, after the murder of State Senator William Goebel of Kentucky, in 1899, ex-Governor Taylor of that State took refuge

[1] 203 U. S. Rep., 222.

arms the government of the United States with this power. Indeed, such a power would place every State under the control and dominion of the general government, even in the administration of its internal concerns and reserved rights. And we think it clear, that the federal government, under the Constitution, has no power to impose on a State officer, as such, any duty whatever, and compel him to perform it; for if it possessed this power, it might overload the officer with duties which would fill up all his time, and disable him from performing his obligations to the State, and might impose on him duties of a character incompatible with the rank and dignity to which he was elevated by the State.

The Supreme Court has decided that a State can try a person extradited from another State for a crime or on a charge other than that upon which he has been extradited. This is importantly different from the rule in cases of extradition from foreign countries in which trial may be had only on the charge which the prisoner has been brought here to answer. In the case of *Lascelles vs. Georgia*,[1] a plausible rogue, named Lascelles, also known as Walter G. Beresford, had been extradited, in 1891, from New York to Georgia to answer to an indictment charging him with being a common cheat and swindler. He had been put to trial and found guilty in Georgia on a charge of "larceny [or stealing] after trust delegated." He had appealed from the judgment of conviction to the Supreme Court of Georgia, and then had taken the case to the national Supreme Court on the ground that he had been tried "for a separate and different offence from that for which he was extradited from the State of New York to the State of Georgia, without being allowed a reasonable

[1] 148 U. S. Rep., 537.

Art. IV., Sec. 2 (continued). No Person held to Service or Labour in one State, under the Laws thereof, escaping into another, shall in Consequence of any Law or Regulation therein, be discharged from such Service or Labour, but shall be delivered up upon Claim of the Party to whom such Service or Labour may be due.

This provision for the delivery to their owners of those who might escape to the free States was one of the special considerations which induced the Southern States to ratify the Constitution.

In the case of *Prigg vs. Pennsylvania* it was shown to the Supreme Court that a man named Prigg had been convicted in the courts of Pennsylvania, under a local law against kidnapping, of having abducted a negro woman from York County, Pennsylvania. The jury had found that the negress was a slave owned by one Margaret Ashmore of Maryland; that she had run away in 1832; that Prigg, acting as agent for Mrs. Ashmore, had caused the apprehension of the negress on a magistrate's warrant, and had taken her before the magistrate, who had refused to order her to be returned to her owner. Thereupon Prigg had taken it upon himself to take the woman back to Maryland. Justice Story stated in his opinion in this case that the kidnapping law, under which Prigg had been convicted, was unconstitutional because inconsistent with the fugitive slave clause of the Constitution. He said:

Historically, it is well known that the object of this clause was to secure to the citizens of the slaveholding States the complete right and title of ownership in their slaves, as property, in every State in the Union into which they might escape from the State where they were held in servitude. The full recognition of this right and title was indispensable to the security of this species of property in all the slaveholding States; and, indeed, was so vital to the preservation of their domestic interests and institutions, that it cannot be doubted that it constituted a fundamental article without the adoption of which the Union could not have been formed. Its true design was to guard against the doctrines and principles prevalent in the non-slaveholding States, by preventing them from intermeddling with, or obstructing, or abolishing the rights of the owners of slaves.

Art. IV., Sec. 3. New States may be admitted by the Congress into this Union; but no new State shall be formed or erected within the Jurisdiction of any other State; nor any State be formed by the Junction of two or more States, or Parts of States, without the Consent of the Legislatures of the States concerned as well as of the Congress.

New States may be admitted by the Congress into this Union. This part of the clause providing for the formation of new States gave Congress power to carry into effect an article in the Ordinance of 1787 establishing the Northwest Territory, which declared that not less than three nor more than five States should be formed out of that immense public domain. Under it, Congress has established all the States formed from the territorial areas of the Louisiana Purchase, ceded in 1804, Spanish Florida, ceded in 1819, and the Mexican Cession, taken over in 1848, and has admitted by a merging process in 1845 the independent State of Texas.

Many troublesome political questions disturbed the councils of Congress when the acts for the admission of States carved out of ceded territory were under consideration. The United States of 1787 included only the area between the Atlantic Ocean and the Mississippi River, bounded on the north by British America and on the south by Spanish Florida. Many of the leading public men of the era before the Civil War always insisted that the provisions of the Constitution applied only to the United States for which it had been made; that all territory subsequently acquired by purchase, conquest, or annexation was subject to the national government, but not entitled to become a part of the United States. Hence arose those fierce debates in Congress which began in 1811, when the act for the admission of Louisiana was under consideration, and were renewed from time to time until the act for the admission of Texas had been adopted.

No new State shall be formed or erected within the Jurisdiction of any other State. Notwithstanding this positive, unqualified prohibition, the State of West Virginia, admitted to the Union in 1863, was formed wholly "within the jurisdiction of" the State of Virginia. Virginia had seceded in 1861, and the majority of the members of its legislature were at Richmond doing all they could to break up the Union. On June

11, 1861, the members from the western part of the State assembled at Wheeling and chose men loyal to the Union for State officers in place of the officials who had cast in their lot with the South. "They did not assume," says Mr. Blaine in his *Twenty Years of Congress*,[1] "to represent a mere section of the State, but in the belief that the loyal people were entitled to speak for the whole State, they declared that their government was the government of Virginia." On August 20, 1861, the new State government, if it can be so called, adopted an ordinance providing "for the formation of a new State out of a portion of the territory of this State." This action was approved by popular vote in the parts of Virginia where such a vote could be taken. A State constitution was framed by a convention and ratified by a similar vote. Congress had no other authority for the act making West Virginia a State. It was a war measure adopted solely for the purpose of crushing the rebellion.

Nor [shall] any State be formed by the Junction of two or more States. The framers of the Constitution seem to have thought that, in time to come, new States might be formed by the amalgamation of existing States. Thus far in American history nothing of the kind has happened.

Nor [shall] any State be formed by the Junction of . . . Parts of States, without the Consent of the Legislatures of the States concerned as well as of the Congress. The territorial area known as the New Hampshire Grants, afterward erected into the State of Vermont, was claimed by both New York and New Hampshire at the time when the Federal Convention was in session. The territory which is now the State of Kentucky was

[1] Vol. I., p. 458.

of Virginia. South Carolina owned a pan-
p extending westward to the Mississippi
the southern part of what is now Tennessee.
rest of Tennessee belonged to North Carolina.
greater part of what afterward was divided up
een the States of Alabama and Mississippi was an
rtlying section of Georgia. Each of the proprietor
insisted upon its rights over its wilderness
. The Constitution makers, therefore, were
to insert this clause which required, in advance
ny act of Congress forming new States out of
s of States, the consent of the States owning great
rial areas.

proud old commonwealths which established the
on may look down condescendingly upon the new
as but the fact remains that the new States have
same rights as the others. This point was made
by Justice McKinley in his opinion in the case of
Pollard's Lessee vs. Hagan,[1] in which the question to
be decided was whether the United States retained any
right or title to the soil under the navigable waters
of Alabama after the admission of that State on
December 14, 1819. He said:

When Alabama was admitted into the Union, on an equal
footing with the original States, she succeeded to all the
rights of sovereignty, jurisdiction, and eminent domain
which Georgia possessed at the date of the cession, except
so far as this right was diminished by the public lands
remaining in the possession and under the control of the
United States, for the temporary purposes provided for
in the deed of cession and the legislative acts connected
with it. Nothing remained to the United States, according
to the terms of the agreement, but the public lands.

[1] 3 Howard's Rep., 212.

and Regulations respecting the Territory or other Property belonging to the United States; and nothing in this Constitution shall be so construed as to Prejudice any Claims of the United States, or of any particular State.

The makers of the Constitution thought it better to give Congress rather than the President the right to control and manage the property of the United States. In Europe, the rule always had been to vest the ownership of national property in the king. The plan of government which the members of the Constitutional Convention worked out, provided for a sovereign people rather than a sovereign individual. Therefore, it was more natural to give this sovereign power to the People's representatives in the law-making body, than to the President, who, by an indirect method of election, had been made somewhat independent of the People.

The rules and regulations which Congress has provided for the government of the insular possessions of the United States—Porto Rico and the Philippines —are framed upon the theory that the inhabitants of territory acquired by the United States do not become citizens when their country is annexed. This point was strongly put by Justice Brown in his opinion in the case of *Downes vs. Bidwell,* [1] in which the legal relations of Porto Rico to the United States after

The decision was that he could, because the island of Porto Rico had become territory appurtenant to and belonging to the United States, but not a part of the United States within the meaning of the revenue clauses of the Constitution.   Justice Brown said:

We are . . . of opinion that the power to acquire territory by treaty implies not only the power to govern such territory, but to prescribe upon what terms the United States will receive its inhabitants and what their *status* [political condition] shall be in what Chief Justice Marshall termed the "American Empire."   There seems to be no middle ground between this position and the doctrine that if their inhabitants do not become, immediately upon annexation, citizens of the United States, their children thereafter born, whether savages or civilized, are such, and entitled to all the rights, privileges, and immunities of citizens.   If such be their *status*, the consequences will be extremely serious. Indeed, it is doubtful if Congress would ever assent to the annexation of territory upon the condition that its inhabitants, however foreign they may be to our habits, traditions, and modes of life, shall become at once citizens of the United States.

The Supreme Court, in the case of *Kansas vs. Colorado*,[1] decided in 1906, laid down the rule for all controversies in which the absolute power of Congress over Federal reservations and other property of the United States, located within the borders of a State, comes in conflict with the equally absolute power of each State to make laws for the government of all of its territory. Such conflicts between the national and local governments do not often arise, because no one disputes the right of the United States to make whatever rules and regulations it chooses for the management of national

[1] 106 U. S. Rep., 46.

parks, forest reservations, forts, post offices, custom houses, and bonded warehouses; nor does any one doubt for a moment that each State has the same power over its own public lands, state roads, state parks, asylums, hospitals, capitol buildings, and other property of similar character. But such controversies do arise when one of the States makes such use of its public property as directly or indirectly affects the value or usefulness of property of the United States located within its borders; or *vice versa*, when the United States makes some use of its property within a State which affects the value of the public property of that State. In the Kansas–Colorado case, the original controversy grew out of a claim that certain irrigation improvements undertaken by the State of Colorado, by diverting the waters of the Arkansas River which had supplied the needs of Kansas farmers, would injuriously affect the latter State. Hence the State of Kansas had brought in the Supreme Court an action in equity in which it asked that the State of Colorado be restrained from continuing the erection of the irrigation improvements. The Attorney General of the United States had asked the Supreme Court to permit the national government to be made a party to this action upon the ground that legislation for the reclaiming of arid lands throughout the United States was the duty of the nation, and that the rights of the States in that particular field of public endeavor were subordinate to the rights of the general government. Justice Brewer, in giving the decision of the Supreme Court in this case, said that Congress had no power to control the reclamation of arid lands within the borders of a State, unless the navigability of the navigable waters of the United States would be affected by

mean that its legislation can override State laws in respect to the general subject of reclamation. While arid lands are to be found, mainly if not only in the Western and newer States, yet the powers of the National Government within the limits of those States are the same (no greater and no less) than those within the limits of the original thirteen, and it would be strange if, in the absence of a definite grant of power, the National Government could enter the territory of the States along the Atlantic and legislate in respect to improving by irrigation or otherwise the lands within their borders. . . .

Congress can make whatever rules and regulations it likes for the government of the Territories. In the case of *Murphy vs. Ramsey*,[1] the Supreme Court sustained the validity of an act of Congress passed in 1882 which required persons who wished to vote in the Territory of Utah, when applying for registration, to take an oath that they were not living in polygamy. This law had been challenged on the ground that it deprived the inhabitants of their constitutional right to vote. Justice Matthews, therefore, stated at length in his opinion the power of Congress over the Territories:

In ordaining government for the Territories, and the people who inhabit them, all the discretion which belongs to legislative power is vested in Congress; and that extends, beyond all controversy, to determining by law, from time to time, the form of the local government in a particular Territory, and the qualification of those who shall administer it. It rests with Congress to say whether in a given case, any of the people, resident in the Territory, shall participate in the election of its officers or the making of its laws; and it may, therefore, take from them any right of suffrage it may previously have conferred, or

re Duncan,[1] "a republican form of government is guaranteed to every State in the Union, and the distinguishing feature of that form is the right of the people to choose their own officers for governmental administration, and pass their own laws in virtue of the legislative power reposed in their representative bodies, whose legitimate acts may be said to be the acts of the people themselves."

But who is to say whether the form of government which exists in any State is or is not "a republican form of government," that is, one under which the people govern themselves? This puzzling question was answered by the Supreme Court in its decision in the case of *Luther vs. Borden*.[2] The militia officers who were defendants in that case had asked the Court to rule that their acts were justifiable because done by the orders of the State government under the old royal charter of 1663, which remained the constitution of Rhode Island until 1843. The plaintiffs had asserted that this was not a good defense; for, under that charter the right to vote being given only to owners or lessees of real estate, the State of Rhode Island did not have the republican form of government guaranteed by the Constitution of the United States, and, therefore, could not prosecute persons who attempted to upset an illegal State constitution. Chief Justice Taney declared that the Supreme Court had nothing to do with such political questions as this contention brought up. He said:

Under this article of the Constitution [Art. IV., Sec. 4], it rests with Congress to decide what government is the established one in a State. For as the United States

... foreign army had invaded ... had been no such invasions as ... United States to intervene. They ... United States could not send ... States to protect them ... because none of their legisla- ... asked for protection. ... with President Lincoln. ... constitutional ...

... The Supreme Court decided in 1857, in the case of ... Missouri, which had adopted a ...

secession ordinance but never actually had been part of the Confederacy, amounted to an invasion of a State. On October 15, 1864, the town of Glasgow, Mo., then occupied by a Federal force guarding military stores, had been attacked and taken by the Confederates. Colonel Harding, in command of the Union soldiers, had set fire to the military stores before abandoning the town, and this fire had destroyed, in a local store, a stock of goods which had been insured against fire. The storekeeper had sued the insurance company, which had defended its refusal to pay the insurance by citing a clause in the policy which provided that the company should not be required to make good any loss or damage by fire which might happen by means of any invasion, insurrection, riot, or civil commotion, or of any military or usurped power. Mr. Boon had insisted that a fire set by Federal soldiers, who were there to protect him against the rebels, had not been caused by an invasion. Justice Strong, however, holding that the Southern troops had invaded the State of Missouri, defined the word "invasion" as follows:

During the battle, and when the government troops had been driven from their exterior lines of defense, it became apparent to Colonel Harding that the city could not be successfully defended, and he thereupon, in order to prevent the said military stores from falling into the possession of the rebel forces, ordered Major Moore, one of the officers under his command, to destroy them.

In obedience to this order to destroy the said stores, and having no other means of doing so, Major Moore set fire to the city hall, and thereby the said building, with its contents, was consumed. Without other interference, agency, or instrumentality, the fire spread along the line of the street aforesaid to the building next adjacent to the city hall, and

... through two intermediate build-
ings ... the plaintiffs, and destroyed the same,
... During this time, said
... such goods, the ...
... surrender had taken place, nor ...
... nor any part thereof, obtained ...
... the city.

... the inquiry is ...
... of the usurping military force or power
... and operative cause of the fire .....
... is inevitable, that the fire which caused
... of the plaintiff's property happened ...
... in consequence of, but by means of the
... military or usurped power.

"... words "domestic violence" in this section mean
... Judge Grosscup of the United States
... Court of Illinois, in his charge to the grand
... the Pullman Strike of 1894, defined the
word "insurrection" as follows:

> ... against civil or political authority.
> ... opposition of a number of persons
> ... of law in a city or state. Now the laws
> ... under penalty any person
> ... or retarding the passage of the mail, and
> ... of the officers to arrest such offenders
> ... the law. It therefore is small
> ... that any person or persons have wilfully
> ... retarded the passage of the mails and that
> ... arrest for such offense ...
> ... a number of persons ... combine a power ...
> ... that defiance ...
> ... insurrection, which is treason ...
> ... established.

... Rep., ...

CHAPTER XXIV

THE Constitution of the United States was drafted mainly by lawyers. Either consciously or unconsciously, they modelled it after the forms of the legal documents with which they were familiar. Indeed the Constitution makers seem to have followed the form of a title deed to real estate from the beginning to the end of their work. The Preamble, like the introductory clause of a title deed, states that the People of the United States are doing a specified act, which, in this case, is the establishment of the Constitution. In the first, second, and third articles, the People of the United States, by this Constitution, grant legislative, administrative, and judicial powers to three great departments of the general government, just as a person selling a house and lot gives or grants to the buyer a right or title of possession. The fourth article contains a statement of the benefits which the people of the States of the United States are to obtain from the general government—benefits constituting the good and valuable considerations which, then as now, had to be stated in every valid and binding deed of real estate. Such a title deed of power to a general government could not be expected to last forever. Plans of public administration have to be made to

when ratified by the **Legislatures of three fourths of the several States**, or by **Conventions in three fourths** thereof, as the one or the other **Mode of Ratification** may be proposed by the Congress; **Provided that no** Amendment which may be made prior to the **Year One** thousand eight hundred and eight shall in any **Manner** affect the first and fourth Clauses in the Ninth Section of the first Article; and that no State, **without its** Consent, shall be deprived of its equal Suffrage **in the** Senate.

The reversionary clause in the title deed of **power** called the Constitution of the United States, is the **Fifth** Article, which states the way and manner in **which the** People of the United States may resume **their supreme** powers in order to amend or change **the rights and** powers of the general government.

"The term reversion," said **Judge Porter of the** New York Court of Appeals in the opinion in the case of *Clute vs. N. Y. C. & H. R. R. Co.*,[1] "signifies a return to a pre-existing or former state or place."

The government of the United States differs from all other political systems, past or present, in this: that by the reversionary clause giving the power of amendment the People of the United States keep the supreme power in their own hands. Under the political system which had prevailed in England prior to the Puritan Revolution, supremacy of power had vested in the king. In the Ship Money Case against John Hampden, tried in the Exchequer Chamber in 1637, twelve judges united in deciding that "no statute [of parliament] can bar the king of his regality; that statutes taking away his royal power in the defence of his kingdom are void; and that

[1] 120 N. Y. Rep., 267, 272.

Progressive Democracy.

"is justified in declaring that the first article of any sincerely intended progressive program must be the amendment of the amending clause of the Constitution." The new machinery, according to Mr. Croly, "must make the Constitution alterable at the demand and according to the dictates of a preponderant prevailing public opinion. Instead of requiring the assent of two-thirds of Congress and the legislatures of three-fourths of the States, the power of revision should be possessed by a majority of the electorate. The only limitations placed on this power should be a method of procedure which allowed sufficient time for deliberation and a certain territorial distribution of the prevailing majority."

The more conservative element in the community dissents from these radical proposals upon the ground that the Constitution is the law formulated and maintained by and for the People of the United States, of yesterday, of today, and of tomorrow. These conservatives insist that the difference between the People's Law, which is permanent, and the representative-made laws of legislative bodies, which meet each public need as it arises, ought to be maintained. In amending the Constitution, the majorities necessary for the submission of amendments to the States and the number of States whose consent is required for their adoption ought to be so great as to make sure that they reflect the will of the People, not that of a bare temporary majority of voters.

Art. VI., Subd. 1. All Debts contracted and Engagements entered into, before the Adoption of this Constitution, shall be as valid against the United States under this Constitution, as under the Confederation.

Fourteenth Amendment. Sec. 4 (first sentence). The validity of the public debt of the United States, authorized by law, including debts incurred for payment of pensions and bounties for services in suppressing insurrection or rebellion, shall not be questioned.

All Debts contracted and Engagements entered into, before the Adoption of this Constitution, shall be as valid against the United States under this Constitution, as under the Confederation. A stipulation that the public debt incurred during the Revolution should be as valid under the new constitutional government as it had been under the Articles of Confederation signified little more than the opinion of the framers of the Constitution that the revolutionary debts ought to be paid by the United States. Massachusetts, Connecticut, Pennsylvania, and one or two other States had paid nearly the whole cost of the War for Independence upon a very distinct understanding that all the States would eventually pay their fair shares of an expense which had been incurred for the common good.

Alexander Hamilton, when Secretary of the Treasury, took the matter up with the First Congress under the Constitution, and carried through a political trade under which the capital of the United States was located on the Potomac to please the Southern States, and the revolutionary debts incurred for the common benefit were assumed by the United States to please the Northern commonwealths.

The validity of the public debt of the United States, authorized by law, including debts incurred for payment of pensions and bounties for services in suppressing insurrection or rebellion, shall not be questioned. During the years immediately after the Civil War, many

American statesmen feared that the Southern States, once re-established in their political rights, would regain their old ascendency in the national councils, and would be able to repudiate the immense public debt which had been incurred in suppressing the rebellion and in rewarding those who had risked their lives that the Union might be preserved. For that reason, it seemed wise to the leaders of the nation to insert in the Fourteenth Amendment a positive prohibition of any possible legislation by which the validity of any part of the public debt of the United States could be questioned.

Art. VI., Subd. 2. This Constitution, and the Laws of the United States which shall be made in Pursuance thereof; and all Treaties made, or which shall be made, under the Authority of the United States, shall be the supreme Law of the Land; and the Judges in every State shall be bound thereby, any Thing in the Constitution or Laws of any State to the Contrary notwithstanding.

This Constitution, and the Laws of the United States which shall be made in Pursuance thereof; and all Treaties made . . . under the Authority of the United States, shall be the supreme Law of the Land. "America," said Chief Justice Marshall in his opinion in the case of *Cohens vs. Virginia,*[1] "has chosen to be, in many respects, and to many purposes, a nation; and for all these purposes her government is complete; to all these objects, it is competent. The people have declared, that in the exercise of all powers given for these objects, it is supreme. It can, then, in effecting these objects,

[1] 6 Wheaton's Rep., 264.

... ...rging them wi...
... ...endants asserts
... ... under th...
... ...d been carrie...
... ...eir contention
... ...roviding for super-
... subordinate to the
... ... has been held
... ...se upon the ground
... ... in pursuance of
...preme law of the land "

... ... that whilst the
... ... which have not
... ...ction of the United
... ...tional laws of the
... supreme law of the
... ...aws of the States,
... ...ligation. This is
... ...s authority of the
... ...ceeded in practise,
... ...hem as it was con-

State must have in order to rank with other sovereigns. The rules, regulations, provisos, and agreements that the political departments of the government insert in treaties with other nations are the laws of the United States quite as much as are the laws enacted by Congress and approved by the President.

In the case of *Ware vs. Hylton*,[1] decided by the Supreme Court in 1796, it was shown that the defendants, on July 7, 1774, had given to a subject of Great Britain their bond for the payment of £2,976 11s. 6d., of good British money. On October 20, 1777, the Virginia legislature had enacted a law to sequester British property, one section of which provided that a citizen of Virginia, owing money to a subject of Great Britain, might make payment to the loan office of the State and obtain, from the loan commissioner, a certificate in the name of the creditor which should discharge him from so much of the debt as had been so paid to the loan office. On April 26, 1780, the defendants had paid into the loan office the sum of $3,111 1/9, equal to £934 14s. Virginia currency, and obtained a certificate discharging the debt in question.

Being sued on the bond which they had given, the defendants had pleaded the payment to the loan office as a defence to so much of the debt. The plaintiffs had then urged that this plea was not a good defence because the treaty of peace with Great Britain, made September 3, 1783, contained an article in these words: "It is agreed that creditors, on either side, shall meet with no lawful impediment to the recovery of the full value, in sterling money, of all *bona fide* debts heretofore contracted." The question before the court, therefore, was whether the claim that a payment had been made

[1] 3 Dallas' Rep., 199, 244.

. . . . had been paid.

. . . . their debts
. . . . that a
. . . .
. . . . are bound to
. . . . the treaty . . . .
. . . . that the
. . . . by the treaty to
. . . . . . that the words in their
. . . . the
. . . . . . of the debt
. . . . . . instrument
. . . .

. . . .

. . . . . is
. . . .
. . . . . .
. . . .

. . . .
. . . .
. . . .
. . . .

Art. VI., Subd. 3. The Senators and Representatives before mentioned, and the Members of the several State Legislatures, and all executive and judicial Officers, both of the United States and of the several States, shall be bound by Oath or Affirmation, to support this Constitution; but no religious Test shall ever be required as a Qualification to any Office or public Trust under the United States.

The meaning and purpose of this stipulation that the chief legislative, executive, and judicial officers of the United States and of the States shall be required to declare under oath or affirmation their allegiance to the Constitution, was summed up by Judge Peyton in the case of *Thomas, Sheriff, vs. Taylor,*[1] heard and decided in the High Court of Errors and Appeals of the State of Mississippi in 1869. At the close of the Civil War, the provisional government of Mississippi had levied a tax on cotton at the rate of two dollars per bale. Mr. Taylor, the defendant, had offered to pay the tax on fifty bales by tendering a State treasury note for $100, which had been issued under a State law passed on December 19, 1861, after Mississippi had seceded from the Union. The sheriff had refused to accept the note. His refusal put squarely before the court the question whether a law made by the Mississippi legislature in 1861 after the State had seceded from the Union was valid and binding. The answer was that the law was not valid because the members of the legislature which had enacted it, had not taken the oath prescribed by the Constitution. Judge Peyton said:

The great question presented by the record is, whether the State of Mississippi and the rightful authority which

[1] 42 Mississippi Rep., 651.

now controls her people are bound by the acts and engagements of the government, which was organized under the ordinance of secession in 1861, and finally overthrown by the military forces of the United States in 1865. . . . The constitution of the State of Mississippi as one of the Confederate States, and the constitution of the Confederate States, both require that the members of the legislature shall, before they enter upon their duties, take an oath or affirmation to support the constitution of the Confederate States.   The members of the [Mississippi] legislature of that year [1861], if they took any oath at all, must have taken an oath or affirmation to support the constitution of the confederate States of America, according to the requirements of said constitution.   The legislation of Mississippi, from the date of the ordinance of secession to the surrender of the Confederate armies, was done either without the sanction of an oath, or under an oath to support a constitution adopted in violation of the Constitution of the Union, and for the express purpose of subverting the government of the United States; either of which, we think, would be sufficient to invalidate the legislation. . . . The Constitution of the United States provides that the senators and representatives in Congress, and the members of the several State legislatures, and all executive and judicial officers, both of the United States and of the several states, shall be bound by oath or affirmation to support that Constitution.   We cannot think that so important a provision in the paramount law of the land was intended to be merely directory, and not absolutely necessary to be complied with.

On June 1, 1789, Congress passed an act prescribing the following form of oath or affirmation:

I, A . . . B . . ., do solemnly swear, or affirm, that I will support the Constitution of the United States.

In 1862, when the Civil War was raging, the form was changed in order to exclude from the public service those who had been disloyal to the Union. The "iron-clad" test oath then adopted was as follows:

I, A . . . B . . ., do solemnly swear, or affirm, that I have never voluntarily borne arms against the United States since I have been a citizen thereof; that I have voluntarily given no aid, countenance, counsel, or encouragement to persons engaged in armed hostility thereto; that I have neither sought, nor accepted, nor attempted to exercise the functions of any office whatever, under any authority, or pretended authority, in hostility to the United States; that I have not yielded a voluntary support to any pretended government, authority, power, or constitution within the United States, hostile or inimical thereto. And I do further swear, or affirm, that, to the best of my knowledge and ability, I will support and defend the Constitution of the United States against all enemies, foreign and domestic, that I will bear true faith and allegiance to the same, that I take this obligation freely without any mental reservation or purpose of evasion, and that I will well and faithfully discharge the duties of the office on which I am about to enter, so help me God.

On July 11, 1868, Congress prescribed the following oath in order to insure the loyalty of public officers who, having been disqualified for office by taking part in the rebellion, had, by the removal of their disabilities, again become eligible for national and State offices:

I, A . . . B . . ., do solemnly swear, or affirm, that I will support and defend the Constitution of the United States against all enemies, foreign and domestic; that I will bear true faith and allegiance to the same; that I take this obligation freely without any mental reservation or purpose of evasion; and that I will well and faithfully discharge the duties of the office on which I am about to enter, so help me God.

One provision of the Fourteenth Amendment, which became a part of the Constitution on July 28, 1868, provided that persons who had held certain national and State offices and had taken an oath to support the Constitution, and afterward had been disloyal, should not be Senators or Representatives in Congress, or presidential electors, or hold any office under the United States or under any State.   This clause, it was thought, excluded from office only a very small number of those who had taken part in the rebellion.   Therefore, on February 15, 1871, Congress passed an act requiring all persons elected or appointed to office, who might be unable to take the oath required by the act of 1862 that they had never "borne arms against the United States," etc., to take the oath of loyalty prescribed by the act of July 11, 1868, which had been enacted three weeks before the adoption of the Fourteenth Amendment.

On May 13, 1884, Congress passed an act requiring all persons in the civil, military, or naval service of the United States, except the President, whose oath of office is prescribed in the Constitution (Art. II., Sec. 1, Subd. 7), to take the oath of loyalty prescribed by the act of 1868, known usually as Section 1757 of the Revised Statutes of the United States.

Art. VII.   The Ratification of the Conventions of nine States, shall be sufficient for the Establishment of this Constitution between the States so ratifying the Same.

This statement of the condition upon which the Constitution of the United States was to become effective is nearly in the form of the conditional clauses which in old times were often inserted in title deeds.

"This article speaks for itself," said Hamilton in *The Federalist*.[1] "The express authority of the people alone could give due validity to the Constitution. To have required the unanimous ratification of the thirteen States, would have subjected the essential interest of the whole to the caprice or corruption of a single member. It would have marked a want of foresight in the convention, which our own experience would have rendered inexcusable.

"Two questions of a very delicate nature present themselves on this occasion: 1. On what principle the Confederation, which stands in the solemn form of a compact among the States, can be superseded without the unanimous consent of the parties to it? 2. What relation is to subsist between the nine or more States ratifying the Constitution, and the remaining few who do not become parties to it?

"The first question is answered at once by recurring to the absolute necessity of the case; to the great principle of self-preservation; to the transcendent law of nature, and of nature's God, which declares that the safety and happiness of society are the objects at which all political institutions aim, and to which all such institutions must be sacrificed. Perhaps, also, an answer may be found without searching beyond the principles of the compact itself. It has been heretofore noted among the defects of the Confederation, that in many of the States it had received no higher sanction than a mere legislative ratification. The principle

[1] No. 43.

... but the moral relations will remain ... The claims of justice ... the other will be in force and must be fulfilled; ... of humanity must in all cases be duly and ... requited, whilst considerations of a common ... and above all the remembrance of the endearing scenes which are past, and the anticipation of a speedy triumph over the obstacles to reunion, will, it is hoped, not urge in vain, moderation on one side, and prudence on the other."

Done in Convention by the Unanimous Consent of the States present the Seventeenth Day of September in the Year of our Lord one thousand seven hundred and Eighty seven and of the Independence of the United States of America the Twelfth. IN WITNESS whereof We have hereunto subscribed our Names.

The closing paragraph of a deed of real estate is a certificate of witnesses that the instrument has been executed by the persons who are declared to have made it. In the same way, the Constitution of the United States closes with a certificate signed by General Washington, who presided over the Constitutional Convention, and thirty-eight other notables of the United States, in which they assert the genuineness of the instrument of government which they were about to propose to the States of the United States. The attestation clause, according to Bouvier's *Law Dictionary*, is "that clause wherein the witnesses certify that the instrument has been executed before them, and the manner of the execution of the same."

Some of the most influential and respectable members of the Convention refused to sign the Constitution as drafted. Colonel Mason, Mr. Wythe, and Governor Randolph of the Virginia delegation were men whose adverse opinion might have been fatal, if Washington had not been on the other side. Patrick Henry opposed its adoption. Hamilton alone of the New York delegation favored it. Samuel Adams of

and 'h ... to the legislatures of the different ... This understanding was ... to ... and ... whole Rhode Island Carolina had ratified the Constitution, the ... United States equaled in number the original ... which, in Congress assembled, had declared the independence of the United States of America.

INDEX

(Titles of legal decisions and names of books are in italics. Italic "J." after the name of a person means Justice of the U. S. Supreme Court; "C. J." Chief Justice of that court. Judges of inferior U. S. Courts are denoted by the word "Fed."; judges of State courts by the names of their States.)

A Selection from the
Catalogue of

G. P. PUTNAM'S SONS

**Complete Catalogues sent
on application**

"The best summary at present available of the political history of the United States."—FRANK H. HODDER, Professor of American History in the University of Kansas.

American Political History
1763-1876

By Alexander Johnston

Edited and Supplemented by
James Albert Woodburn

Professor of History and Political Science, Indiana University;
Author of "The American Republic," "Political
Parties and Party Problems in the
United States," etc.

In two parts, each complete in itself and indexed. Octavo. Each, net, $2.00

1. **The Revolution, the Constitution, and the Growth of Nationality. 1763-1832.**

2. **The Slavery Controversy, Secession, Civil War, and Reconstruction. 1820-1876.**

These volumes present the principal features in the political history of the United States from the opening of the American Revolution to the close of the era of the Reconstruction. They give in more convenient form the series of articles on "American Political History" contributed to Lalor's "Cyclopedia of Political Science, Political Economy, and Political History," by the late Professor Alexander Johnston.

"These essays, covering the whole field of the political history of the United States, have a continuity and unity of purpose; introduced, arranged, and supplemented as they have been by Professor Woodburn (who contributes a very necessary chapter on the Monroe Doctrine
well-balanced history

G. P. PUTNAM'S SONS

New York   London

A
History of Mediaeval
Political Theory in
the West

By R. W. Carlyle, C. I. E., and
A. J. Carlyle, M. A.

Vol. IV (Completing the Series) 6- net*

This treatise will be found by students of mediaeval history, and of the evolution of political science, a companion volume to such works as Bryce's "Holy Roman Empire," Gierke's "Theory of the State," and to all mediaeval history.

Volume I considered the period from the Second Century to the Ninth; Volume II, Political Theory of the Roman Lawyers and Canonists, 10th-13th Centuries. This volume, the record from that point.

G. P. Putnam's Sons
New York   London

Lightning Source UK Ltd.
Milton Keynes UK
UKHW012249110219
337137UK00006B/917/P